# Aspects of Modern Monetary and Macroeconomic Policies

*Other titles by Philip Arestis include:*

Philip Arestis & Malcolm Sawyer (*editors*)
THE POLITICAL ECONOMY OF ECONOMIC POLICIES

Philip Arestis (*editor*)
MONEY AND BANKING: ISSUES FOR THE TWENTY-FRIST CENTURY

Philip Arestis
MONEY, PRICING, DISTRIBUTION AND ECONOMIC INTEGRATION

Philip Arestis & Malcolm Sawyer (*editors*)
RELEVANCE OF KEYNESIAN ECONOMIC POLICIES TODAY

Philip Arestis, Michelle Baddeley & John McCombie (*editors*)
WHAT GLOBAL ECONOMIC CRISIS?

Philip Arestis & Elias Karakitsos
POST-BUBBLE US ECONOMY
Implications for Financial Markets and the Economy

Philip Arestis, Jesus Ferreiro & Felipe Serrano (*editors*)
FINANCIAL DEVELOPMENTS IN NATIONAL AND INTERNATIONAL MARKETS

Victoria Chick (*author*), Sheila Dow & Philip Arestis (*editors*)
ON MONEY, METHOD AND KEYNES
Selected Essays

*Other titles by Eckhard Hein include*:

Eckhard Hein, Arne Heise & Achim Truger (*editors*)
WAGES, EMPLOYMENT, DISTRIBUTION AND GROWTH
International Perspectives

# Aspects of Modern Monetary and Macroeconomic Policies

Edited by

Philip Arestis, Eckhard Hein and Edwin Le Heron

palgrave
macmillan

First published 2007 by
PALGRAVE MACMILLAN
Houndmills, Basingstoke, Hampshire RG21 6XS and
175 Fifth Avenue, New York, N.Y. 10010
Companies and representatives throughout the world

PALGRAVE MACMILLAN is the global academic imprint of the Palgrave Macmillan division of St. Martin's Press, LLC and of Palgrave Macmillan Ltd. Macmillan® is a registered trademark in the United States, United Kingdom and other countries. Palgrave is a registered trademark in the European Union and other countries.

ISBN 13: 978–0–230–00793–2 hardback
ISBN 10: 0–230–00793–7 hardback

This book is printed on paper suitable for recycling and made from fully managed and sustained forest sources.

A catalogue record for this book is available from the British Library.

Library of Congress Cataloging-in-Publication Data

Aspects of modern monetary and macroeconomic policies / edited by Philip Arestis, Eckhard Hein and Edwin Le Heron.
p. cm.
Includes bibliographical references and index.
ISBN 13: 978–0–230–00793–2 (cloth)
ISBN 10: 0–230–00793–7 (cloth)
1. Money policy. I. Arestis, Philip, 1941– II. Hein, Eckhard, 1963– III. Le Heron, Edwin, 1956–

HG230.3A72 2007
339.5′3–dc22 2006047142

10 9 8 7 6 5 4 3 2 1
16 15 14 13 12 11 10 09 08 07

Printed and bound in Great Britain by
Antony Rowe Ltd, Chippenham and Eastbourne

# Contents

# List of Tables and Figures

**Tables**

**Figures**

# Notes on the Contributors

**Philip Arestis** is Professor and University Director of Research, Cambridge Centre for Economic and Public Policy, University of Cambridge, UK.

**Angel Asensio** is 'Maître de Conférences', Centre d'Economie de Paris Nord (CEPN), Université Paris 13 – CNRS, France.

**Jörg Bibow** is Assistant Professor of Economics, Skidmore College, Saratoga Springs, New York, USA, and Research Associate, Levy Economics Institute of Bard College, Annandale-on-Hudson, New York, USA.

**Peter Flaschel** is Professor of Economic Theory, Department of Economics and Business Administration, Bielefeld University, Germany.

**Claude Gnos** is Associate Professor, University of Burgundy and Head of the Centre for Monetary and Financial Studies, Dijon, France.

**Eckhard Hein** is Senior Researcher at the Macroeconomic Policy Institute (IMK) in the Hans Boeckler Foundation, Duesseldorf, and Visiting Professor at Carl von Ossietzky University Oldenburg, Germany.

**Peter Howells** is Professor of Monetary Economics, Bristol Business School, University of the West of England, Bristol, UK.

**Elias Karakitsos** is Professor and Chairman of Global Economic Research and is Associate Member, Cambridge Centre for Economic and Public Policy, University of Cambridge, UK.

**Theodore Koutsobinas** is Assistant Professor at the Department of Statistics, Actuarial Studies and Financial Mathematics, University of the Aegean, Samos, and Teaching Fellow, Graduate Program, Department of Statistics, Athens University of Economics and Business, Athens, Greece.

**Edwin Le Heron** is 'Maître de Conférences' in Economics, Sciences Po Bordeaux, France, and Researcher at the SPIRIT (Science de Politique, Relations Internationale et Territoire). He is also President of the ADEK (the French Association for the Development of Keynesian Studies).

**Basil Moore** is Professor Extraordinary of Economics at Stellenbosch University, South Africa.

**Christian Proaño** is a PhD Student at the Department of Economics and Business Administration, Bielefeld University, and at the Macroeconomic Policy Institute (IMK) in the Hans Boeckler Foundation, Duesseldorf, Germany.

**Malcolm Sawyer** is Professor of Economics, University of Leeds, UK.

**Elisabeth Springler** is Assistant Professor at the Institute for Monetary and Fiscal Policy, Vienna University of Economics and Business Administration, Austria.

**Achim Truger** is Senior Researcher at the Macroeconomic Policy Institute (IMK) in the Hans Boeckler Foundation, Duesseldorf, Germany.

[illegible] [illegible] Latin [illegible] [illegible]

[illegible]

# 1
# Introduction

*Philip Arestis, Eckhard Hein and Edwin Le Heron*

Over the last 30 years or so the developments in the area of monetary and macroeconomic policies have been quite substantial. Within the new consensus macroeconomics (NCM), monetary policy is upgraded while fiscal policy is downgraded. This new monetary policy has been the main instrument of policy under the guise of inflation targeting, an approach pursued by a number of central banks worldwide. There are a number of aspects relating to this new monetary and macroeconomic policy approach. It is the intention of this edited book to focus on some of these developments, as we try to show in this introduction.

In the opening chapter, entitled 'Does Inflation Targeting Increase the Deflationary Bias in the World Economy?', Basil Moore, argues that the bank rate is now widely recognized as the main instrument of monetary policy, set exogenously by the central bank to achieve its stabilization targets with its level maintained unchanged between monetary policy committee meetings. Once the bank rate is recognized as the central bank's main policy instrument, whose level is set pro-cyclically over the business cycle, the IS curve metamorphoses into the downward-sloping aggregate demand function in interest rate-output space. If the assumption of demand-constrained output and employment is upheld, why is it that central banks have an innate bias towards tight money, Moore asks? There are several reasons, but the most important is because monitoring and influencing price stability is now regarded as the central bank's critically important responsibility. Central banks must attempt to insure that internal and external balance is preserved. In most economies price stability can only be approached by setting higher interest rates, and pursuing more restrictive monetary policies makes it impossible for economies to operate without an output gap.

Peter Howells poses the question: 'What is Endogenous when Monetary Policy is Transparent?' The conventional presentation of monetary policy in the Post Keynesian literature is that the central bank sets the rate of interest at which it is prepared to provide liquidity to the banking system and then (with some possible qualifications) supplies reserves on demand. The demand for additional reserves comes from banks' willingness to respond to the demand for credit, which originates in the 'state of trade'. In this simple reversal of the neoclassical presentation, the money supply is endogenous while the rate of interest is the exogenous variable. But attempts to increase transparency in monetary policy making place a premium on agents being able to infer the next movement in the official interest rate from prevailing macroeconomic data. In the extreme case, where the central bank follows an interest rate rule, interest rates are determined by inflation and the output gap. In these circumstances, 'exogenous' is a potentially misleading description when applied to the interest rate. If anything is exogenous, it is the inflation target.

Theodore Koutsobinas addresses 'Monetary Policy Formation in the Long-term Margin: A Kahn–Tobin Framework', to provide an analytical framework of chain asset substitution on the basis of arbitrage in financial markets. This process explains the 'mystery' behind the effectiveness of monetary policy in administering the very short-term interest rate. It explains the possibility that monetary policy may prove ineffective in the case of downward stickiness of the long-term interest rate. In this vein, this chapter re-examines the 'bills-only' debate in an analytical context and supports the adoption of an alternative form of 'bills-bonds' approach in which the long-term end of the curve is crucial according to the earlier generation theoretical contributions of Tobin and Kahn. An attractive feature of the approach followed in this chapter is that chains of asset substitution on the basis of arbitrage processes are obtained by using maximization techniques on arbitrage profit without relying on assumptions about the nature of expectations, whether rational or behavioural.

In 'Bank Lending and Regulation in Insider Financial Systems: A Theoretical Assessment', Elisabeth Springler attempts to integrate the effects of modern banking regulation, in particular changes imposed by the Basle II regulatory framework, into an endogenous money supply model. With this theoretical starting point, the chapter begins by pointing out the characteristics of the Basle II banking regulatory framework, which are relevant to the argument. The chapter then proceeds with an analysis of the relevant features of endogenous money for economies with financial systems of the bank-based type. The latter are characterized by the important role of banks for the external financing of firms' investment and strong institutional ties between creditor and debtor. The discussion focuses on the potential lending constraints that might arise when implementing features of asymmetric information into endogenous money supply theory which takes account of changes in the regulatory framework.

Angel Asensio discusses 'Monetary and Fiscal Policy Interactions in a Keynesian Context: Revisiting Macroeconomic Governance'. He points out that governance in the NCM carries several drawbacks when implemented in Keynesian non-ergodic regimes, especially when unemployment is interpreted in terms of the 'natural' rate. Under such circumstances the policy mix proposed may anchor the system far from full employment. Even within a Keynesian explanation of unemployment hysteresis-type difficulties do not vanish, for policy makers also have to deal with uncertainty. In contrast with the economic policy rules of the NCM, a Keynesian pragmatic and progressive approach is proposed, based on intermediate targets designed with respect to the confidence that authorities have in the chances of success. Monetary and fiscal policy interactions are discussed in such a context. Even if monetary policy is thought doubtful in its impact on effective demand, it still matters through avoiding increases in interest rates when fiscal policy aims to stimulate effective demand.

Claude Gnos investigates 'Monetary Policy from a Circuitist Perspective'. The contribution of this perspective is twofold, according to Gnos. First, circuit theory helps to clarify the usual reference made both by orthodox and heterodox theories to excess nominal demand when they come to define inflation. It is concluded that the source of inflation is to be found in interferences and mismatches between the formation, spending and transfer of money incomes. In this view, inflation and deflation may – and indeed do – coexist. Second, circuit theory dismisses the traditional approaches of money regulation that amount to quantitative rules applying to the quantity of money (money-supply targeting) or to the rate of interest rates (in the case of nowadays inflation targeting), and favours a reform of the structural features of banking. A twofold division of banks' monetary and financial activities is proposed, along with the implementation of a specific department recording of the retained profits that firms devote to the accumulation of capital. This renewed structure would allow banks to manage monetary and financial flows in such a way that inflation and deflation would be avoided, without imposing any specific constraint on the economic agents' behaviour.

Philip Arestis and Elias Karakitsos switch attention to the more 'international' dimension of monetary matters. In 'A Policy-Game Framework for the Dollar-Euro Exchange Rate', they are concerned with the instability inherent in currency models. They focus on the relationship between the dollar and the euro to deal with the question of stability/instability. This question can only be answered when the business cycles of the US and the Euro area can be investigated in terms of their synchronization or de-synchronization. The authors utilize such a framework in this chapter in an attempt to study the dollar–euro exchange rate at the theoretical level without forgetting at the same time the realities of the wider real world.

The rest of the chapters concentrate on the practice of monetary and macroeconomic policies. Edwin Le Heron discusses 'The New Governance in Monetary Policy: A Critical Appraisal of the Fed and the ECB' to suggest that for the last fifty years, four monetary policy regimes have prevailed: the full *discretion* of the government with the Keynesian regime until 1974; the monetary *rule* of the monetarist regime, 1974 to 1982; the *credibility* of the rule developed by the new classical economists during the 1980s; and the *confidence* strategy of the NCM after 1990. The great novelty of the credibility regime was the institutional importance of the design of full central bank independence. But the belief in an automatic rule disappeared with the NCM, so that the independent central bank needed a new legitimacy. Governance, then, which refers to the relationship between the central bank and the government, assumes new importance in the form of credibility versus confidence. The latter distinction appears to be much more useful for understanding these changes. The paper develops the new governance in monetary policy through a comparison of the ECB (credibility strategy) and the Fed (confidence strategy).

Peter Flaschel and Christian Proaño deal with 'AS–AD Disequilibrium Dynamics and the Taylor Interest Rate Policy Rule: Euro-Area Based Estimation and Simulation'. The chapter estimates a Keynesian AS–AD disequilibrium model for the Euro area, which builds on sticky wage and prices adjustments, a dynamic IS-equation and a static form of Okun's Law. The model, thus, employs two Phillips curves that relate wage and price inflation dynamics to corresponding factor utilization rates, linked together by a simple form of Okun's Law. It adds goods market disequilibrium dynamics, driven by the multiplier process, the real rate of interest and income distribution. For policy analysis it uses a Taylor interest rate rule. The empirical estimates for the Euro area support the proposed theoretical structure. Simulation results, based on the estimated parameters, show strong, though cyclical convergence, where the role of monetary policy concerning the asymptotic stability and the volatility of the considered dynamics are by and large as expected, but not always without ambiguities.

Jörg Bibow turns attention to 'How the Maastricht Regime Fosters Divergence as Well as Instability'. This chapter investigates the phenomenon of persistent macroeconomic divergence that has occurred across the euro area in recent years. Optimal currency area theory would point towards asymmetric shocks and structural factors as the foremost candidate causes. The alternative hypothesis pursued by Bibow focuses on the working of the Maastricht regime itself, and on monetary policy in particular, highlighting that the regime features powerful built-in de-stabilizers that foster divergence as well as instability. Supposed adjustment mechanisms have turned out in practice to undermine the operation of the currency union by making it ever less 'optimal', that is, less subjectable to a 'one-size-fits-all' monetary policy and a common nominal exchange rate in view of the resulting business cycle de-synchronization and related build-up of financial imbalances. The threats of instability and divergence reinforce each other. Without regime reform these developments could potentially spiral out of control, threatening the long-term survival of the European Monetary Union, it is argued.

In 'Germany's Post-2000 Stagnation in the European Context – A Lesson in Macroeconomic Mismanagement', Eckhard Hein and Achim Truger question the mainstream diagnosis of Germany's recent stagnation as well as the prescribed remedies. They show that the 'institutional sclerosis' view of Germany's stagnation is unfounded and that, therefore, the political measures proposed and actually taken have been misguided. Instead, they claim that macroeconomic mismanagement, mainly imposed by the Maastricht regime, explains the German absolute and relative stagnation compared with the Euro area as a whole and with the USA. If the problem of macroeconomic mismanagement is not addressed and solved, irrespective of occasional cyclical upswings, they predict a continuing stagnation tendency for the German economy. And they argue that this is not only a German problem, but a matter of European concern, because the macroeconomic policies which have caused the German constellation will have major negative feedback effects on the other Euro area countries.

In the final chapter, Philip Arestis and Malcolm Sawyer deal with macroeconomic policies in the UK. They ask: 'Macroeconomic Policy in the UK Under New Labour: The End of Boom and Bust?' The chapter first considers macroeconomic performance under the new Labour government since 1997. It then considers the nature of fiscal and monetary policy since 1997 and the effects, which those policies may have had on macroeconomic performance. Finally, the question is asked as to whether Gordon Brown, Chancellor of the Exchequer throughout the period, has been a lucky chancellor in terms of whether the relatively good macroeconomic performance since 1997 can be ascribed to his policies or to the general national and global macroeconomic environment.

The genesis of the project out of which this book has emerged can be located in the 9th conference of the German Research Network 'Alternative Conceptions of Macroeconomic Policies under the Conditions of Unemployment, Globalisation and High Public Debt' on 'Macroeconomics and Macroeconomic Policies – Alternatives to the Orthodoxy'. The conference was organized in cooperation with the Post Keynesian Economic Study Group, UK, and the Association pour le Développement des Études Keynésiennes, France, and took place in Berlin, 28–29 October 2005. Further papers from the conference are published in two books (Hein, Heise and Truger 2006; Hein and Truger 2007), and in a special issue of *INTERVENTION. Journal of Economics*. We would like to thank the contributors to this volume for their co-operation and the participants in the conference for the stimulating discussions. Special thanks go to Barbara Schnieders for her assistance in the editing process and to the Hans Boeckler Foundation for organizational and financial support for the conference and the publications. Furthermore, and as always, we are exceedingly thankful and grateful to Amanda Hamilton and her staff at Palgrave Macmillan for her encouragement and support throughout the life of this project. Without the generous support of the people just mentioned this project would not have reached the stage of publication.

## References

Hein, E., Heise, A., Truger, A. (eds) (2006) *European Economic Policies – Alternatives to Orthodox Analysis and Policy Concepts* (Marburg: Metropolis).

Hein, E., Truger, A. (eds) (2007) *Money, Distribution and Economic Policy: Alternatives to Orthodox Macroeconomics* (Cheltenham: Edward Elgar).

# 2

# Does Inflation Targeting Increase the Deflationary Bias in the World Economy?*

*Basil Moore*

## Introduction

This chapter consists of two parts: The first develops the application of process analysis to closed economies (Moore 2006). Economies are complex systems where all variables are continuously changing. Process analysis attempts to explain and, when possible, predict the short-run ordinal movement of selected variables. Complex systems have no tendency to reach an equilibrium configuration where all change has ceased. In consequence for complex system equilibrium analysis is useless, and easily leads to erroneous conclusions.

The second part consists of an application of process analysis to open economies operating under flexible exchange rate regimes, where monetary policy is pursued under inflation-targeting regimes. In such regimes central bankers derive respect and influence primarily from their demonstrated past ability to attain their inflation targets. This can easily lead to the adoption of policies with a deflationary bias, since Central banks are rewarded for hitting their inflation targets, but are not held responsible for the accompanying low growth rates of aggregate demand and high unemployment rates, which are typically attributed to other causes.

## Fatal problems of conventional IS–LM analysis

Post Keynesian economists have now embraced endogenous money and exogenous interest rates for 30 years. Nevertheless the IS–LM diagram, with its explicit assumption of monetary exogeneity and

*This chapter is based on Moore (2006).

interest rate endogeneity, remains widely accepted by most mainstream economists, and still appears in most money and banking and macroeconomic textbooks.

Post Keynesians insist that interest rates do not, as the textbooks maintain, adjust to equilibrate saving and investment or the supply and demand for 'loanable funds' (Moore 1988). Bank rate (BR) is now widely recognized as the main instrument of monetary policy, set exogenously by the central bank (CB) to achieve its macroeconomic stabilization targets and maintained stable at that level between CB interest rate meetings. By an arbitrage process other short-term market rates are held equal to BR plus an asset differential, reflecting expected differences in liquidity, maturity, collateral and tax status, and borrower risk among securities. Long-term rates are also determined by an arbitrage process, and are equal to the capital markets' expectations of future values of BR plus a positive maturity premium, reflecting debtor preferences to issue assets of shorter maturity than creditor preferences to hold short-term securities.

Most financial market participants now recognize that the money supply is credit-driven and not controlled by the textbook base-deposit multiplier relationship. Nevertheless most academic textbooks continue to seriously lag practitioners in the teaching of financial phenomena. In IS–LM analysis the LM curve is defined as all positions where the demand for money is equal to the supply of money, as consistent with both the liquidity preference and the loanable funds theory. The LM curve is viewed as upward-sloping in interest-income space, because the demand for money rises with income, and the CB is assumed able to control the money supply as its policy instrument. Once the money supply is recognized as endogenously credit-driven, and BR is seen as the CB's chief exogenous policy instrument, the LM curve becomes a horizontal line at the BR set by the CB (Moore 1988).

The IS curve, defined as all positions where planned saving (S) is equal to planned investment (I), is similarly false, but for different reasons: S = I is simply an accounting identity. As the accounting record of investment, saving is identical to investment by definition at every level of income, interest rate and time period. Saving does not exist as an independent relationship. Whenever some units invest, the same or other units necessarily save an equal amount, since total assets must equal total liabilities. Saving should be viewed as abstention from consuming current income, and so identical to current investment.

In spite of the fact that to save is a transitive verb, in developed economies most 'saving' is non-volitional (Moore 2006). Planned saving is never equal to planned investment (except by very rare accident). The IS curve is literally nonsense. The message of mainstream analysis 'changes in the money supply cause changes in the level of income and interest rates' reverses the true direction of causality between income and money, and provides a classic example of the 'reverse causation' error caused by the confusion of identities with behavioural relationships.

In summary Hicks's IS–LM diagram as a model for modern macroeconomies is nontransparent, confusing and incorrect. As a guide to understanding the interaction between money, interest rates, and money income IS–LM analysis is a misleading fiction and must be banished from the textbooks (Moore 2006).

## The BR–AD relationship

The underlying important truth buried in the conventional downward-sloping IS curve is the recognition that aggregated demand (AD) is inversely related to the level of interest rates. This downward-sloping relationship of the AD curve is central to the understanding of monetary policy, and contrary to the positive short-term relationship frequently observed empirically between changes in BR and changes in investment. Once BR is recognized as the CB's main policy instrument whose level is set pro-cyclically over the business cycle, it ceases to be surprising that BR and AD and investment are positively related over the short run. The IS curve metamorphosis's into a downward-sloping AD function in interest rate-output space. It is then unsurprising that in the short run BR and investment are positively correlated. The CB raises BR whenever it anticipates a rise in 'animal spirits' and an increase in investment spending. A change in BR is an excellent proxy for the CB's expectation of the change in immeasurable 'animal spirits'.

In Figure 2.1 the level of BR set by the CB is measured on the vertical axis and the level of AD is measured on the horizontal axis. The IS curve is now renamed the AD curve, whose slope summarizes the interest-elasticity of aggregate demand. The position and shape of the AD curve shifts widely pro-cyclically leftwards and rightwards with changes in 'animal spirits'. The BR set by the CB in period t ($BR_t$) is associated with the current particular set of 'animal spirits' as seen by the CB, and generates a particular change in aggregate demand ($\Delta AD_t$). As BR is reduced towards zero AD increases indefinitely, and the AD curve asymptotically approaches the horizontal axis. When most firms

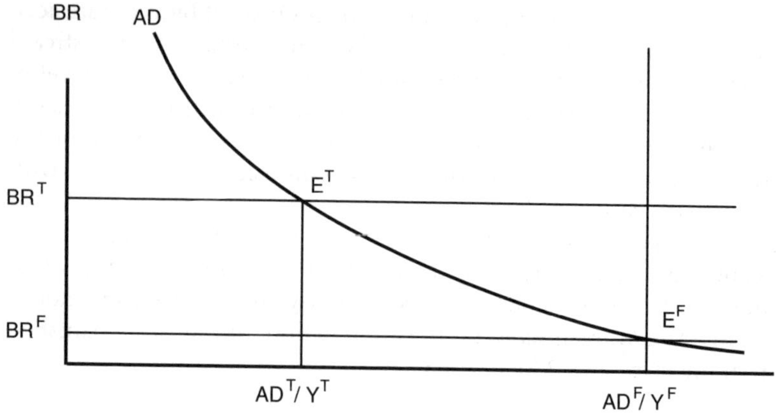


*Figure 2.1* The BR–AD diagram

are quantity-takers total output is demand-driven. Changes in AD (ΔAD) then result in identical changes in aggregate supply (AS) and ΔAS ≡ ΔGDP.

Figure 2.1 highlights the underlying reason why output is characteristically demand-constrained in most market economies: CBs typically set BR at too high a level (e.g. $BR^T$) which generates a level of AD ($AD^T$) far above the level of BR that generates full employment ($BR^F$) and required for full employment output ($AD^F$). Alternatively stated CBs fail to set BR at a sufficiently low level ($BR^F$) to induce a level of AD sufficient to induce the full employment output level ($Y^F$). This very simple insight is of central importance for the general analysis of monetary policy.

If economies are in fact demand-constrained as Post Keynesians vociferously maintain, why do CBs have such a destructive bias towards tight money? CBs are not managed by fools. The central reason is their fear of inflation. Maintaining price stability is now regarded as the CB's single most important macro responsibility. CBs also attempt to insure that internal and external balance is preserved, but price stability takes precedence. In most economies where there is no incomes policy, price stability can only be achieved by setting higher interest rates, pursuing more restrictive monetary policies and reducing AD, making it impossible for economies to operate without a large output gap.

## Process analysis: the BR–ΔAD diagram

Economies are complex systems which never approach equilibrium. To analyze complex systems comparative-static equilibrium analysis must be replaced with process analysis (Moore 2006). The goal of process analysis is to explain and forecast how complex systems change over historical time, in particular the effects of how deficit spending is financed, and how the manner of finance influences the rate of growth of AD.

In process analysis no attempt is made to uncover a system's future 'equilibrium state'. All variables are dated and the current value of all variables is taken as predetermined. The attempt is made to explain and predict the ordinal change in all variables considered, over the shortest period for which data are available. Economies consist of both slow-changing and fast-changing variables. Different variables differ widely in the chronological period over which change occurs and is measured.

The current price of all assets represents the markets' collective discount of what the price is expected to be in the subsequent market period. When the current price is equal to the markets' expected price in the next period the expected change in price is zero, allowing for discounting and all transactions costs. For many fast-changing variables experienced speculators are able to forecast ordinal short-run changes in prices with some confidence based on past market observation.

For fast-changing variables it is impossible to accurately forecast the ordinal change over even very short chronological periods. Price changes over any short-run period represent the net cumulative change of thousands of transactions. When the future change in price cannot be known in advance the market has conventionally been termed 'efficient'. 'Efficient' does not imply the market price is 'correct', in the sense of being the 'true' price. 'Efficient' markets differ from 'inefficient' markets principally because prices change more rapidly in response to changes in expectations. The complexity of summing the net effect of a series of stochastic changes enormously increases the uncertainty of the final outcome, and renders the net cumulative change over very short-run periods unpredictable, as in the case of stock prices and exchange rates.

Comparative static equilibrium analysis is not merely useless for complex systems it is typically positively misleading.[1] Complex economic variables have no tendency to approach any future 'equilibrium' configuration or growth rate. Changes in current autonomous spending have no predictable cardinal 'multiplier' effect on future income. When firms are price-setters and quantity-takers, the short-run rate of change in prices is predetermined primarily by the past rate of change in costs of production. In complex economies change is continuously

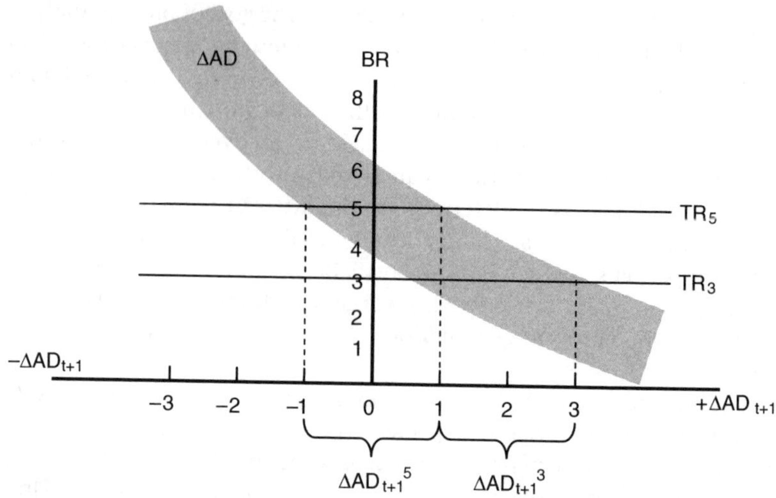


*Figure 2.2* The BR–ΔAD diagram

endogenously generated. Since saving is the accounting record of investment, actual saving is always identical to actual investment. But planned saving is never equal to planned investment, except by extremely unlikely accident. Providing inventories remain at their target levels, so long as there is no quantity-rationing, the change in AS (ΔAS) is determined by the sum of the change in AD (ΔAD) in every period.

Figure 2.2 presents the BR–AD diagram of Figure 2.1 revised for process analysis. It attempts to explain and forecast the ordinal change in AD (the BR–ΔAD diagram). The level of BR is measured on the vertical axis, and the ordinal percentage change in AD from its current value to its value in the subsequent period is measured on the horizontal axis. The current level of AD and hence GDP is viewed as predetermined. The analysis attempts to explain and forecast the ordinal change in AD over the subsequent period.

In Figure 2.2 the position of zero change in current AD is denoted on the horizontal axis at the origin. Positive or negative changes in AD from its current value are measured to the right or left of the origin (+/−$\Delta AD_{t+1}$). The time unit is the shortest period for which changes in the dependent variable (GDP) are observed and recorded. For variables in the National Income Accounts, the chronological time unit is ordinarily one quarter or one year, depending on data availability. For individual commodities price and quantity change can be measured over much shorter periods: quarterly, monthly, weekly, daily or even hourly.

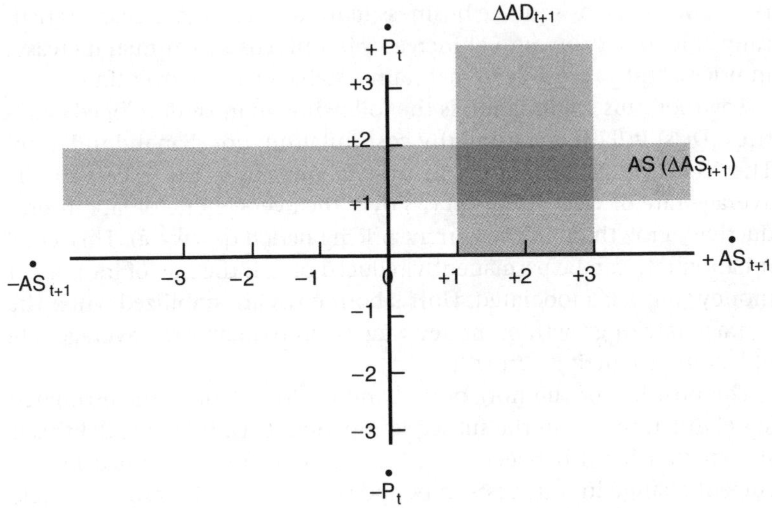


*Figure 2.3* The AD–AS diagram

For homogeneous assets, like equities and foreign currencies, that are traded on well-organized markets with low transactions costs, change may be measured in days, hours, minutes, or even by an approximation to continual change in real time (Goodhart and Demas 1990).

The downward-sloping AD relationship portrays the broad inverse relationship between the current value of BR ($Br_t$), and the change in AD in the subsequent period ($\Delta AD_{t+1}$). In complex systems all relationships are time-dependent and exhibit only 'demi-regularities' (Moore 2006). The AD relationship is drawn as a fractal band that takes up space, not a deterministic single-value relationship. The width of the AD band denotes the variability of the demi-regularities that characterize complex relationships. The ΔAD band shifts widely pro-cyclically upwards (rightwards) during periods of expansion, and downwards (leftwards) during periods of recession, as induced by changes in non-measurable expectations about the future ('animal spirits').

The aggregate supply relation summarizing the price-setting and quantity-taking behaviour of business firms is drawn in Figure 2.3 as the horizontal band ($\Delta AS_{t+1}$). The 'core' inflation rate in the current period is predetermined by the excess of the average rate of increase in money wages over the average rate of growth of labour productivity in the previous period (Blinder *et al.* 1998). Increases in money wages in excess of the rate of growth of average labour productivity must either raise unit costs, or squeeze business mark-ups. Firms are characteristically able to pass on annual increases in unit costs as annual increases in prices, and so are able to maintain a stable mark-up over time.

The root cause of inflation is the following. In most developed countries (DCs) inflation is primarily cost inflation, not demand inflation. The 'core' inflation rate ($\dot{p}$) in unit labour costs, the excess of the average rate of wage inflation ($\dot{w}$) over the average rate of labour productivity growth ($\dot{a}$) in the current pricing period ($\dot{p} = \dot{w} - \dot{a}$). This 'core' inflation rate can be permanently reduced only if the rate of increase of money wages is moderated. Unit labour costs are stabilized when the average rate of growth of money wages approximates the average rate of labour productivity growth.

The position of the horizontal band $(\Delta AS)_{t+1}$ depicts the estimated 'core' inflation rate in the subsequent period (t+1). In Figure 2.3 this is shown as a band between 1 and 2 per cent pre-determined by the current change in unit costs in period (t). The inflation rate is entirely cost-determined and independent of current changes in aggregate demand in the present period ($\Delta AD_t$). The position and interest-elasticity of the ΔAD band, and the BR set by the CB (shown as 3 per cent in Figure 2.2) determine the change in AD in period (t+1) (shown as 2 per cent with a fan range of 1 to 3 per cent in Figure 2.2).

In Figure 2.3 the more deeply shaded intersection of the AD and AS bands denotes the average expected range of changes in inflation (1 to 2 per cent) and output (1 to 3 per cent) in period (t) to occur in period (t+1). It does not denote an 'equilibrium' band of inflation and output change.[2] Changes in output are completely demand-determined ($\Delta AD_{t+1}$) by changes in 'animal spirits' and by the level of BR (set by the CB in the current pricing period). Changes in prices are considered entirely cost-determined.

'Animal spirits' (agents' changing expectations of changes in other agents' future expectations) vary greatly pro-cyclically and shift the AD relationship widely rightwards and leftwards. The CB varies BR procyclically in pursuit of its stabilization goals. When the CB expects the ΔAS relation to shift right by more than a certain amount, it raises BR. When the CB expects the ΔAD to shift left by more than a certain amount, it lowers BR. Both the timing and the ordinal and cardinal change in BR are made at the discretion of the CB.[3]

The CB's 'policy reaction function' describes how the CB has changed BR in the past, in response to the observed deviation of the economy from its stabilization goals (Moore 1988). The CB's 'policy reaction function' is now widely termed the 'Taylor Rule' (TR), after an important paper by John Taylor which empirically estimated the past rate-setting behaviour of the Federal Reserve System (Taylor 1993). In Figure 2.2 the TR is drawn as a horizontal line at the BR set by the CB ($BR_t$). When the CB sets BR at 5 per cent ($TR_5$), the expected change in AD (ΔAD) over the subsequent quarter is zero (with a fan range from +1 to −1 per cent). When the CB sets BR at 3 per cent ($TR_3$), the expected change in AD (ΔAD) over the subsequent quarter is +2 per cent (with a fan range from +1 to +3 per cent).

## The ΔBR–ΔAD diagram

The chief empirical problem for the analysis of complex systems is that the *ceteris* never remain *paribus*. When interest rates are changed, it is informative to decompose the change in AD into the change associated with the previous level of BR, and the change associated with the current change in BR. Unfortunately there is frequently insufficient information to distinguish the effects of changes in BR on AD from the effects of the levels of BR on AD. When BR is changed more frequently than once a quarter the effects of changes in BR on AD cannot be estimated directly, since changes in GDP are only measured quarterly.

In Figure 2.4 the Taylor Rule curve is shown for a one per cent increase ($+\Delta BR_E$) and one per cent decrease in BR ($-\Delta BR_R$). A rise in BR *ceteris paribus* induces a reduction in AD, and a fall in BR induces an

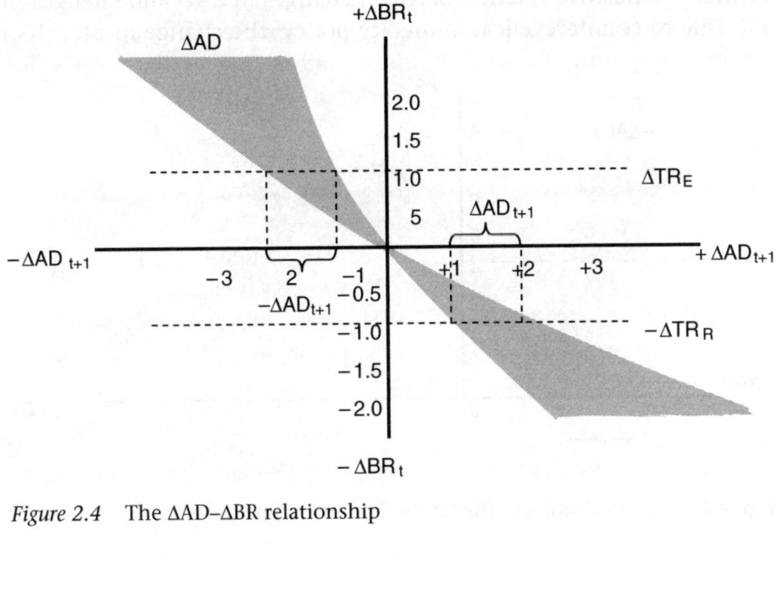


*Figure 2.4* The ΔAD–ΔBR relationship

increase in AD. The implicit assumption, which is appropriate only for laboratory experiments, is the *ceteris paribus* assumption. In the absence of changes in the causal variable (BR), the dependent variable (GDP) then remains unchanged. But this assumption ignores the fact that the real world is not a laboratory, changes in 'animal spirits' are continuously changing, and are the prime underlying determinant of changes in both AD and BR.

In consequence changes in investment (ΔI) and AD (ΔAD) in the short run vary empirically positively and not inversely with changes in BR (ΔBR). AD varies pro-cyclically with swings in 'animal spirits' even when BR is unchanged. Figure 2.4 is not based on the real world, but is drawn under the highly restrictive assumption that BR is set at that particular rate which ensures that AD remains unchanged (5 per cent in Figure 2.2). Such a restrictive assumption must be imposed for AD to remain constant over the cycle, and to ensure ΔAD is negatively related *ceteris paribus* to the change in BR. But in laboratory experiments all other variables are held constant. In the real world shifts in 'animal spirits' cause the ΔAD relation to vary widely pro-cyclically over the cycle. The position, shape of and change in the AD band (ΔAD) are time–dependent in their response to changes in BR.

In Figure 2.5 the ΔAD relation shifts upward during expansions ($\Delta AD_E$) and downward during recessions ($\Delta AD_R$), as CBs vary BR pro-cyclically. Even when the interest elasticity of ΔAD is very substantial, as shown by the high interest elasticity of the ΔAD curve, this generally results in a positive relation between changes in ΔAD and changes in BR. Due to countercyclical monetary policy, the change in BR ($\Delta BR_t$)

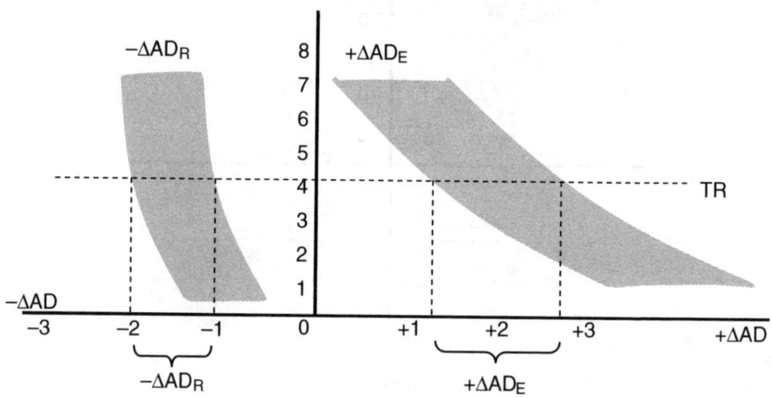


*Figure 2.5* Cyclical shifts in the BR–ΔAD relationship

can be regarded as an excellent proxy for the CB's expectations of a change in animal spirits. So an increase in BR signals the CB expects a future increase in inflation, output and aggregate demand. Changes in AD are therefore likely to be positively empirically correlated with changes in BR. ΔBR and ΔAD rise and fall together in expansions and recessions.

Figure 2.6 shows how ΔBR and ΔAD shift pro-cyclically over the cycle. During expansions when the ΔAD relationship is expanding (shifting right), CBs increase BR (+ΔBR). During contractions the ΔAD relationship is declining (shifting left), CBs reduce BR. The inverse effect of interest rate changes on AD are theoretically assumed to be substantial, as indicated by the high interest-elasticity of the $\Delta AD_E$ and the $\Delta AD_R$ relationships in Figure 2.6. But the observed empirical association of changes in BR with changes in AD is merely a reduction in the rate of expansion of $+\Delta AD_E$ during economic expansions and not an absolute decrease. Similarly during recessions reductions in BR reduce the rate of decline of $-\Delta AD_R$ but do not normally result in absolute increases in AD. Even when the interest elasticity of investment is extremely high, as shown by the large effects of ΔBR on the change in AD, it is usually dominated by the concurrent pro-cyclical shifts in the ΔAD relationship, due to accompanying shifts in 'animal spirits'.

The above analysis explains why it has proven so extremely difficult to generate significant negative coefficients on interest rates in invest-

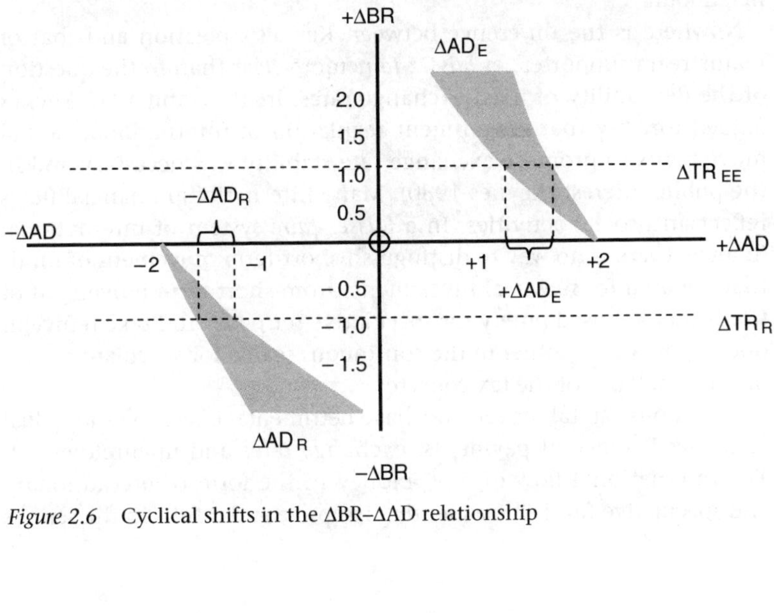


*Figure 2.6* Cyclical shifts in the ΔBR–ΔAD relationship

ment demand equations. The empirical relationship between changes in interest rates and changes in investment spending is predominantly positive, in both expansions and recessions. The central explanation is that the single most important causal variable in an uncertain world, changes in 'animal spirits', are non-measurable and so must be omitted from the model's formal analysis. Since the omitted variable is strongly positively related to ΔBR, this imparts a huge negative omitted variable bias to estimated interest rate coefficients.

## Keynes's insistence on the deflationary bias of flexible exchange regimes

Neoclassical theory underplays the necessity for CBs to continuously maintain system liquidity due to fundamental uncertainty about future events. This greatly impedes understanding of the core problems facing international finance: illiquidity, 'unstable' exchange rates and increasing debt obligations. Keynes developed his vision of how the existing international payments system creates a global deficiency of aggregate demand in greater length in his post-*General Theory* writings which are much less widely known. He emphasized that when governments lack the political will to stimulate domestic AD, due either to a self-imposed belief in the desirability of a 'free' market or a 'balanced' budget, or to the fear of missing self-imposed inflation 'targets', each country's international advantage can easily become at variance with that of its neighbours.[4]

Nowhere is the difference between Keynes's position and that of mainstream supporters of *laissez-faire* more clear than in the question of the desirability of fixed exchange rates. In 1941 and 1942 Keynes argued forcibly that government regulation of international capital movements to promote exchange rate stability was necessary and in the public interest (Keynes 1980). Many international financial flows reflect anti-social activities. In a *laissez-faire* system of international finance, there is no way to distinguish short-term movement of funds that are used for new real investments from short-term movement of funds that are used purely for speculative purposes and take refuge in one nation after another in the continuous search for speculative gains or the avoidance of the tax collector.

Exogenous capital movements have detrimental effects on individual countries balance of payments, exchange rates and unemployment. The international flow of 'hot' money in the form of precautionary and speculative funds is frequently disruptive and results in the serious impoverishment of nations whose current accounts would otherwise have been balanced:

> Loose funds... sweep round the world disorganizing all steady business. Nothing is more certain than that the movement of capital funds must be regulated. (...) There is no country which can in the future safely allow the flight of funds for political reasons, or to evade domestic taxation or in anticipation of the owner turning refugee. Equally, there is no country that can safely receive fugitive funds which cannot safely be used for fixed investments and might turn it into a deficiency country against its will and contrary to the real facts. (Keynes 1980: 87)

So long as countries trade with the rest of the world, they must avoid expansionary domestic policy that threatens external imbalance to protect their exchange rates. All countries that engage in international trade must maintain the expected future conversion rate of their currency close to the current values. When the exchange rate is expected to fall CBs must pay a risk premium to attract funds to compensate foreign portfolio holders of their securities for anticipated capital losses.

Since all currencies represent a store of wealth in asset portfolios all countries must be concerned about the current size of their foreign exchange reserves and the future value of their exchange rates. When a country's current foreign exchange outflows consistently exceed its foreign exchange receipts, under existing trade regimes it has few choices: It must either pay out foreign currency from its reserves, borrow foreign currency to cover its negative balance, let the exchange rate depreciate, or devalue its currency.

The world is a closed economy so total surpluses must equal total deficits. One country's surpluses imply an identical deficit for other countries. To combat cost inflation, CBs in all countries with balance of payments (BOP) deficits are forced to pursue restrictive policies and maintain interest rates at high levels. But in creditor countries with surpluses, CBs are not forced to pursue offsetting expansionary policies. They are free to permit their surpluses to accumulate forever. All pressure to adjust is then placed on the deficit countries, which are forced to pursue more restrictive policies. This asymmetry has been termed the 'Keynes Effect', and results in a strong restrictive bias to world AD.[5]

Creditors must bear the exchange rate risk that in the future the debtor country may find itself unable to service its total foreign borrowing, in which case creditors will be repaid at only some fraction of the face value. As a result many LDCs typically face very high borrowing costs, and find it extremely difficult to finance real capital imports in excess of their export proceeds. Their cyclical expansions are characteristically deflated by draconian monetary policy, designed to depress rapid AD growth, reduce their debt ratios, and the growth rate of their GDP.[6]

## The continuous trade-off between internal and external balance

The continuous conflict between internal and external balance is rendered much more transparent using process analysis. In Figure 2.7 the current level of AD and the BOP are taken as predetermined. The verti-

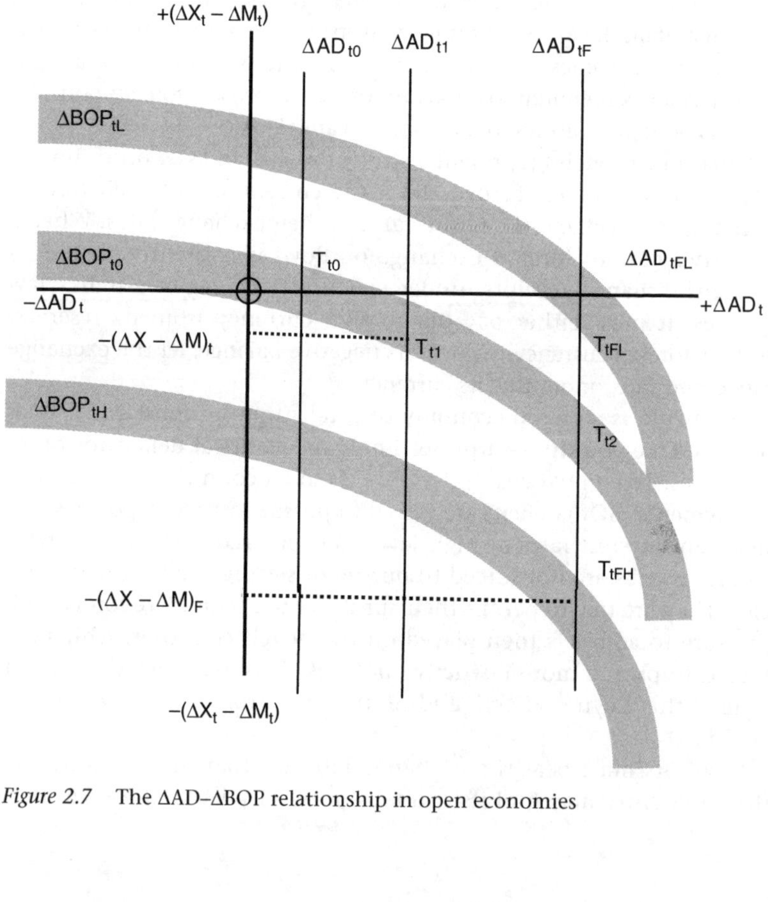


*Figure 2.7* The ΔAD–ΔBOP relationship in open economies

cal axis measures the positive or negative change in the BOP surplus or deficit ($\Delta X_t - \Delta M_t$), and the horizontal axis measures the positive or negative change in aggregate demand (+/– $\Delta AD_t$). Imports are positively related to changes in domestic AD, while exports are positively related to changes in foreign AD. The fractal band $\Delta BOP_{t0}$ slopes downward to illustrate the extent to which the BOP deteriorates when domestic AD and imports increase. Given the current exchange rate ($E_{t0}$) and current Bank Rate ($BR_{t0}$), an increase in domestic AD causes imports to increase, and worsens the balance of payments, as shown by the downward slope of the BOP relationships ($\Delta BOP_{t0}$). As the exchange rate is lowered this increases exports and reduces imports so the $\Delta BOP$ curve shifts upward from $\Delta BOP_{tH}$ to $\Delta BOP_{tL}$.

The BOP is in balance where exports are equal to imports and the $\Delta BOP_{t0}$ relationship intersects the horizontal axis ($T_{t0}$). The economy is held by tight monetary policy at $\Delta AD$ sufficiently below full capacity output so the value of imports equals the value of exports, and the current account is balanced. The current change in aggregate demand ($\Delta AD_{t0}$) is below the economy's potential capacity ($\Delta AD_{tF}$). The CB recognizes that lowering BR would increase employment and raise $\Delta AD_0$ towards $\Delta AD_F$. But the current account deficit would increase ($T_{t2}$), and the resulting outflow of foreign exchange would lower the level of reserves, reduce the exchange rate, and directly raise import prices and the inflation rate. In order to achieve its inflation target the CB decides to forego a more expansionary monetary policy, and acquiesces to higher levels of unemployment and excess capacity and a modest current account deficit ($T_{t1}$). As the exchange rate is reduced, this increases exports and reduces imports. In consequence AD increases, and the BOP curve shifts upward from $\Delta BOP_{tH}$ to $\Delta BOP_{tL}$.

In open economies operating under floating exchange rate regimes, where capital mobility is high, an increase or decrease in BR induces short-term capital inflows or outflows, depending upon the change in the interest rate differential with the centre economies. This causes the exchange rate to appreciate or depreciate, unless the rise in BR leads to a collapse in bond and equity prices and to overshoot or undershoot its expected value in the next period. These induced short-term capital flows continue over time in response to continually changing expectations about real holding-period returns across countries and periods, including anticipated capital gains and losses.

If the interest rate in the centre is taken as given, lower interest rates in the periphery reduce the interest rate differential of the country *vis-à-vis* the rate in the centre. These reduced differentials lead to capital outflows and cause the exchange rate to depreciate. By lowering the foreign price of exports and raising the domestic price of imports, exchange rate depreciation raises the domestic demand for exports and for import-competing domestic goods, and reduces the foreign import demand. A lower exchange rate shifts the $BOP_t$ relationship upwards, e.g. to $\Delta BOP_{tL.}$ This raises AD, increases the net BOP surplus, and makes possible a positive BOP at higher levels of domestic aggregate demand.

The increase in foreign demand for exports and increased domestic demand for import-competing goods induced by a depreciation of the exchange rate raise the interest-elasticity of AD above the level of closed economies, enabling the economy to reach full employment levels of AD ($\Delta AD_{tF}$) consistent with internal balance ($T_{tFL}$). Lower exchange rates raise the level of AD consistent with external balance (the intersection of the $\Delta BOP_{tL}$ relation with the horizontal axis), and the level of income consistent with internal balance (the intersection of $\Delta BOP_{tL}$ with $AD_F$). Lower exchange rates permit internal and external balance to be attained simultaneously ($T_{tFL}$).

In open economies one unintended effect of flexible exchange rate regimes is to enormously increase the influence of monetary policy on AD and the inflation rate. In closed economies higher interest rates (BR) raise the cost of borrowing, lower asset prices, and reduce AD. The ΔAD relation shifts downward depending on the interest-elasticity of AD. But in closed economies the 'core' inflation rate is largely determined by the extent to which the average rate of money wage growth exceeds the average rate of growth of labour productivity. In economies where unions have strong bargaining power in many industries, the average rate of money wage increase is relatively independent of the general unemployment rate.

In open economies an increase in BR induces short-term capital inflows, which cause the exchange rate to appreciate and overshoot its expected value in the next period, until real rates of return are equalized among different countries. Short-term capital inflows and outflows change continuously over time. In complex systems variables change continuously. As a result expected real rates of return on different assets (including capital gains and losses) are never equalized across all countries for all holding periods.

The appreciation of the exchange rate by raising the foreign price of exports and reducing the domestic price of imports reduces the demand for exports, increases the demand for imports, and causes the balance of payments to deteriorate. This raises the interest-elasticity of GDP and so increases the reduction in AD that accompanies any given rise in BR in closed economies. With a restrictive monetary policy higher interest rates increase the current account deficit at full employment ($AD_F$) and render it impossible for the CB to achieve internal balance and full employment.

Due to short-term capital inflows and outflows impacting on the value of the exchange rate, the effects of a change in BR on ΔAD are much greater in open economies. This permits CB's to more easily attain their inflation targets. But as will be shown, inflation targeting introduces an additional restrictive bias into the world trading economy.

## Inflation targeting

In closed economies a reduction in BR reduces borrowing costs, raises asset prices and expands aggregate demand depending on the interest-elasticity of AD (e.g. a moderate movement of AD to e.g. $T_{t1}$ in Figure 2.7). But in open economies lower levels of BR in addition induce capital outflows, which result in the depreciation of the exchange rate, and raise the domestic price of imports. The reduction in BR causes capital outflows, exchange rate depreciation, increases in the price of imports and temporary increases in the inflation rate, until the exchange rate stabilizes at a lower level, depending upon the openness of the economy. This causes a rise in the inflation rate due to the higher cost of imported goods that accompany exchange rate depreciation.

A fall in the exchange rate leads to a current but temporary increase in the inflation rate, providing all induced secondary cost and price increases are avoided. But even a temporary rise in the inflation rate makes it more difficult for CBs pursuing expansionary monetary policy to achieve their short-term inflation targets. In consequence, CBs are frequently reluctant to pursue more expansionary monetary policy because they anticipate they will breach their inflation target, irrespective of the existing degree of unemployment and excess capacity.

In open economies only the centre country in whose currency all trade takes place can permit negative current account positions to continue indefinitely. All other countries must accept the external balance discipline and restrict AD to maintain the current value of the exchange rate. Apart from the centre all countries not enjoying the luxury of current account surpluses must pursue restrictive policies and generate a substantial output gap to keep domestic AD well below full capacity, so as to prevent their external balance from deteriorating. Restrictive policy usually takes the form of higher interest rates, but it may include higher taxes, restriction of government spending and the imposition of tariffs and quotas on imports. The alternative is to allow the exchange rate to depreciate in floating exchange rate regimes or to permit the exchange rate to fall in fixed exchange rate regimes.

In flexible exchange rate systems creditors often find it difficult to distinguish whether BOP deficits indicate the exchange rate is overvalued and so is more likely to fall in the future, whether the CB is keeping interest rates high to reduce future inflation and so the exchange rate may rise further in the future, or whether the deficits are due to investors borrowing to deficit-finance attractive investment projects. Their expectations of high future rates of return may or may not be justified ex post.

The general response to a worsening of a current account deficit is for central banks (CB) to raise the level of BR to attract additional net short-term funds and increase the existing exchange rate. Higher exchange rates depress the level of domestic AD by decreasing both foreign demand for exports and domestic demand for import-competing goods. By reducing the price of imports exchange rate appreciation directly reduces the inflation rate, and so enables CBs to more easily attain their inflation targets.

But in open economies more restrictive monetary policy, although it temporarily reduces the inflation rate, conflicts fundamentally with the goals of internal balance: higher employment and more rapid output growth. Countries persistently running large BOP deficits frequently have no choice but are forced to restrict domestic demand and reduce their demand for imports to protect their exchange rates.

Developing countries (DCs) are generally more heavily dependent on imported capital goods than mature economies. As the growth rate rises, some agents desire to undertake additional capital formation financed by new debt issue in response to higher expected returns on investment projects. For many DCs the marginal propensity to import borrowed capital goods rises above unity when the economy is in the boom phase of the cycle.[7] Creditors must bear the exchange rate risk that the country in the future may find itself unable to service all its foreign borrowing. In consequence most DCs typically face high borrowing costs, and find it difficult to finance capital imports greatly in excess of their export proceeds.[8] Their cyclical expansions are typically deflated by more deflationary monetary policies designed to depress their demand for capital imports and reduce their debt ratios. This in turn further depresses the rate of growth of GDP and increases unemployment.[9]

## Conclusion

When the CB has elevated the attainment of its inflation target to the central criterion of the success of its time on watch, the introduction of inflation targeting in effect prevents the CB from ever pursuing expansionary policies, even when they may be clearly appropriate. Under cost inflation reducing BR greatly increases the probability that the CB will temporarily overshoot its inflation targets. Therefore, inflation targeting induces CBs to pursue more restrictive policies. Inflation targeting obscures the central truth that in most developing economies inflation is cost inflation due primarily to money wage increases in the formal sector exceeding average labour productivity growth. It leads to inflation being regarded as caused by excess AD, rather than as cost inflation caused by excessive money wage increases. Inflation targeting leads to a bias in favour of high interest rates, depressing the level of real income, asset values, employment growth and the rate of growth of real GDP, and making it less possible for the economy to achieve internal balance, full employment and rapid growth.

## Notes

1. By focusing on the final state-change in all variables, equilibrium analysis ignores all events that occur during the transition process but disappear after change ceases (Stock and Watson 2003).
2. In complex real world economies there is no 'equilibrium' level of income, 'natural' rate of unemployment, 'normal' rate of interest, or 'warranted' rate of growth of output that are determined solely by real variables. Monetary change is non-neutral in its effects on both nominal and real output (Moore 2006).
3. The various theoretical reasons why changes in aggregate demand ($\Delta$AD) are inversely related to changes in Bank Rate are outlined in detail in Moore (2006).
4. Keynes's analysis makes clear how the huge current account deficits of the US throughout the 1990s have provided a critically important direct stimulus to AD for the rest of the world. The huge US deficits have provided an expansionary bias, and prevented the world from falling into deeper and more widespread unemployment. Conversely China's current account surplus exerts a restrictive effect, by imposing current account deficits on the rest of the world, who must then pursue restrictive policies to protect their exchange rates.
5. In 1941 Keynes proposed an International Clearing Union (ICU), designed to encourage both deficit and surplus countries to reduce their balance of payment imbalances by appropriate expansionary and restrictive policies. This was to be effectuated by the ICU imposing a tax on the net surplus balance *and* on the net deficit balance of both deficit and surplus countries. In spite of his eloquence, he was unable to persuade the largest creditor

country, in 1946 the US, that it should now pay a new tax on the net surplus amount in its BOP (Keynes 1980). See also Keynes (1936).

6. The import of capital goods results in an increase in domestic capital formation, and so actually constitutes an increase rather than a decrease in national saving (Moore 2006).
7. In South Africa the marginal propensity to import has typically exceeded 100 per cent during boom periods. This suggests one explanation why in a country like South Africa, with unemployment rates estimated at between 30 and 40 per cent, the CB keeps short-term interest rates at double-digit levels. Such interest rates would be unthinkable in any developed economies, if their unemployment had reached double-digit levels.
8. The importation of capital goods actually results in an increase in domestic capital formation and saving. Proper capital accounting would record this as an increase and not a decrease in national saving (Moore 2006).
9. In South Africa short-term rates are currently about 10 per cent. The Reserve Bank is unwilling to reduce BR because it believes this might jeopardize its commitment to keep the inflation rate within its 3–6 per cent target, in spite of unemployment and underemployment rates of 30–50 per cent.

## References

Blinder, R., Canetti, E., and Labour, D. (1998) *Asking about Prices: A New Approach to Understanding Price Stickiness* (New York: Russell Sage).

Goodhart, C. and Demas, A. (1990) *Reuters Screen Images of the Foreign Exchange Market: the Deutschmark/Dollar Spot Rate*, Financial Markets Group Discussion Papers No. 196, August 1990.

Keynes, J.M. (1936) *The General Theory of Employment, Interest and Money* (London: Macmillan).

Keynes, J.M. (1980) *The Collected Works of J.M. Keynes, XXV Activities 1940–1944: Shaping The Post War World* (London: Macmillan).

Moore, B. (1988) *Verticalists and Horizontalists: The Macroeconomics of Endogenous Money* (London: Cambridge University Press).

Moore, B. (2006) *Shaking the Invisible Hand: Complexity, Endogenous Money and Exogenous Interest Rates* (London and New York: Palgrave Macmillan).

Stock, J. and Watson, M. (2003) 'Forecasting Output and Inflation: The Role of Asset Prices', *Journal of Economic Literature*, 41 (3): 788–829.

Taylor, J. (1993) 'Discretion versus Policy Rules in Practice', *Carnegie Rochester Series on Public Policy*, 39: 195–214.

Walsh, C. (2003) *Monetary Theory and Policy* (Cambridge, MA: MIT Press).

Woodford, M. (2003) *Interest and Prices: Foundations of the Theory of Monetary Policy* (Princeton: Princeton University Press).

# 3
# What is Endogenous when Monetary Policy is Transparent?

*Peter Howells*

## Introduction

In the conventional Post Keynesian account of money supply determination (and the conduct of monetary policy), it is the rate of interest set by the central bank that is exogenously determined while the quantity of money is determined by the demand for bank loans, which in turn is dependent on the 'state of trade'. Over the years, this simple statement of what Fontana calls 'one of the main cornerstones of Post Keynesian economics' (Fontana 2003: 291) has generated a certain amount of debate and subsequent refinement. Controversial issues have included (i) the role of the demand *for money*; (ii) the precise range of expenditures bearing upon the demand for credit; (iii) the importance of banks' liquidity preference; and (iv) the extent to which central banks themselves contribute to endogeneity by passively supplying reserves. Palley's recent comment that 'For the last decade, the post-Keynesian approach to endogenous money has become bogged down in a debate between what have been called the 'accommodationist' and 'structuralist' approaches' (Palley 2002: 152) is a reference to (iii) and (iv).

Nonetheless, throughout the debate, the convenient shorthand that the interest rate is exogenous while the quantity of money is (in some sense) demand-determined has persisted more or less untouched. And it is easy to see why since it offers a complete reversal of the neoclassical orthodoxy and enables us to draw a strong and simple contrast. It allows us to borrow the familiar interest-money space of the money-market equilibrium diagram and turn the vertical money supply curve through ninety degrees. This was the image that Basil Moore used nearly twenty years ago in the title of his seminal work, *Horizontalists and Verticalists* (1988).

The problems with this simple contrast are now well-known:

- If we are using interest-money space then the interest rate on the vertical axis is the bond rate or (more realistically these days) a spread term. Whatever it is, it must be the opportunity cost of money, while the rate that the central bank is setting ('exogenously') is the cost of borrowed reserves.
- Again, if we are borrowing the neoclassical framework, then any suggestion that the money supply is perfectly elastic at the going rate of interest should be shown as the locus of intersections between rightward-shifting demand and (vertical) supply curves. It is not a 'horizontal money supply' curve in the conventional sense of the term.
- If some part of money's endogeneity is due to banks being able to economize on reserves (the so-called 'structuralist' argument) then the incentive to innovate must be a rise in the rate of interest and in these circumstances the 'supply' curve would have an upward slope.
- There is the question of how the flow of new deposits created by the demand for *credit* is reconciled with the community's demand for *money*. If, as seems likely, relative interest rates are involved, then it is difficult to know, *a priori*, what the money 'supply' curve should look like so long as we have the bond rate (or similar) on the vertical axis.

These, and other problems, are discussed at some length in Fontana (2003) as part of a justification for an altogether more sophisticated graphical representation.[1] The point we wish to make here, however, is that while there remain a number of controversies surrounding the endogeneity of money, there is widespread agreement that the *exogenous* variable is the rate of interest set by the central bank.

> The exogenous variable for the entire process of money creation is the price of credit, which is, through the intermediation of banks, under the control of the central bank (Fontana 2003: 296).[2]

However, it is now four years since Charles Goodhart warned against this practice.[3]

> An exogenous variable is one which is not set in response to other past or current developments in the economy, e.g. it is fixed at some level irrespective of other developments, or is varied randomly according to the throw of a dice or the occurrence of sunspots, or whatever. It would be extraordinarily rare, and stupid, for economic

> policy to be set in such an 'exogenous' way. Instead, virtually all economic policy is set in most part in response to other current, or past, or expected future economic developments. The question then is whether the regular feedback relationships involved in such reaction functions are appropriate. (Goodhart 2002: 20)

Properly described, the official rate of interest is a 'policy-determined' variable. It occupies a sort of half-way house: not quite endogenous since it requires the agency (and discretion) of the central bank for its determination; not quite exogenous, since the chosen rate will certainly *reflect* current and anticipated economic conditions.

In the rest of this chapter, we suggest that recent trends in monetary policy making have shifted this 'policy-determined' variable towards the endogenous end of the spectrum, and, indeed, could, if they were taken to extremes, fully endogenize the interest rate. The driving force behind this trend is the current desire, on the part of many central banks, to void interest rate changes of all surprise by making policy fully 'transparent'. The ultimate way to do this is to publish an interest-setting rule, in which the official rate of interest would be fully and openly determined by the state of the economy. In such a world, it is the inflation target that is better described as exogenous. Just how close we might be to this situation is something that we discuss in the third section. But before we can debate it in detail, we need to review the recent trend toward transparency in policy making. In doing so, we shall see that there are several meanings of transparency, each with a distinct method of measurement. Only one of these *necessarily* leads us to think of a mechanical policy rule with the consequent endogenizing of the interest rate. This is the subject of the next section.

## The quest for transparency in monetary policy making

Since the Bank of England adopted a policy of explicit inflation targeting in 1992, there has emerged a remarkably rapid consensus that 'transparency' in the conduct of monetary policy improves policy outcomes. The clearest illustrations of this (from many that we could select) are firstly the debate between Otmar Issing (1999) and Willem Buiter (1999) over the institutional arrangements at (the then new) ECB. While there was a lively disagreement between them about how 'open' ECB policy making could be, given the procedures laid down, there was no disagreement whatsoever that openness was 'a good thing'.[4] The fact that its own transparency has become an issue at the Federal Reserve in the last few years (Greenspan 2001) is yet another illustration that central banks feel very sensitive on this issue.[5]

But 'transparency' can mean a number of things even when applied specifically to monetary policy making. Eijffinger and Geraats (2002), for example, produced a comprehensive index (for nine central banks) of central bank transparency applied to the *political, economic, procedural, policy* and *operational* aspects of central banking. On this, let us call it 'comprehensive', view of transparency the more information that a central bank is prepared to release, the more transparent it is likely to be since the additional information is almost bound to reveal something useful about one or other of these many aspects of central banking.

Implicit in this view of transparency is an approach to its measurement which is very reminiscent of the central bank independence literature of some 15 years ago. It involves listing a variety of characteristics (relating to institutional structure, procedures etc.) which *a priori* one would expect to add to the useful information about a central bank's behaviour, attaching a score (or range of scores) to each characteristic and then summing the score achieved by each central bank. Table 3.1 summarizes the results of a number of such studies.

Apart from the fact that the different studies involved widely differing numbers of central banks, the most remarkable feature of the

*Table 3.1* Central bank transparency – rankings by study of characteristics

| | Fry *et al.* (2000) | Eijffinger and Geraats (2002) | De Haan and Amtenbrink (2002) | Bini-Smaghi and Gros (2000) |
|---|---|---|---|---|
| Australia | 15= | 7= | — | — |
| Canada | 13= | 4 | 3 | — |
| D Bundesbank | 25= | — | 6 | 5 |
| Euro zone | — | 5= | 4 | 2 |
| France | 40= | — | — | — |
| Italy | 12 | — | — | — |
| Japan | 5 | 7= | — | — |
| New Zealand | 4 | 1 | 1 | 4 |
| Sweden | 1= | 3 | — | — |
| Switzerland | 8= | 9 | — | — |
| UK | 3 | 2 | 2 | 1 |
| US | 1= | 5= | 5 | 3 |

*Note*: '=' indicates the ranking was shared with another central bank.

results is that the (old) Bundesbank scores low in every study. We have already remarked on its high reputation as a central bank and these results introduce our next point, namely, that just collecting evidence of 'openness' may not tell us anything very useful about the critical aspects of policy making.

When pressed on their interest in making policy more transparent, central banks themselves have a very clear view about what matters. They are interested in its ability to help private sector agents understand the model of the economy with which the policy-makers are operating. This has two benefits. Firstly, it helps anchor the public's expectations about future policy moves (Bean 1998: 1796). This is important because the transmission mechanism often involves medium- or long-term interest rates, while the policy instrument is invariably a very short-term rate. What links the two is often said to be 'expectations' and from this it is argued that agents' expectations are more likely to be correct if they fully understand the thinking behind the authorities' actions (Blinder *et al.* 2001; De Haan and Amtenbrink 2002; Woodford 2001; Freedman 2002).

Secondly, if agents understand the model with which the bank is working, it is less likely that interest rate changes will come as a 'shock' to market agents. In the words of the (now) Governor of the Bank of England:

> A transparent monetary policy implies that announcements of changes in interest rates by the MPC might come as rather little surprise. The news would not be in the outcome of the meetings of the MPC, but in the economic statistics published during the month. Markets would be able to *anticipate* the likely reaction of the MPC and the decisions of the MPC would follow a *predictable policy reaction function* ... transparency should lead to policy being predictable. It is all part of the view that a central bank should be boring. (King 1997: 440, emphasis added)

As a measure of transparency understood in this 'anticipation' sense, the characteristics approach is unhelpful. Firstly, it lacks a firm theoretical basis for linking the institutional reforms to an increased understanding of central bank decision making. We are left with the feeling that, for example, publishing the minutes of meetings (a highly-rated characteristic in most indices of transparency) *must* add to agents' ability to understand central bank decisions (and *fuller* minutes must therefore help toward a *fuller* understanding...) simply because they reveal more information. Thus, on this view, the Bank of England *must have* become progressively more transparent after 1992, simply because of its successive reforms. For example, the first quantified target was announced in October 1992;[6] the first *Inflation Report* published in February 1993; the minutes of Chancellor–Governor meetings were published beginning in May 1994; the minutes (of the MPC meetings) were enhanced after June 1997 by being fuller and adding an Appendix commenting on recent economic data, etc.

But the question is not whether more (and/or better) information is available. The question is what steps, taken by the monetary authorities, *help people to anticipate the central bank's next move*. While more information may always be useful to someone, it may be that for the purpose of anticipating interest rate changes, additional information is simply unnecessary beyond a certain point. It has always been Thornton's contention, for example, that agents need very little information in order to understand policy decisions, provided that the central bank behaves in a consistent fashion (Thornton 2003). We have already remarked (footnote 4) that secrecy did not prevent the Bundesbank from building up an impressive record of policy making.

The extent to which policy making is transparent, in the specific sense that agents can anticipate changes in the official rate, is much better judged by looking at the behaviour of money market interest rates close, in time, to changes in the official rate. This approach has spawned a substantial literature.[7]

These studies are, in effect, bringing together two sets of ideas each of which independently goes back some way.[8] On the one hand there is the theoretical argument that secrecy in policy making influences the volatility of asset prices. Goodfriend (1986) and Dotsey (1987), for example, showed that secrecy in policy making lowered the unconditional volatility of interest rates. However, lowering the *unconditional* variance of asset prices implies *raising* the conditional variance. Secrecy reduces the feasible information set of agents; it makes the authorities' reaction function less transparent. As a result, secrecy induces larger and more frequent forecasting errors. In the case of monetary policy, for 'asset prices' read 'interest rates'. The other, more voluminous, literature concerns the link between official rates (or other monetary policy announcements) and market rates. Included here is the work of Shiller, Campbell and Shoenholtz (1983), Hardouvelis (1984) for monetary policy news in general; and Cook and Hahn (1989), Radecki and Reinhart (1994), Dale (1993), Hardy (1996) for interest rates.

For the USA, Kuttner (2001) and Poole, Rasche and Thornton (2002) have all documented the ability of money markets to anticipate monetary policy changes, the latter showing that anticipation has improved since the Federal Reserve began announcing its target for the Federal Funds rate in 1994. One of the earliest market-based studies of transparency was undertaken by Daniel Hardy for the IMF in 1998. Interestingly in the present context, this showed that German money markets had little difficulty in anticipating Bundesbank interest rate decisions in spite of the Bank's aloofness. Again for the IMF, Ross (2002) looked at the performance of the ECB after three years of operation and compared it with the Federal Reserve and the Bank of England. He found that 'all three central banks are relatively predictable institutions', suggesting that the long list of reforms at the Bank of England, summarized above, have given it little advantage.

For the UK two papers, by Chadha and Nolan (2001) and Caporale and Cipollini (2001), approach the question of transparency through the volatility of market rates. The former tested for a direct relationship between interest rate volatility in the UK and transparency measured by (i) the publication of minutes of the MPC meetings, (ii) the effects of announcements on the interest rate decisions of the MPC and (iii) the publication of the *Inflation Report*. None of these factors seemed to affect volatility significantly. They also experimented with dummy variables accounting for days on and before announcement day and found mixed significant effects from these dummies on volatility over selected periods in the UK. They conclude that their results are 'simply picking up the fact that markets are continually adapting to new information' (Chadha and Nolan 2001: 20). Caporale and Cipollini (2001) found that in Euroland and the US volatility is higher before the change in policy rate than after the decision, which may indicate that agents adjust to information before the policy change relatively more than after the change.

Yet another paper, by Haldane and Read (2000), looked at the effect of monetary policy 'surprises' on the yield curve in a number of countries. For the UK they found that the effects of policy news on the short end of the yield curve have diminished since the introduction of inflation targeting (though they remain high by comparison with the US and with Germany). This, they put down to the increasing transparency of policy. Since their dataset covers the period from 1984 to 1997, the increase in transparency to which they ascribe the reduction in surprises must be largely the result of the switch to inflation targeting and the publication of chancellor–governor minutes thereafter. It tells us nothing, of course, about the reforms associated with and following Bank of England independence.

Such attempts as there have been to assess the effect on money market anticipations of the later (after 1997) reforms at the Bank of England, have not generally had a very positive view. Wadwhani (2001) and Bell (2005) both notice an *increase* in the level of money-market surprises following on the move to operational independence, but are both optimistic that the reduction in surprises will be resumed once markets have had time to learn how the MPC 'works'. Lasaosa (2005) finds no signs of the learning as yet and Biefang-Frisancho and Howells (2006), updating the Haldane/Read study confirm the positive impact of the switch to inflation targeting but little effect from any subsequent innovations.

Taken together, then, we can say that tests of transparency based on the behaviour of money market professionals are fairly consistent in finding quite a high level of transparency in the policy decisions of major central banks. Clearly, and importantly from our point of view, agents are moderately successful at inferring the next movement in interest rates from current macro data. Of some additional interest is the doubt these studies cast on the importance of recent reforms aimed explicitly at increasing transparency. There is no evidence that agents found the mind of the Bundesbank difficult to read and not much evidence that the Bank of England's decisions have become easier to anticipate as a result of any innovations subsequent to the adoption of an explicit inflation target.

## Anticipating interest rate changes

While the studies in the second section tend to confirm that agents *do* anticipate official interest rate changes quite well, they do not tell us *how* they do it. In this section we consider some possibilities.

The simplest way to ensure that agents can make consistently accurate forecasts of central bank decisions is for the central bank to explicate its reaction function. In present circumstances, the obvious way to do this would be to adopt an explicit rule linking the official rate to those macro variables which the central bank believes to be most relevant to achieving its objective. Where the latter is, for most central banks now, an inflation target, the former would be a Taylor (or 'Taylor-type') Rule, as follows:

$$i_t = \pi_{t-1} + \theta_1 (\pi - \pi^*)_{t-1} + \theta_2 \left(\frac{(y - y^*)}{y^*}\right)_{t-1} + (i_t - \pi_t)^* \qquad (3.1)$$

where $i_t$ is the official rate set by the central bank, $\pi_{t-1}$ is the inflation rate in the previous period, $(\pi - \pi^*)_{t-1}$ is the deviation of inflation rom its target rate in the previous period, $\left(\frac{(y - y^*)}{y^*}\right)_{t-1}$ represents the deviation of output from its natural rate and $(i_t - \pi_t)^*$ is the target real rate of interest. $\theta_1$ and $\theta_2$ are constants and were set by Taylor (1993) at 0.5. The interpretation is that, in an ideal world, the official rate would be set at a level consistent with the inflation target and 'natural' rate of output growth. To maintain this real rate, the nominal rate must be adjusted by adding the current rate of inflation. Further adjustments are then made as follows. If the current rate of inflation is above the target rate, then the nominal rate should be increased by 50 basis points for every 1 per cent of the deviation. The effect is to raise the real interest rate above its long-run 'neutral' level. At the same time, a similar adjustment (50 basis points per unit) is made in respective of the extent to which actual output differs from potential. This imparts a forward-looking character to the rule in so far as *current* demand pressure is thought to have some bearing on the future inflation rate.

'Taylor-type' rules are similar in that inflation and the output gap (or some other measure of demand pressure) are the key variables in the reaction function, but the coefficients and/or the lags differ from those in Taylor's original specification.[9] One obvious modification is to replace the first term on the right-hand side by a forecast of the future path of inflation (giving rise to Svensson's (1997) observation that 'inflation targeting' is better described in practice as 'inflation forecast targeting').

No central bank admits to setting interest rates in this way. *If* it did, then a central bank would have no need of a committee and no need of a meeting (with minutes, voting records, etc.) in order to take a decision. (Though it would not prevent a committee *appearing* to be making a discretionary decision while in practice, and covertly, using a rule.) In Svensson's memorable words:

> Thus, if a central bank wants to commit itself to a simple instrument rule, it should announce the simple instrument rule and then mechanically follow it. This has the further implication that once the decision about the instrument rule is made, the decision process of the bank is exceedingly simple and mechanical. For the Taylor rule, it just consists of regularly collecting data on inflation and output, collecting either external estimates of potential output or constructing internal estimates, and then calculating the output

> gap. (Estimating potential output is a nontrivial matter, though, and a major challenge in practical monetary policy.) Once these inputs in the Taylor rule are available, calculating the instrument-setting is completely mechanical. In particular, there is no room for judgment (except that judgment may enter in the estimation of potential output). As McCallum (2000) has expressed it, policy decisions could be turned over to 'a clerk armed with a simple formula and a hand calculator'. (Svensson 2003: 3)

The most convincing evidence that no central bank has yet gone quite this far, comes from the market-based studies that we discussed in the second section which show that while anticipation may be quite good, it is far from perfect – as it would be if the rate of interest followed such a rule mechanically.

However, while the central bank may not explicitly follow such a rule, its exercise of discretion may still lead to results which are very similar to those that would follow from such a rule and money market agents may find it efficient to behave *as if* the central bank were following such a rule. In these circumstances, one might argue that the interest rate has effectively become endogenous.

There is now an extensive literature on the extent to which the Taylor Rule describes the conduct of monetary policy by central banks in recent years; so extensive that we can only pick out some highlights. For the USA, for example, Clarida, Galì and Gertler (1998) and Judd and Rudebusch (1998), have found that variants of Taylor-type rules fit the data reasonably well, once we allow for the Fed's policy of 'interest rate smoothing' (making a series of small adjustments when the rule might suggest a single larger one). Judd and Rudebusch's (1998) study interestingly divides the data for 1970 to 1997 into three periods corresponding to the leadership of the Federal Reserve by, in turn, Burns, Volcker and Greenspan. The rule fits the data quite well in the Greenspan era while under Burns it tends to overpredict and under Volcker to underpredict. Carlstrom and Fuerst (2003) bring the data up to 2003. This reveals that official rates were above those dictated by the rule from 1995 to 1999 but that the close fit was subsequently re-established.

For the UK (1972–97), Nelson (2000) finds that the rule fits the data quite well since the switch to inflation targeting in 1992. For the 1970s, the estimated long-run response of the nominal interest rate to inflation was well below unity. Moreover, the real interest rate was permitted to be negative for most of this period. In the 1980s, control of inflation was more successful and the estimates suggest a tighter monetary policy. This tightening was manifested in an increase in the average prevailing level of real interest rates, though the estimated response to the domestic inflation rate was lower than a Taylor Rule would require. Indeed, the estimates in the paper suggest that the long-run response of nominal interest rates to inflation remained below unity until the period of inflation targeting, 1992–97. For this most recent period, the long-run estimated responses of the UK nominal interest rate to inflation and the output gap are remarkably close to the values of 1.5 and 0.5 respectively, found by Taylor (1993) to be a good description of recent US monetary policy.

Clarida, Galí, and Gertler (1997) looked at the record of the Bundesbank from 1970 to 1996 and found that its interest rate decisions were 'encompassed' by the parameters in the original Taylor Rule. It typically pushed up nominal short-term interest rates by about 130 to 160 basis points (and thus the real rate by some 30 to 60 basis points) for every 1 percentage point rise in expected inflation one year ahead, holding the output gap constant, and that it reduced the nominal (and real) short rate by about 25 to 50 basis points for every 1 percentage point shortfall in output relative to potential, holding expected inflation constant. There are significant differences, however, between the rules based on Bundesbank behaviour and the original Taylor Rule with respect to the equilibrium real interest rate which appeared to vary between 3.25 and 3.75 per cent – while in the original Taylor Rule the neutral rate was assumed to be 2 percent.

In a 1999 paper for the Bank for International Settlements, Gerlach and Schnabel showed that a conventional Taylor Rule captured the behaviour of average interest rates in the EMU area in the 1990–1997 period, with the exception of the period of exchange market turbulence in 1992–93, extremely well. Inevitably, this gives us very little guide as to what may have happened after the major discontinuity represented by the formation of EMU and the passing of responsibility for policy to the ECB. As regards the ECB, the jury is out.

An early study, by Sauer and Sturm (2003), suggested that the ECB was insufficiently active (compared with the prescriptions in the Taylor Rule). It was accommodating changes in inflation and hence was in danger of following a destabilizing policy. They did, however, caution against drawing conclusions from such a short-term study, especially since the data contained few periods in which the actual rate of inflation was very far away from the target allowing us few opportunities to judge the ECB's true level of commitment.

The study of policy in the EU by Gerlach-Kristen (2003) is interesting in that it estimates interest rate reaction functions under the hypothesis that interest rates, inflation and the output gap have a unit root. Hence its use of a cointegration approach to capture the movements of short-term nominal rates. The cointegrating vector links the nominal short interest rate to inflation, the output gap and the long interest rate. The main finding is that interest rate reaction functions estimated using the cointegration approach are, in contrast to traditional Taylor Rules, stable in sample and forecast better out of sample. However, the model was estimated on quarterly data from 1988 to 2002 which means that the results are an imperfect basis for drawing conclusions about the conduct of policy since monetary union in 1999.

## Conclusion

On the evidence in the previous section, we have some way to go before we can say that the official interest rate is mechanically determined by a limited number of variables within the economic system – which would be necessary if we were to describe the interest rate, literally, as endogenously determined. Inflation and output (in the form of an output gap) may be the main influences on the rate, but the setting of the rate requires an agency role for the central bank.

> Mechanical policy rules are not credible... No rule could be written down that describes how policy would be set in all possible outcomes. Some discretion is inevitable. But that discretion must be constrained by a clear objective to which policy is directed... (King 1999: 13)

That said, the evidence does suggest a very strong sense of uniformity and consensus amongst central banks that making it clear that inflation is the first priority and then setting the nominal rate at least *with regard to* the current path of inflation and the pressure of aggregate demand, produces better monetary policy outcomes than was generally the case in the past. Inevitably, given this consensus, agents have a fighting chance of anticipating correctly the next most likely policy move in any given set of circumstances.

And the evidence in the second section suggests that they do that really quite well. Thornton (2003) has always argued that what makes a central bank transparent (and credible too) is consistent behaviour. The record of the Bundesbank, referred to several times in this chapter, lends some support to that, as indeed does the evidence in the second section that many of the changes in operating procedures towards 'openness' have had little effect. No doubt, if central banks continue to operate consistently within the framework that they have adopted in the last few years, agents' anticipation will improve further and they will act even more *as if* the interest rate were endogenous. In the meantime, what we need is another term for the interest rate: not quite endogenous, but more so than Goodhart's 'policy-determined variable' suggests.

## Notes

1. It is worth stressing in the present context that while much of the success of Fontana's approach in handling a number of controversial issues surrounding the endogeneity of money is undoubtedly down to its increased complexity (*inter alia,* four quadrants, stepped supply curves), its coherence stems from abandoning the preoccupation with interest-*money* space and being written explicitly in *flow* terms.
2. See also Moore (1988: 258; 1989: 66; 2003: 120).
3. In print, that is. He had been counselling against it in conferences and seminars for much longer.
4. It is interesting that the ECB should be so sensitive about its transparency credentials when it was modelled so explicitly on the Deutsche Bundesbank which was one of the world's most secretive central banks. The fact that the Bundesbank was also one of the most successful of central banks (at least in its maintenance of price stability) should give pause for thought to those who embrace transparency so enthusiastically as a necessary condition for successful monetary policy.
5. See also the survey referred to in Geraats (2002) in which 74 per cent of central banks said that transparency was an important aspect of their operations.
6. See Bowen (1995) for a discussion of the thinking behind the switch to inflation targeting and the institutional changes which accompanied it.
7. Money-market rates are chosen from a very wide range of alternatives on the grounds (i) that they are very closely connected to movements in the official rate and (ii) one would expect money market agents to be particularly well-informed about likely interest rate movements given the very large funds for which they are responsible and the scale of profit/loss associated with the correct/erroneous anticipation.
8. One might argue for three sets of literature. Looking for signs that markets anticipate official announcements is very reminiscent of the 'event study' approach to testing the semi-strong form of the efficient market hypothesis. The market is semi-strong form efficient if the news (of earnings, takeover bid etc.) is in the price by the time of its official announcement.
9. For further discussion of variations on Taylor's original specification, see Kozicki (1999) and Svensson (2003).

## References

Bean, C. (1998) 'The New UK Monetary Arrangements: A View from the Literature', *Economic Journal*, 108 (451): 1795–809.

Bell, J. (2005) 'Monetary Policy News and Market Reaction to the *Inflation Report* and MPC *Minutes*', *Bank of England Quarterly Bulletin*, 45(3): 169–78.

Biefang-Frisancho Mariscal, I. and Howells, P.G.A. (2006) 'Monetary Policy Transparency: Too Good to be True?', *Oxford Economic Papers*, forthcoming.

Bini-Smaghi, L. and Gros, D. (2000) *Open Issues in European Central Banking* (London: Macmillan).

Blinder, A.S., Goodhart, C.A.E., Hildebrand, P., Lipton, D. and Wyplosz, C. (2001) *How do Central Banks Talk?* (Geneva: International Center for Monetary and Banking Studies).

Bowen, A. (1995) 'Inflation Targetry in the United Kingdom', in A. Haldane (ed.), *Targeting Inflation* (London: Bank of England).

Buiter, W. H. (1999) 'Alice in Euroland', *Journal of Common Market Studies*, 37(2): 181–209.

Caporale, M.C and Cipollini, A. (2001) 'The Euro and Monetary Transparency', Discussion Paper, South Bank University.

Carlstrom, C.T. and Fuerst, T.S. (2003) 'The Taylor Rule: A Guidepost for Monetary Policy?', Federal Reserve Bank of Cleveland, *Economic Commentary*, July: 1–4.

Chadha, J. and Nolan, C. (2001) 'Inflation Targeting, Transparency and Interest Rate Volatility: Ditching "Monetary Mystique" in the UK', *Journal of Macroeconomics*, 23 (3): 349–66.

Clarida R., Galì, J., and Gertler, M. (1997) *Has the Bundesbank Followed a Taylor Rule? A New Test and Some Implications*, IMF Seminar Series 1997–10A.

Clarida, R., Galì, J. and Gertler, M. (1998) 'Monetary Policy Rules in Practice: Some International Evidence,' *European Economic Review*, 42: 1033–68.

Cook, T. and Hahn, T. (1989) 'The Effect of Changes in the Federal Funds Rate Target on Market Interest Rates in the 1970s', *Journal of Monetary Economics*, 24: 331–51.

Dale, S. (1993) 'The Effect of Changes in Official UK Rates on Market Interest Rates since 1987', *The Manchester School*, 61: 76–94.

De Haan, J. and Amtenbrink, F. (2002) *A Non-transparent European Central Bank? Who is to Blame?*, Paper given at the conference on Monetary Policy Transparency, held at the Bank of England, 10 May.

Dotsey, M. (1987) 'Monetary Policy, Secrecy and Federal Funds Rate Behaviour', *Journal of Monetary Economics*, 20: 463–74.

Eijffinger, S.C.W. and Geraats, P.M. (2002) 'How Transparent are Central Banks?', CEPR Discussion Paper No. DP3188.

Fontana, G. (2003) 'Post Keynesian approaches to endogenous money: A time framework explanation', *Review of Political Economy*, 15 (3): 291–314.

Freedman, C. (2002) 'The Value of Transparency in Conducting Monetary Policy', *Federal Reserve Bank of St Louis Review*, July/August: 155–9.

Fry, M., Julius, D., Mahadeva, L., Roger, S. and Sterne, G. (2000) 'Key Issues in the Choice of Monetary Policy Framework', in L. Mahadeva and G. Sterne (eds), *Monetary Policy Frameworks in a Global Context* (London: Routledge).

Geraats, P.M. (2002) 'Central Bank Transparency', *Economic Journal*, 112 (483): 532–65.

Gerlach, S. and Schnabel, S. (1999) *The Taylor Rule and Interest Rates in the EMU Area: a Note*, BIS Working Paper No. 73.

Gerlach-Kristen, P. (2003) *Interest Rate Reaction Functions and the Taylor Rule in the Euro Area*, IMF Working Paper No. 258.

Goodfriend, M. (1986) 'Monetary mystique: Secrecy and Central Banking', *Journal of Monetary Economics*, 17: 63–97.

Goodhart, C.A.E. (2002) 'The Endogeneity of Money', in P. Arestis, M. Desai and S. Dow (eds), *Money, Macroeconomics and Keynes: Essays in Honour of Victoria Chick*, vol. 1 (London: Routledge).

Greenspan A (2001) *'Transparency in Monetary Policy'*, speech given at the Federal Reserve Bank of St. Louis, Economic Policy Conference, St Louis, Missouri (via videoconference) October 11th.

Haldane, A.G. and Read, V. (2000*) Monetary Policy Surprises and the Yield Curve*, Bank of England Working Paper No. 102.

Hardouvelis, G.A. (1984) 'Market Perceptions of Federal Reserve policy and the Weekly Monetary Announcements', *Journal of Monetary Economics*, 14: 225–40.

Hardy, D.C. (1996) *Market Reaction to Changes in German Official Interest Rates*, Deutsche Bundesbank Discussion Paper No. 4/96.

Issing, O. (1999) 'The Eurosystem: Transparent and Accountable, or "Willem in Euroland"', *Journal of Common Market Studies*, 37 (3): 503–19.

Judd, J.P. and Rudebusch, G.D. (1998) 'Taylor's Rule and the Fed: 1970–97', *Federal Reserve Bank of San Francisco Review*, 3: 3–16.

King, M. (1997) 'The Inflation Target Five Years On', *Bank of England Quarterly Bulletin*, 37 (4): 431–42.

King, M. (1999) 'Challenges for Monetary Policy: New and old', in *Proceedings* (Federal Reserve Bank of Kansas City): 11–57.

Kozicki, S. (1999) 'How Useful are Taylor Rules for Monetary Policy?', Federal Reserve Board of Kansas City, *Economic Review*, Summer: 5–33.

Kuttner, K.N. (2001) 'Monetary Policy Surprises and Interest Rates: Evidence from the Fed Funds Futures Market', *Journal of Monetary Economics*, 47(3): 523–44.

Lasaosa, A. (2005) *Learning the Rules of the New Game? Comparing the Reactions in Financial Markets to Announcements Before and After the Bank of England's Operational Independence*, Bank of England Working Paper No. 255

McCallum, B. (2000) 'The Present and Future of Monetary Policy Rules,' *International Finance*, 3: 273–86.

Moore, B.J. (1988) *Horizontalists and Verticalists* (Cambridge: Cambridge University Press).

Moore, B.J. (1989) 'The Endogeneity of Money', *Review of Political Economy*, 1(1): 64–93.

Moore, B.J. (2003) 'Endogenous Money', in J.E. King (ed.), *The Elgar Companion to Post Keynesian Economics* (Cheltenham: Edward Elgar).

Nelson, E. (2000) *UK Monetary Policy 1972–97: A Guide using Taylor Rules*, Bank of England Working Paper No. 120.

Palley, T.I. (2002) 'Endogenous Money: What it is and Why it Matters', *Metroeconomica*, 53 (2): 152–80.

Poole, W., Rasche, R.H. and Thornton, D.L. (2002) 'Market Anticipations of Monetary Policy Actions', *The Federal Reserve Bank of St Louis Review*, 84 (4): 65–94.

Radecki, L.J. and Reinhart, V. (1994) 'The Financial Linkages in the Transmission of Monetary Policy in the United States', in *National Differences in Interest Rate Transmission* (Basel: Bank for International Settlements), pp. 291–337.

Ross, K. (2002) *Market Predictability of ECB Monetary Policy Decisions: A Comparative Examination*, IMF Working Paper No. 02/233.

Sauer, S. and Sturm, J.-E. (2003) *Using Taylor Rules to Understand ECB Monetary Policy*, CESifo Working Paper No. 1110.

Shiller, R.J., Campbell, J.Y. and Shoenholtz, K. (1983), 'Forward Rates and Future Policy: Interpreting the Term Structure of Interest Rates', *Brookings Papers on Economic Activity*, 1: 173–217.

Svensson, L.E.O. (1997) 'Inflation Forecast Targeting: Implementing and Monitoring Inflation Targets', *European Economic Review*, 41: 1111–46.

Svensson, L.E.O. (2003) 'What is Wrong with Taylor Rules: Using Judgment in Monetary Policy Through Targeting Rules', 41 (2): 426–77.

Taylor, J.B. (1993) 'Discretion versus Policy Rules in Practice', *Carnegie-Rochester Conference Series on Public Policy*, 39: 195–214.

Thornton, D.L. (2003) 'Monetary Policy Transparency: Transparent about What?', *The Manchester School*, 71 (5): 478–97.

Wadhwani, S.B. (2001) 'Some Reflections on the MPC', *Bank of England Quarterly Bulletin*, 41 (3): 351–6.

Woodford, M. (2001) *Monetary Policy in the Information Economy*, paper given at the Federal Reserve Bank of Kansas City conference 'Economic Policy for the Information Economy', Jackson Hole, Wyoming, August.

# 4
# Monetary Policy Formation at the Long-Term Margin: A Kahn–Tobin Framework*

*Theodore T. Koutsobinas*

## Introduction

During the last years, there is an increasing interest among central bank policy makers in the 'portfolio rebalancing effect', which stems from the imperfect substitutability of financial assets, and which can be generated by central bank open market operations (Andrés *et al.* 2004). The discussion over the 'portfolio rebalancing effect' echoes the earlier-generation debate between the 'bills-only' and the 'bills-bonds' approach. The 'bills-only' approach represents the 'conventional' position as it was shaped in the old debate that took place in the 1950s. According to the proponents of the 'bills-only' framework, the objectives of central bank policy should be achieved by open market operations in bills, but not in bonds. Thus, following this argument, the emphasis is on short-term treasury instruments rather than on long-term ones. Since the period in which this debate took place, the Federal Reserve Board applied almost always the 'bills-only' approach. The only exception was the application of the policy of 'operation-twist' in 1961.

Contrary to the traditional wisdom in that era, there were two theoretical approaches which, despite their differences, emphasized the importance of the long-term interest rate. The one theoretical approach was advanced by Tobin (1961) on the basis of his work on imperfect asset substitution (see Andrés *et al.* 2004). However, although Tobin

*I would like to thank Claudio Sardoni, Sheila Dow, Giuseppe Fontana and other participants at the Berlin Conference held in October 2005 on *Macroeconomics and Macroeconomic Policies – Alternatives to the Orthodoxy* for their comments on a preliminary version of this paper.

(1997) recognized the importance of Keynesian expectations and fundamental uncertainty he did not develop his work on them. On the contrary, the role of uncertainty in asset substitution was used in another theoretical contribution provided by Kahn (1972). This latter approach exemplifies the Post Keynesian framework on monetary theory according to Hicks (1983).

Despite the differences that existed between the approaches followed by Tobin and Kahn, there were important lessons in them regarding the effectiveness of monetary policy. According to Tobin, standard monetary policy operates in assets that are as far as possible away from the long-term margin that is important for the real economy. On the other hand, the theoretical framework that was advanced by Kahn emphasizes the ineffectiveness of monetary policy as a result of exogenous expectations that are shaped by variations in liquidity-preference.

Today, the New Keynesian models or dynamic stochastic general equilibrium models (DSGE) (see Walsh 2003 for an extensive treatment) represent advances of the earlier models that Tobin and Kahn criticized. Thus, contemporary New Keynesian models are vulnerable to the criticism that Tobin and Kahn conducted to earlier-generation models. Thus, in New Keynesian models, deviations of the long-term interest rate from the expectation of the path of the current short-term interest rates as predicted by the expectations theory of the term structure of interest rates are not allowed. Thus, these models are consistent only with the assumption of perfect substitutability of real and monetary assets at a common interest rate plus an exogenous term that was put forth earlier by Tobin (1982).

In addition, there is a new interest today to develop Tobin's view that different securities should be treated differently (Kashyap 1999: 190). Bernanke (2002) argued that monetary policy should attempt to lower interest rates 'further out along the term structure of interest rates'. This could be achieved not only through influencing expectations of the term structure of interest rates but also preferably, according to Bernanke, through central bank purchases of long-term bonds that reduce long-term interest rates relatively to the expected path of short-term interest rates. This in turn reflects Tobin's and Kahn's central message – namely, that the influence of central bank policy on aggregate demand should take place through its effect on the entire variety of asset yields.

The current interest for monetary policy operation at the long-term margin calls for the revival and the development of theoretical approaches such as Tobin's and Kahn's that, contrary to traditional wisdom, emphasized the impact of the long-term interest rate. The chapter is organized as follows: first, I re-examine the 'bills-only' debate in the light of the theoretical contributions of Tobin and Kahn. On the basis of this dual theoretical discussion, an analytical framework is developed to examine what form of policy measures (and under which circumstances) can replace the application of the traditional 'bills-only' approach. I discuss the conclusions of this analytical framework in the light of evidence from the application of the monetary policy of 'portfolio rebalancing' in Japan and from the development of inflation-indexed bonds. Finally, I develop a theoretical framework that uses arbitrage as a process that explains chain asset substitution. This arbitrage process is discussed in the light of Kahn's marginal equilibrium. The theoretical framework that is advanced on the basis of the arbitrage process provides an explanation for the 'mystery' of the impact of free market operation associated with the very short margin of government securities on the real economy. It also reveals the limitations of central bank operations in the long-term margin associated with the influence of liquidity-preference and fundamental uncertainty. A particular attractive feature of the examination of the arbitrage process is that it can be put forth as a maximizing problem for arbitrageurs and, therefore, yield robust results.

## The 'bills-bonds' approach: the analytical framework of Tobin and Kahn

Both the analytical frameworks that were advanced by Tobin and Kahn are consistent with the 'bills-bonds' approach and offer alternative explanations of the importance of the yield of long-term (i.e., ten-year) government bonds. Of course, there were differences among them. For example, Tobin proposed that the long-term government yield can be viewed as revealing information and, therefore, can be used as a proxy for the expected inflation rate. On the other hand, Kahn treated the yield of the long-term government bond as the return of a liquidity-preference-dependent asset in a multi-asset framework. In the former case, in which the role of expected inflation is considered, the 'fair-value' model that was used by Federal Reserve Board (FRB) lately (Fed 1997) bears a similarity with Tobin's view since the real return on equity is equal to the nominal yield adjusted for the expected change in inflation. On the other hand, as a liquidity-dependent asset, bonds reveal information about the state of liquidity preference and the underlying market expectations, a view that is consistent with Kahn's (1972) approach.

In any case and despite their differences, the notion of the long-term interest rate is fundamental in these two theoretical approaches. Thus, they undermine the conventional belief on the effectiveness of the 'bills-only' approach. The latter refers to Federal Reserve Open Market Committee trading in the open market confined to very short-term Government securities, preferably 91-day Treasury bills. This is a move to affect bank reserves, and hence overall credit and the money supply, only through short-term interest rates. This intervention is conducted also in the hope that that long-term interest rates could be influenced further, although only indirectly and after a time lag. In essence, this implies that eventually the market in long-term Government securities is free.

As was mentioned above, the conventional 'bills-only' approach was followed with only one exception by the Federal Reserve Board (FRB) in the post-war era. This exception is associated with the application of the 'operation-twist' in 1961. At that time, the economy was recovering from recession but the balance of payments was troublesome. In this economic situation, treasury authorities associated the state of the economy with long rates while they considered the balance of payments depending on short rates, or 'hot money'. So an attempt was made to twist the yield curve by selling bills while buying bonds. This form of intervention, however, proved to be faulty because the market resisted it. Thus, while initially long rates became lower and reached 3.73 per cent from 3.89 per cent, they eventually rebounded to 4.06 per cent. This result proved that long-term rates are able to ignore the control of Federal Reserve Board and to behave to a certain degree independently of it.

This discussion highlights certain conclusions. First, the conventional 'bills-only' approach as it is applied by central banks is ineffective as a valuation tool and as an intervention measure. This result is consistent with both the analyses of Tobin and Kahn. Thus, in a more recent restatement of his views, Tobin (1996) argues that standard monetary policy operates in assets that are as far as possible away from the long-term margin that is important for the real economy. On the other hand, for Kahn, liquidity preference variations influence the shape of the yield curve and, therefore, monetary policy becomes ineffective. Secondly, in the light of the evidence of the episode of the 'operation-twist' the critical question which is raised is whether there is an alternative form of policy measures that can substitute successfully the application of the 'bills-only' approach. For Tobin, open market operations in indexed bonds would be closer to doing what the Federal

Reserve really is or should be trying to do – a closer substitute for real assets at the margin for investments (Tobin 1996). However, the implications of Kahn's analysis lead to a different answer, especially during periods when substantive changes in liquidity-preference take place. In such a situation, there is no reason to believe beforehand that monetary policy will prove to be effective despite following Tobin's suggestion to use in developing markets with synthetic financial assets such as inflation-indexed bonds as an instrument for conducting monetary policy.

This ineffectiveness of monetary policy happens because, according to Kahn, the dependence of the expected long-term interest rate on the time pattern of short-term interest rates holds only after price adjustment takes place and after investors become 'marginal' between financial assets (see Kahn 1972: 74). In a situation of substantive variations of liquidity-preference, expectations change and portfolio asset balances vary accordingly. In this case, the expected long-term interest rate depends on expectations, which are different from those that were present originally. Thus, changes in liquidity-preference influence the state of investors' marginal equilibrium in which there is no movement between different types of assets (i.e., from stocks to bonds) and the evaluation of the monetary measures of the value of assets is such that the latter are equal.

Thus, the role of uncertainty and of the 'lack of conviction' among investors is important and influences decisions in portfolio allocation (see Kahn 1972: 76–8). In this framework, movements of asset prices of different financial assets towards a different direction than the one wished by central banks as a result of the influence of changes in the state of confidence are possible. This situation is complicated by the fact that there is interdependence between the demand and the supply of different categories of assets (Kahn 1972: 80).

On the other hand, the interest rate on overnight loans of federal funds is the market rate, which the Fed controls by buying or selling Treasury bills at its intervention rate. Tobin (1999) emphasized the impact of this free market operation associated with the very short margin of government securities on the real economy. He considered this impact remarkable even a 'mystery,' since the federal funds rate is the shortest of all interest rates and the most remote from rates of assets and debts in terms of which the financing of real investment takes place by companies. Tobin (1999) offers two possible explanations for the massive impact of this 'tiny' and 'remote' margin of interest rates: monetary policy expectations and chains of asset substitution. In this chapter, the influence of speculative expectations with regard to the expected rates of appreciation of assets assumed by investors as put forth by Kaldor (1982) will not considered. Thus, only the impact of chains of asset substitution will be examined.

Moreover, Tobin claims that expectations of future monetary policy such as a string of federal funds rate reductions are not really operative without the presence of chains of assets substitution and portfolio reshufflings that affects the whole spectrum of market interest rates. Tobin (1996) argues that the Fed should intervene at a margin of market of interest rates that is more close to the real economy – that is, the long-term margin. He mentions that open market operations at the long-term margin took place in the past although he does not make any reference to their success or failure. However, this type of intervention could be desirable, in his view, in certain cases. One such case is the presence of a liquidity trap that makes ineffective the intervention at the very shortest of interest rates such as it was the case with Japan in the late 1990. Situations like this one justify, according to Tobin (1999), operations at the long-term margin of interest rates. In this connection, the development of inflation-indexed government bonds is beneficial for monetary policy because they are closer to real goods than are nominal bonds. Thus, for Tobin, innovative theorization about the tactics and structure of monetary operations is required since fiscal policies are no longer eligible for countercyclical stabilization and international financial markets can cause instability in both national financial markets and economies.

## Monetary policy in Japan: the 'portfolio rebalancing effect'

According to conventional wisdom, monetary policy is thought to have its main effects by affecting expectations of future short-term interest rates. This channel is the basis of many monetary policy prescriptions both away from and at the zero bound (see Krugman 2000). But central bankers and policy analysts have also considered financial-market effects that may be secondary away from the zero bound but may appear larger at the zero bound (see Bernanke 2000; Bernanke and Reinhart 2004). One such effect is the 'portfolio rebalancing effect', which stems from the imperfect substitutability of financial assets (see Tobin 1969, 1982, and, earlier, 1961). A central bank potentially generates such effects through its open market operations.

The Bank of Japan initiated quantitative monetary policy easing in March 2001, and it expected portfolio-rebalancing effects to help improve the economy (Auerbach and Obstfeld 2004). But, as accepted by Governor Fukui (2003), this objective proved to be ineffective. One reason why the portfolio-rebalancing operations were ineffective was that the capital positions of the private-sector financial intermediaries had been impaired by an accumulation of nonperforming loans following a fall in asset prices in a prolonged recession. As a result, financial institutions may have become more reluctant to take on portfolio risk (Kimura and Small 2004; Muto 2003). Such reluctance was seen as dampening the institutions' demands for risky assets and, thereby, weakening the portfolio-rebalancing effects noted above. Nevertheless, consistent with Kahn's concerns, this analysis that refers to the evidence of Japan's portfolio-rebalancing operations clearly counsels caution against accepting the view that a massive large-scale purchase of long-term government bonds by the Bank at the zero bound provides unambiguously positive net benefits to financial markets. Although the dramatic increase in the outright purchases of long-term government bonds may be useful in demonstrating commitment to fight deflation, a central bank should accept the hard reality that there is a potential adverse side effect of such purchases. Thus, one of the safest conclusions is that such purchases should be used only to supplement the commitment effects, such as an attempt to influence expectations of future short rates (Okina and Shiratsuka 2003).

## Inflation-indexed bonds

Tobin (1999) supported the idea of developing markets with synthetic financial assets such as inflation-indexed bonds for the purpose of conducting monetary policy. The introduction of Treasury Inflation Indexed Securities (TIIS) in January 1997, which are also called TIPS, refer to government bonds the payments of which are indexed to actual inflation during the lives of bonds. Following the lead of several countries, the US Treasury issued at that time its first trance of inflation-protected securities. These debt instruments were patterned after Canada's Real Return Bonds (RRBs). TIPS offer investors protection against inflation in two ways:

(1) The principal amount that buyers initially invest in TIPS is adjusted quarterly, on a lagged basis, using the US Consumer Price Index (CPI). At maturity, the buyers receive an accrued principal repayment that reflects the inflated value of their initial investment;

(2) In addition, the semi-annual coupons paid on TIPS are also adjusted for inflation by applying the Note's stated 'real' coupon rate to the inflation-adjusted principal amount as of the coupon date (see DePrince and Ford 1998: 47).

At the launching period, the Treasury Secretary Rubin decided to proceed with the issuance of TIPS for two reasons. First, evidence existed that investors impounded an inflation premium into the yields on conventional Treasury securities to compensate for the uncertainty associated with future inflation. By issuing TIPS, this uncertainty was hoped to be resolved. Second, TIPS would be directed toward a specific clientele, which would reduce the yield further (DePrince and Ford 1998). However, this was not justified by subsequent evidence. While markets in other countries were receptive to the issuance of inflation-indexed government bonds, the market reaction to TIPS in the US has been subdued up till today for various reasons. Other countries, the UK and Canada, in particular, have observed relatively stronger markets for their inflation-indexed debt because there were concerns among investors in those countries that the governments would attempt to manage their national debts by resorting to inflationary tactics. But, in the case of US domestic reasons were more accountable. For example, tax procedures constrained the market interest in the TIPS to investors who can hold them in tax-deferred accounts. On top of that, secondary market activity was persistently light. This was marked by two visible features of the market: the dollar size and the derivatives market. The dollar size of the market initially across all of the TIPS issued was US$ 107 billion (McCulloch and Levis 1998), a very small percentage of the market value of all Treasury securities issued during this time period. The derivatives market for the TIPS was also inactive, as very few futures contracts were traded on the Chicago Board of Trade. In fact, this relative illiquidity may have resulted in a higher yield on the TIPS than would otherwise be the case, even though most, if not all, of the inflation uncertainty is effectively eliminated. An additional domestic factor refers to the level of inflation in the US, which in recent years has been relatively low; consequently, investors have not felt the need for inflation protection. It turns out, however, that term premiums are very hard to estimate for inflation-indexed bonds, a difficulty that exists even for conventional (nominal) yield curves because uncertainty about the term structure translates into 'some' uncertainty regarding the precise level of the equilibrium real rates (Bomfin 2001). One possible explanation for this evidence is consistent with Kahn's emphasis on liquidity-preference in a multi-asset framework because the latter implies that inflation-indexed bonds cannot capture the effect of variable liquidity-premia across assets as it is the case with conventional yield curves.

## The role of the arbitrage process in chain asset substitution

Tobin did not offer an explanation of the 'mysterious' process in terms of which chains of asset substitutions take place. Yet the explanation of this process is fundamental and critical for the development of innovative thinking about the structure of monetary operations. In this chapter, the impact of arbitrage across values of different assets is introduced and utilized analytically in order to provide a sound explanation of the generation of the chain asset substitution process. It must be noted that price-adjustment or arbitrage under Keynesian fundamental uncertainty is specified differently from the notion of arbitrage in neoclassical financial theory. For example, the essence of arbitrage in neoclassical financial theory as proposed by Ross (1976) lies on the existence of a constant riskless rate of return and on the existence of a constant positive linear pricing rule, which prices correctly the effect of various exogenous factors that influence the price of an asset. In addition, in neoclassical financial theory arbitrage is viewed as applying to assets that are perfect substitutes. On the contrary, under Keynesian fundamental uncertainty, there are many pricing rules as different states of expectations may prevail over-time that are influenced by different degrees in the state of confidence. In addition, the existence of only one constant pricing rule is inconsistent with the presence of premia, which are varying over time as Summers (1985) notes. Equivalently, in Post Keynesian financial theory, there is no room for a constant risk-free interest rate because the liquidity premia or 'illiquidity-discounts' of different assets are time-varying in the sense that the latter are influenced by changes in uncertainty perception and in the state of confidence over time. As such, assets with different and varying 'illiquidity-discounts' are considered imperfect substitutes while arbitrage in neoclassical financial theory applies only to assets that are specified as perfect substitutes. Thus, price-adjustment or arbitrage towards equilibrium as a state of rest under Keynesian fundamental uncertainty does not involve a transition from 'incorrect' to 'correct' pricing for every asset but a transition from a dizequilibrium situation in which investors value unevenly the expected values of certain assets to a situation in which they equalize the expected values of all assets and become indifferent across them.

On the other hand, the assumption that the central bank can control the short-term interest rate following a real interest rate rule (Taylor 1993) has become the conventional wisdom in the recent past. This assumption undermines naturally the influence of the liquidity preference along the short end of the curve. Yet this is not the case when we turn our attention to the consideration of the long end of the yield curve where the influence of central bank is uncertain. In a multi-asset framework, there are many different long-term interest rates and, as Romer admits, the influence of monetary policy on these interest rates is very weak (see Romer 2000: 168). With respect to a multi-asset framework the key question is whether the existence of multiple interest rates that correspond to bonds of variable term to maturity can be always compatible with the application of a real short-term interest rule. The fact that the influence of monetary policy on long-term interest rates is weak, and that on the contrary the impact of the liquidity-preference on long-term interest rates is more powerful, due to strong fundamental uncertainty, points out to the existence of practical difficulties in the application of a real interest rate rule.

Nevertheless, the control of the short-term interest rate by central banks is an important feature of the allocation mechanism across assets because it is a key interest rate that it is not flexible. However, rigidity is not witnessed only in the case of short-term interest rates fixed by central banks. The case of downward stickiness of the long-term interest rate as a result of the influence of liquidity-preference has been a fundamental aspect of Keynes's analysis (Keynes 1936) and has been stressed as an important departure from conventional wisdom (Kahn 1972; Leijonhufvud 1968). In what follows, the issue that will be examined is whether the presence of sticky interest rates such as the exogenously administered short-term interest rate by central banks or the liquidity-preference dependent long-term interest rate plays a fundamental role in the asset substitution process.

In order to develop this analytical framework, it is assumed that there are two types of agents that are involved in financial markets: investors and arbitrageurs. The incorporation of these categories of market players in financial markets allows the introduction of both expectations and chain asset substitution in our analysis. Investors demand different assets according to their forecasts that are influenced by expectations, whether rational or behavioural. On the other hand, arbitrageurs do not hold any expectations. Their behaviour is simply derived from their incentive to maximize the expected return from differences in market rates. It must be noted that in the case in which expectations or monetary policy determine the price of one or more assets, this will be mirrored in the arbitrage process. For example, if given expectations determine the price of one asset and central bank policy determines the price of another asset, the arbitrage process that involves the prices of two different assets can be used as an analytical tool to describe successfully the asset substitution effect. Thus, one attractive feature of the model is that if there are sticky interest rates that are caused either by expectations (i.e., liquidity-preference induced expectations) or by exogenous intervention of central banks, these forces will be mirrored in the arbitrage process.

There are certain rules of thumb in the form of signals for the identification of arbitrage opportunities. A first signal is the presence of differences between market rates of assets of variable term to maturity because these differences determine the profit opportunities of arbitrageurs. Of course, the greater these differences are, the greater are the arbitrage opportunities. By definition, arbitrage involves the purchase of assets on one market and the immediate or simultaneous resale on another market in order to profit from a price discrepancy. This implies a simultaneous adjustment of the prices of two different assets. But, there exists the special case of sticky prices in which the price discrepancy may continue to persist. In this situation, there are forces that prevent the market rate of one asset to adjust to the market rate of another asset. As a consequence, the arbitrageurs must intensify their involvement (whether this is a purchase or sale) on the asset, which features a flexible and more easily adjustable market rate. For example, when arbitrageurs witness the presence of a sticky market rate of one asset they perceive it as a signal that the flexible market rate of another asset must be adjusted to the level of the sticky market rate. Thus, the presence of a sticky market rate is a signal that market activity must be intensified in a certain direction, namely, towards adjusting faster the more flexible market rate.

Thus, the maximization process in an arbitrage process necessarily involves asset substitution. Moreover, it can take concrete forms as it can occur consecutively in a chain of asset substitution from short-term assets to long-term assets (i.e., from three-month to six-month bills to one-year, three-year, five-year, ten-year bonds or longer) or vice-versa. This happens because there is eventually an incentive for arbitrageurs to conduct asset substitution consecutively in a chain process. This incentive is associated with the fact that arbitrageurs are exposed to small risk-premium variation between assets with little term to maturity differences.

The arbitrageurs are in essence noise traders who observe the stickiness of the interest rate of one asset, $i_t^*$ in the market and then use $i_t^*$ as a benchmark or reference rate in some adjustment mechanism to determine their trading investment path. It is assumed that $i_T$ represents the stream of interest rates of bonds of different term to maturity. For example, the interest rates of bonds of different term to maturity, say t and t+m, are $i_t$ and $i_{t+m}$, which are positive values. Arbitrage is initiated when the values of two interest rates with different terms to maturity remain different even if discounting (i.e., at the conventionally assumed risk-free interest rate) for differences in term to maturity takes place. This implies, for example, that an arbitrage process can take place when there is a difference between $i_t$ and $i_{t+m,(t)}$, which is the interest rate of bond of maturity t+m discounted at maturity t. In the case of sticky interest rates, the notation for these interest rates is $i^*_t$ and $i^*_{t+m,(t)}$. Since there are two rates that are relevant for arbitrageurs, there are two states (i.e., F1 and F2) depending on which rate is sticky. Thus, an example of such an auxiliary adjustment mechanism is a geometrically decreasing distributed lag, which may be represented in continuous form by the state of nature constraints to the maximization solution below with $\gamma$ being positive between 0 and 1.

The problem of maximizing arbitrage profit is as follows:

$$\max V = \int_0^\infty (i_t - i_{t+m,\,(t)})\, e^{-rt}\, dt \qquad (4.1)$$

s.t.

$$F1:\ di_t/dt = \gamma\,(i_t^* - i_{t+m,\,(t)})$$

$$F2:\ di_{t+m,\,(t)}/dt = \gamma\,(i_{t+m,\,(t)}{}^* - i_t)$$

Where the degree of the geometrically decreasing function, $\gamma$ depends on y as determined by:

$$\frac{d(i_t - i_{t+m,\,(t)})}{dt} = y\,\frac{d(i_t - i^*_{t+m,\,(t)})}{dt},\ \text{where, } y > 1 \qquad (4.2)$$

The rationale of equation (4.2) is that the rate of adjustment is faster in the presence of sticky prices because arbitrageurs need to trade more the asset, which has a flexible market rate at a given time period in order to equalize the interest rates. This leads in the acceleration of the chain of asset substitution. The proof regarding the acceleration of the rate of adjustment is provided in the appendix.

The analytical framework that was advanced in this chapter has a few attractive characteristics. First, it provides a solution to the mystery for the massive impact of this 'tiny' and 'remote' margin of interest rates that refers to the short-term interest rate that is exogenously administered by central banks and may spur a chain of asset substitution. More precisely, it has been shown that monetary policy is successful because in the presence of a sticky short-term interest rate the chain of asset substitution that is generated by arbitrage is largely facilitated by the acceleration of the adjustment process. But speaking of sticky interest rates in a broader context reminds us about the other side of the coin. Thus, the existence of downward stickiness long-term interest rates as a result of the influence of expectations induced by liquidity-preference may likewise cause an arbitrage process and a chain of asset substitution that may run against the objectives of monetary policy.

There are two other circumstances that need to be mentioned in the context of this analytical framework. First, there is the possibility of two sticky prices being present. In this state, the analytical framework that is presented here cannot generate an arbitrage process. But this is resolved by making reference to a second situation in which it is assumed that arbitrageurs are considered to be heterogeneous rather than homogeneous. Some arbitrageurs may prefer to arbitrage at the short end of the yield curve while others may opt to operate at the long end of the yield curve. If sticky rates are present at both ends of the yield curve, the heterogeneity of arbitrageurs facilitates two chains of asset substitution that are generated simultaneously towards different directions. Thus, a situation may be encountered in which there are two contrasting simultaneous chains of asset substitution: one running from short-term end to the long-term end and another running from the long-term end to the short-term end. The end result depends on the relative forces of these contrasting chains of asset substitution. If these forces are similar, there is a possibility for the appearance of a kinked yield curve.

## Concluding remarks

In this chapter, an explanation of the success of monetary policy in terms of processes of chains of asset substitution was put forth in order to provide a plausible explanation to the 'mystery' surrounding the effectiveness of monetary policy that was posed by Tobin. A novel feature of the analysis was that this explanation was based on an analytical framework that generated chains of asset substitution in terms of arbitrage in financial markets. It was shown that the downward stickiness of the long-term interest rate is possible to initiate an arbitrage process that leads to failure with regard to the realization of the objectives of monetary policy. This result provides an analytical justification for the adoption by monetary authorities of some form of 'bills-bonds' approach that is consistent with the importance of the long-term interest rates for the effectiveness of monetary policy and that was supported initially in the works of Tobin and Kahn. Another novel feature of the approach of this chapter was that the results of chains of asset substitution on the basis of arbitrage processes were obtained in an objective manner by using maximization techniques on arbitrage profit without regard to assumptions about the nature of expectations, whether rational or behavioural.

As was mentioned earlier, the influence of speculative expectations with regard to the expected rates of appreciation of assets assumed by investors was not considered here. Thus, future research will necessarily involve the explanation of chains of asset substitution in terms of both arbitrage and speculative expectations. In addition, the analysis needs to be expanded in order to provide more precise accounts of the influence of sticky prices along different parts of the yield curve.

## Appendix

The interest rates of bonds of different term to maturity, say $i_t$ and $i_{t+m}$ are always positive even if they approximate zero bound. Interest rates are a strictly increasing function of term to maturity. The presence of a sticky interest rate at term to maturity $t+m$, appropriately discounted at period $t$ so that term maturities are consistent is, $i^*_{t+m,\,(t)}$. This implies that:

$$di_{t+m,\,(t)} > di^*_{(t+m),\,t}\,. \tag{A4.1}$$

Since:

$$di^*_{t+m,\,(t)} = 0.$$

Given (A4.1), the presence of a flexible interest rate, $i_t$ implies that:

$$di_t - di^*_{t+m,\,(t)} > di_t - di_{t+m,\,(t)}. \tag{A4.2a}$$

Or equivalently:

$$d\,(i_t - i^*_{t+m,\,(t)}) > d\,(i_t - i_{t+m,\,(t)})\,. \tag{A4.2b}$$

Allowing for time-variation, where *t* is positive we obtain from (A4.2):

$$\frac{d(i_t - i^*_{t+m,\,(t)})}{dt} > \frac{d(i_t - i_{t+m,\,(t)})}{dt} \tag{A4.3a}$$

This can be written also in a formulation that is relevant for the rate of adjustment γ, which is used in the maximization process of arbitrage profit:

$$\frac{d(i_t - i^*_{t+m,\,(t)})}{dt} = \gamma\,\frac{d(i_t - i_{t+m,\,(t)})}{dt},\ \text{where, } \gamma > 1 \tag{A4.3b}$$

## References


Andrés, J., López-Salido J.D. and Nelson, E. (2004) *Tobin's Imperfect Asset Substitution in Optimizing General Equilibrium*, The Federal Reserve Bank of St. Louis, Working Paper 2004–003A.

Auerbach, A.J. and Obstfeld, M. (2004) *The Case for Open-Market Purchase in a Liquidity Trap*, http://emlab.berkeley.edu/users/auerbach/zerotrap24.pdf.

Bernanke, B.S. (2000) *Japanese Monetary Policy: A Case of Self-Induced Paralysis?*, Presentation at the ASSA meetings, Boston MA, January 9.

Bernanke, B.S. (2002) *Deflation: Making Sure 'It Doesn't Happen Here'*, Remarks before the National Economic Club, Washington, D.C., November 21. www.federalreserve.gov/boarddocs/speeches/2002/20021121/default.htm

Bernanke, B.S. and Reinhart, V.R. (2004) *Conducting Monetary Policy at Very Low Short-Term Interest Rates*, paper presented at the International Center for Monetary and Banking Studies Lecture, Geneva, Switzerland, 14 January.

Bomfin, A.N. (2001) *Measuring Equilibrium Real Interest Rates: What Can We Learn from Yields on Indexed Bonds?*, Federal Reserve Board Working Paper No. 53.

DePrince, A.E. Jr. and Ford, W.F. (1998) 'The US Treasury's Inflation-Protected Securities (TIPS): Market Reactions and Policy Effects', *Business Economics*, 33(1): 47–53.

Federal Reserve Board (1997) *Humphrey-Hawkins Testimony. Monetary Policy Report to the Congress*, July.

Fukui, T. (2003) *Challenges for Monetary Policy in Japan*, speech at the Spring Meeting of the Japan Society of Monetary Economics, on the occasion of its 60th anniversary, 1 June.

Hicks, J.R. (1983) 'IS-LM: An Explanation', in J.P. Fitoussi (ed.), *Modern Macroeconomics* (Oxford: Blackwell), pp. 49–63.

Kahn, R.F. (1972) 'Some Notes on Liquidity Preference', in *Selected Essays on Employment and Growth* (Cambridge: Cambridge University Press).

Kaldor, N. (1939) 'Speculation and Economic Stability', *Review of Economic Studies,* 7(1): 1–27; reprinted in N. Kaldor (1960), *Essays on Economic Stability and Growth, Collected Economic Essays*, Vol. II (London: Duckworth).

Kaldor, N. (1982) *The Scourge of Monetarism* (Oxford: Oxford University Press).

Kashyap, A. (1999) 'Government Debt, the Composition of Bank Portfolios and the Transmission of Monetary Policy: Discussion', in K.A. Chrystal (ed.), *Government Debt Structure and Monetary Conditions* (London: Bank of England).

Keynes, J.M. (1936) *The General Theory of Employment, Interest and Money* (New York: Harcourt and Brace and World); reprinted in D.E. Moggridge (ed.), (1973) *Collected Writings of J.M. Keynes*, vol. VII (London: Macmillan).

Kimura, T. and Small, D. (2004) *Quantitative Monetary Easing and Risk in Financial Asset Markets*, Finance and Economics Discussion Series, 2004–57, Divisions of Research & Statistics and Monetary Affairs, (Washington D.C.: Federal Reserve Board).

Krugman, P. (2000) 'Thinking about the Liquidity Trap', *Journal of the Japanese and International Economies*, 14 (4): 221–37.

Leijonhufvud, A. (1968) *On Keynesian Economics and the Economics of Keynes: A Study of Monetary Theory* (New York: Oxford University Press).

McCulloch, J.H. and Levis, A.K. (1998) *The Inflation Premium Implicit in the US Real and Nominal Term Structure of Interest Rates,* Ohio State University Working Paper No. 98–12, updated in 2000.

Muto, T. (2003) *Structural Changes in the World Economy and Challenges Facing Japan's Economy*, speech at the JCIF International Finance Seminar, June 17.

Okina, K. and Shiratsuka, S. (2003) *Policy Commitment and Expectation Formations: Japan's Experience under Zero Interest Rates*, IMES Discussion Paper Series, Bank of Japan, No. 2003-E-5.

Romer, D. (2000) 'Keynesian Macroeconomics without the LM', *Journal of Economic Perspectives,* 14 (2): 149–69.

Ross, S.A. (1976) 'The Arbitrage Theory of Capital Asset Pricing', *Journal of Economic Theory,* 13: 341–60.

Summers, L. (1985) 'Economics and Finance', *Journal of Finance*, 40: 633–5.

Taylor, J.B. (1993) 'Discretion versus Policy Rules in Practice', *Carnegie-Rochester Conference Series on Public Policy*, 39: 195–214.

Tobin, J. (1961) 'Money, Capital, and Other Stores of Value', *American Economic Review (Papers and Proceedings)*, 51: 15–29.

Tobin, J. (1969) 'A General Equilibrium Approach to Monetary Theory', *Journal of Money, Credit and Banking,* 1: 15–29.

Tobin, J. (1982) 'Money and Finance in the Macroeconomic Process', *Journal of Money, Credit and Banking,* 14: 171–203.

Tobin, J. (1996) 'Interview with James Tobin', *The Region, Banking and Policy Issues Magazine* (Minneapolis: Federal Reserve Bank of Minneapolis), December.

Tobin, J. (1997) 'A General Overview of the General Theory', in G.C. Harcourt and P.A. Riach (eds), *A Second Edition of The General Theory*, Vol. 2.

Tobin, J. (1999) *Monetary Policy: Recent Theory and Practice*, Cowles Foundation Paper No. 975, Yale University.

Walsh, C.E. (2003) *Monetary Theory and Policy*, 2nd edition (Cambridge, MA: MIT Press).

# 5

# Bank Lending and Regulation in Insider Financial Systems: A Theoretical Assessment

*Elisabeth Springler*

## Introduction

Numerous studies have been conducted to evaluate the impact of the Basel II framework of banking regulation on specific groups of companies, including small and medium-sized enterprises. Additionally, quantitative impact studies have shown the effects at a macroeconomic level. Despite these fields of intensive research which rely heavily on econometric data evaluation, a concise integration of these methods of economic policy into monetary theory is still outstanding. Therefore, this chapter attempts to fill this theoretical gap by integrating the effects of modern banking regulation into an endogenous money model. The aim of thc new Basel II accord is to minimize bank risks by paying special attention to adequate credit risk assessment. Other risks, such as market risks and operational risks, are also integrated into the new capital adequacy ratios; but these play only a minor role in the overall economic analysis since the changes in the assessment of these risks from Basel I to Basel II framework were relatively minimal. Consequently, this chapter focuses on the effects of the introduction of new methods of credit risk assessment in Pillar I (capital adequacy ratio) of Basel II and investigates how bank lending is affected by addressing the following question: From a theoretical point of view, do modern forms of banking regulation lead to credit constraints within economies with insider financial systems? As Basel I led to an increase in securitization, which in turn minimized the influence of central bank policies on commercial banks' behaviour, the second research question addressed in this chapter is whether the new accord achieves its aim of further increasing the influence of central banks policies.

We begin by pointing out the characteristics of the Basel II banking regulatory framework which are relevant to this analysis. The following section also consists of an analysis of the relevant features of endogenous funds for economies with insider financial systems. Such systems can be regarded as bank-based financial systems that are characterized by the important role of banks for external investment financing of companies and strong institutional ties between creditors and debtors.[1] The potential effects of Basel II are subsequently investigated on two levels. Firstly, the proposals of Basel II, in particular Pillar I (capital adequacy ratios), are discussed from a macroeconomic point of view which enables conclusions for monetary policy to be drawn. Secondly, microeconomic features are investigated through the implemention of aspects of banking theory into a structuralist endogenous money model. This discussion focuses on potential lending constraints that might arise when implementing features of asymmetric information into endogenous money theory and creating an adapted endogenous money model. Aware of the theoretical problems arising when integrating microeconomic aspects of banking theory as well as elements of asymmetric information into an endogenous money model, a detailed assessment of this implementation precedes the investigation.

## Setting the scene: endogenous money and Basel II

### Characteristics of the Basel II regulatory framework

After the liberalization of most banking sectors in Western Economies, which started in the 1980s following the influential works of McKinnon (1973) and Shaw (1973), and which have been ongoing in economies with a socialist tradition ever since the transformation process started, financial markets changed to form a new financial order. This process, in turn, led to national and international banking regulation undergoing a major restructuring process. Eatwell and Taylor (2000: 209) characterized these developments as follows:

> ...the conscious removal of controls that was a necessary part of the privatization of foreign risk and form the process of internationalization itself. Liberalization has created a seamless financial world, with regulators confined inside increasingly irrelevant national boundaries.

Nevertheless, the period of pure liberalization was replaced by thoughts of re-regulation and the enforcement of self-regulation[2] mechanisms, as financial instability persisted in the 1990s and caused both underdeveloped and developed economies to suffer.[3] It should be noted here that re-regulation proposals did not involve reversing former liberalization procedures, but aimed to introduce proper means of prudential banking supervision and financial markets supervision on an international level to stabilize financial systems. The former mechanisms of banking regulation, such as administrated interest rate ceilings and credit rationing for certain industries, were still thought to cause qualitative and quantitative credit distortions and, as McKinnon (1973) calls it, 'financial repression'.[4] The newly introduced measures of financial regulation, mainly those of the Group of Thirty, OECD guidelines and EU regulation mechanisms (Frenkel and Menkhoff 2000; Strulik 2000), including the proposals of the Committees of the Bank of International Settlements, have been the subject of intense discussion among economists and economic politicians all over the world (Akyüz 2000). Nevertheless, the proposals of the committees of the Bank of International Settlements, the Basel II framework, will be enforceable by law in the member states of the European Union, and has also been adopted in the US by the ten to 12 largest American banks. The members of the Basel Committee agreed on implementing more advanced methods of risk management of Basel II by the end of 2007. By the end of 2006, most of the elements for the implementation of the new framework should be available (Chorafas 2004: 3). The European Parliament has adopted the Basel II directive for the member states and claims the implementation will be complete no later than 1 April 2008.

In total, the Basel II framework consists of three pillars which aim to ensure a proper capital adequacy ratio (Pillar I) of banks by covering more risks than Basel I, to help supervise capital ratios by introducing prudential supervision (Pillar II) for national supervisory authorities and aim to encourage financial disclosure (Pillar III) by strengthening market discipline and transparency. In this analysis, Pillar I of Basel II – the capital adequacy ratio – will serve as an example for changes in banking regulation. It should be noted, however, that the impacts of the implementation of Pillar II (measures of prudential supervision) and Pillar III (market disclosure) and their influence on national financial systems[5] and monetary policy also deserve investigation. When focusing on Pillar I of the Basel II framework, changes from a general capital adequacy of 8 per cent for all loans given by commercial banks to a more sophisticated scheme of risk sensitivity becomes the main point of discussion. To implement this advanced risk sensitivity, commercial banks can choose between three different methods: the standardized, the foundation internal ratings-based and the advanced internal ratings-based approaches.[6] This means that, in contrast to the previous required minimum capital of 8 per cent, the bank now has to hold capital according to the groups of debtors which are classified into 5 categories (0 per cent, 20 per cent, 50 per cent, 100 per cent and 150 per cent). For some portfolios, such as loans to other states with ratings of AAA to AA–, no minimum capital is required (0 per cent), while for loans to states with ratings below B–, up to 150 per cent of the 8 per cent have to be kept as a minimum capital requirement. For non-banks, the risk assessments consist of four categories starting with a risk weighting of 20 per cent of the 8 per cent up to 150 per cent of the 8 per cent. Banks, therefore, have to underlie loans to companies with higher risk (or lower ratings) with 12 per cent capital, whereas for companies with the lowest risk weighting 1.6 per cent is sufficient (Bank for International Settlements 2003).

With these changes in risk-weighted bank lending, the overall minimum capital adequacy ratio a commercial bank has to hold can either increase or decrease relative to the situation under Basel I – depending upon the risk sensitivity of the loans portfolio of the commercial banks. Therefore, changes in minimum capital adequacy ratios can have a similar effect on bank lending to minimum reserve requirements, although they apply to different positions in the banks' balance sheet. As lending increases the risk-weighted assets, the bank reduces its margin against the capital ratio. Therefore, these developments in capital adequacy ratios can be seen as a new method to indirectly control the money-creation process of commercial banks. While minimum reserve requirements have been reduced (in the United States and France, for example,) or even abandoned completely in many countries (including Canada, Sweden and the United Kingdom) (Clinton 1997; Sellon and Weiner 1997), capital requirements become more important in monetary policy as the Basel II Accord has not only been adopted by the European Union and G 10 countries, but by more than 100 countries – at least to some extent.

How will banks react to these changes in risk-sensitivity approaches under the new Basel II minimum capital adequacy standards? The third quantitative impact study, in which 350 credit institutions of different sizes and from more than forty different countries were assessed (Chorafas 2004: 13), aimed to investigate the impact of Basel II, Pillar I on the general capital adequacy ratio. The study concludes that wholesale and investment banks in particular will have to increase their capital adequacy ratios as risk sensitivity becomes more diversified. Chorafas (2004: 15) details the results for 46 banks participating in the third quantitative impact study, showing that banks using a standardized approach will have to increase capital ratios by 17 per cent and banks using the foundation internal rating approach will have to increase capital ratios by 6 per cent. Only banks using the advanced internal ratings approach will not face any change in capital requirements. Therefore, this analysis assumes that banks will increase their capital ratios as a result of Basel II.

## Structuralist versus horizontalist approaches towards endogenous money

The view that money is endogenous in the economic process is, according to Pollin (1991), now widely accepted among economists and central bankers with different theoretical economic backgrounds. Pollin traces the roots of this acknowledgement back to Alan Holmes, a former New York Federal Reserves senior vice president, who stated in 1969 that 'in the real world banks extend credit, creating deposits in the process, and look for the reserves later' (cited by Pollin 1991: 367). Apart from the general consensus that central banks are not in full control of money supply, several approaches to how endogenous money is integrated into monetary theory can be distinguished.[7] The model developed in this analysis follows Post Keynesian tradition. To answer the research questions raised in this chapter it is necessary to focus on an endogenous money framework within Post Keynesian economics that highlights the relationship between banks and companies and enables us to distinguish institutional features to show the effects of the capital adequacy ratio of Basel II on insider financial systems. Disagreement in endogenous money models within Post Keynesian economics starts with the second part of Alan Holmes' statement, when he claims that banks will look for reserves later.

This raises two main questions: Firstly, how and when do banks look for reserves? Different assumptions about the role of commercial banks in managing these reserves also lead to different central bank behaviour. Secondly, is the amount of newly created deposits equal to the amount of money individuals are willing to hold? Two approaches within the Post Keynesian theory are based on these questions: the accommodationist approach and the structuralist approach. Table 5.1 summarizes the main theoretical differences between the structuralist and horizontalist approaches that have been addressed in detail by Moore (1988, 1994, 1997), Cottrell (1994) and Arestis and Howells

*Table 5.1* Theoretical disagreement between structuralists and accommodationists

| | *Structuralists* | *Horizontalists or accommodationists* |
|---|---|---|
| 1. Central bank fully accommodates reserve requirements of commercial banks? | No | Yes |
| • Liquidity preference theory compatibility? | Yes | No |
| ○ Borrowed and non-borrowed funds perfect substitutes? | No | Yes |
| ○ Functioning of Keynesian multiplier? | Yes | No |
| • Liquidity management | Yes | No |
| • Open market operations are useful? | Partly | Yes |
| 2. Amount of newly created deposits equals the amount of demanded deposits? | No | Yes |
| • Independent money supply curve | Yes | No |
| • Convenience lending | No | Yes |
| • Money stock vs money flow problem | No | Yes |

(1996). A set of theoretical differences between the two approaches derives from the question of how the central bank reacts to the requested monetary base of the commercial banks. Both horizontalists and accommodationists claim that central banks always fully accommodate the requests of commercial banks. This results in a perfectly horizontal credit money supply curve. Since this leads to the complete inability of financial authorities to control money, liquidity preference does not fit in the scheme (Chick and Dow 2002; Brown 2003). Conversely, the structuralist approach proposes a compromise by stating that the central bank does not fully accommodate the commercial banks' requests for reserves. Banks' institutional setting and liability management therefore has an influence on the reserves demanded, as well as on the shape of the credit and money supply curve, as Palley (1996) has pointed out. On the one hand, this results in a stronger position of the central bank in the short term since the central bank can have an influence on commercial banks by restricting the growth of non-borrowed funds – which in turn leads to a less than perfect balance between borrowed and non-borrowed funds in the structuralist approach – and of reserves as a consequence. This is also the condition under which liquidity preference holds true. On the other hand, the central bank's position is weakened in the long term since liability management enables banks to create reserves themselves. Open market operations, which serve as useful tools in monetary policy from a horizontalist point of view, have less relevance in the structuralist view due to the importance of the institutional setting (pointed out clearly by Chick and Dow 1996; Niggle 1991). They shift the credit and money supply curves outward. Fontana (2003) and Fontana and Venturino (2003) demonstrated these developments within a time framework.

Which of the two frameworks enables an investigation of the effects on monetary policy and bank lending induced by changes in the Basel II framework? As pointed out above, the Basel II framework was implemented, besides the introduction of a more sophisticated mathematical tool to weight the credit risk of borrowers, to ensure a regulatory tool for monetary policy; thus, the theoretical framework needs to account for liability management of commercial banks. Although increases in capital ratios do not directly affect the demand for deposits as reserve requirements affects it, liability management still is the crucial factor influencing the behaviour of commercial banks. Secondly, as Dymski (1988) points out when developing a Keynesian banking model, the control of money supply and hence the control of liquidity is a crucial feature for a microeconomic approach to banking which is used in this chapter when introducing asymmetric information into an endogenous money model. For this reason, this analysis will focus on a structuralist endogenous money model.

## Implications on a macroeconomic level and effects on monetary policy

Based on the model of Palley (1994) – which also has been applied by Fontana (2003), and Fontana and Venturio (2003) for the implementation of a time framework – Figure 5.1 integrates the effects of Pillar I of Basel II into a structuralist endogenous money framework. The equations used in Figure 5.1 are described in detail in Palley (1994) and are not discussed here. Only changes in functions due to the introduction of new capital requirements are discussed in the following analysis.

In general, changes in the capital adequacy ratio can lead to two different reactions on the part of banks. As pointed out above, quantitative impact studies have shown that most banks will have to increase overall capital ratios. This is also assumed in the following analysis. Changes in bank behaviour which might lead to shifts in loan portfolios are therefore not considered. In the case of the estimated increase in banks' capital reserves, commercial banks will face a

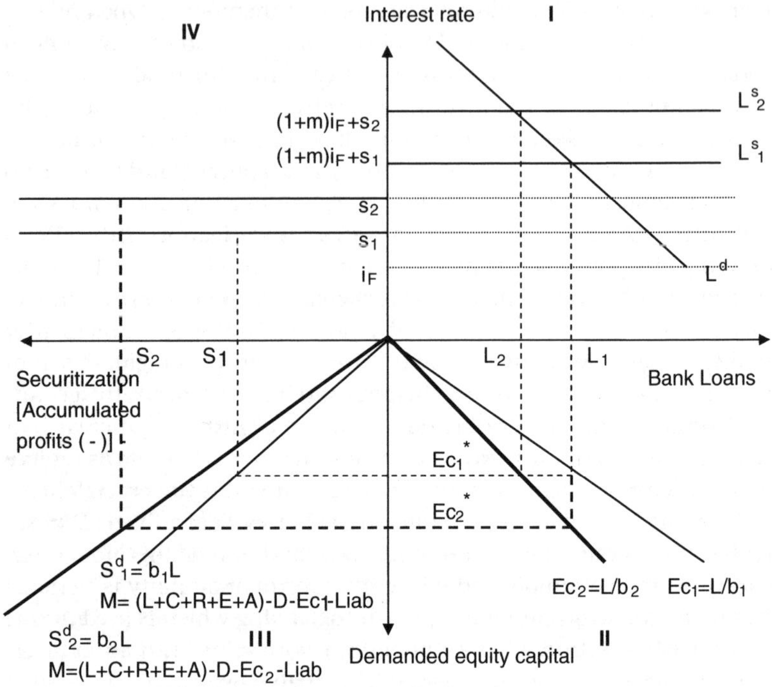


*Figure 5.1* Structuralist endogenous money model and capital requirements

reduction in accumulated profits or will try to offset capital requirements by using methods of securitization ('true sales'). Figure 5.1 illustrates two scenarios by describing the situation for a commercial bank under Basel I and comparing it to the situation under Basel II requirements. For the endogenous money model this applies to a point-in-time analysis in two scenarios. For the purposes of this discussion, the following standardized aggregate bank balance sheet is assumed which does not include a detailed analysis of the group 'other assets' and 'other liabilities', because the analysis in this chapter concentrates on the interrelation between loans and equity capital based on the assumption that neither the behaviour of the commercial bank in terms of holding excess reserves nor the central bank's policy in necessary currency holdings and reserve requirements changes. Therefore, the following aggregate balance sheet does not link specific assets groups to specific groups of liabilities, but instead aims to give an overview of the most relevant positions in the bank balance sheet for

*Table 5.2* Bank balance sheet

| *Assets* | *Liabilities* |
|---|---|
| Other assets: bonds, stocks, commercial papers, treasury bonds, equities etc. (A) | Other liabilities: money market papers, deferments, reserve assets such as provisions for pensions etc. (Liab) |
| Currency holdings (C) | Deposits (D) |
| Reserve requirements (on deposits and time deposits) (R) | |
| Excess reserves (E) | Equity capital (Ec) |
| Loans (L) | – Core capital: shareholders' equity<br>– Supplementary capital: reserves<br>Balance sheet profits/losses (M) |

the analysis in this chapter. The only interrelation between assets and liabilities is marked with an arrow:

The multi-quadrant analysis in Figure 5.1 incorporates, in quadrant I, the relationship between credit money supply and demand ($L^s$ and $L^d$). Since causality runs from loan demand to loan supply, quadrant II emphasizes the effects on the bank's balance sheet and shows the effects on equity capital (Ec) demanded due to a change in capital ratios demanded under Basel I ($b_1$) compared to the new framework ($b_2$). Therefore b stands for the method of introducing capital adequacy ratios under banking regulation. The ratios are applied in an aggregate way; this means that $b_2$ represents the general increase in the ratio based on the assumption that the bank's loan portfolio remains unchanged in terms of risk sensitivity. The following equation applies for the demanded volume of equity capital: $Ec = L/b$. As quadrant II shows, a shift from $b_1$ to $b_2$ leads to an increase in the volume of equity demanded from $Ec_1{}^*$ to $Ec_2{}^*$. The curve turns inward instead of creating a parallel shift since it is assumed that the risk sensitivity ratio b increases with the loan volume. To accommodate the increased demand for equity capital, the commercial bank has two main possibilities: It can either increase securitization – off-balance sheet activity – or reduce accumulated profits in order to increase equity capital. Therefore, quadrant III shows the demand for securitization ($S^d$) in the equation: $S^d = bL$. As with the function of demanded equity capital, the curve for demand for securitization also turns in this case, but outward. A reduction in commercial banks accumulated profits (M) as a result of increased demand for equity capital would have a similar effect in quadrant III. The volume of accumulated profits can be seen as M = (L+C+R+E+A)-D-Ec-Liab. C stands for the volume of currency held by the commercial bank. Similarly, R stands for the volume of reserves a commercial bank has to hold due to the reserve requirements that apply for deposits. The variables A and Liab represent the positions 'other assets' and 'other liabilities' of the bank balance sheet. The volume of excess reserves held by commercial banks is indicated by E. Therefore, quadrant IV reflects the increasing volume of securitization demand – from $S_1$ to $S_2$ – which is accommodated by the market with securitization supply at fixed costs. These are interpreted as interest rate (s) commercial banks have to pay for securitization. In turn, in order to keep accumulated profits at the same level, increased interest rates are transferred to the borrower – as can be seen by the increase in the interest rate for loans in quadrant I. Similarly, s can be interpreted as the cost of an increase in equity capital. Shifts from $b_1$ to $b_2$ therefore lead to an increase from $s_1$ to $s_{2,}$ and banks charge interest rates as a mark-up (m) over the federal funds interest rate ($i_F$).

Overall, commercial banks' stability is not necessarily increasing – when defining stability as a decrease of commercial banks' risk – since commercial banks might increase risk in liability management operations to meet the increased capital requirements of the loans given. Therefore, it seems as if the risks of credit transactions are replaced by risks of liability management transactions, without increasing the potential of central banks to influence commercial banks' behaviour via monetary policy. Palley (2006) points out that a potential solution for this problem is the introduction of asset-based capital requirements as tools of central bank monetary policy. This concept also seems to be adequate in the context of this chapter.

## Implication on a microeconomic level: introducing asymmetric information

Discussing the effects of Basel II on a microeconomic level implies introducing elements of banking theory and banking behaviour into the endogenous money model. As shown in second section, one major argument against banking regulation  mainly against interest rate ceilings – has been quantitative distortions due to credit rationing. To evaluate the effects of Basel II in an endogenous money model therefore implies the discussion of effects on bank lending. More specifically, the relationship between asymmetric information – adverse selection in this case – and potential credit rationing has to be clarified.

This section aims to integrate assumptions of asymmetric information into the Post Keynesian structuralist endogenous money model described above. Discussions about a potential integration arise out of the postulate of *fundamental uncertainty*, which seems to be incompatible with the probabilistic approach of asymmetric information. Within Post Keynesian economics, fundamental uncertainty, together with the concept of historical time and the assumption of non-ergodicity, form the basic theoretical premises which lead to problems in integrating asymmetric information into the analysis. The idea of fundamental uncertainty traces back to Keynes's General Theory of Employment, Interest and Money. With reference to Keynes's attempt to define asymmetric definition, Van Ees and Garretsen (1993) and Crotty (1996) state that asymmetric information would replace the concept of fundamental uncertainty by known and measurable probabilities and would therefore contradict the premise of non-ergodicity. Similarly, Rousseas (1986: 17) argues against the conversion of uncertainty into *risk* which would, according to him, treat uncertainty as certainty. Davidson (1991) qualifies this strict opposition against probability theory, but claims once again that risk is not a synonym for uncertainty.

Nevertheless, this incompatibility between the concept of fundamental uncertainty and asymmetric information has also been heavily opposed by economists including Dymski (1993, 1996) and Fazzari and Variato (1994, 1996).[8] Dymski (1996: 379) argues that the two concepts can be integrated and claims that

> the presence of uncertainty and finance constraints, in turn, depend on the primitive assumptions made about information, time and market coordination. It is also shown that whether intermediary structure matter depends first on whether finance constraints exist, and then on whether financial intermediaries have any special ability to counteract the effects of asymmetric information with information gathering or monitoring.

This would mean that asymmetric information and therefore ergodic probability, as Davidson puts it, serve as additional information about the institutional setting. Dymski (1996) subsequently defined the integration of asymmetric information as the adding of an ex ante risky environment on the level of microeconomic behaviour to the macroeconomic concept of fundamental uncertainty. Asymmetric information would therefore be synonymous with exogenous uncertainty, whereas fundamental uncertainty can be defined as endogenous uncertainty. This analysis follows this line of argumentation and treats asymmetric information as a relevant factor determining individual behaviour and the relationship between creditor and debtor. The integration, therefore, focuses on defining an appropriate setting for analysis and will not introduce models of probability to decrease risk, but instead discusses the causal mechanisms within the assumption of fundamental uncertainty. Furthermore, in order to point out the differences between Post Keynesian and New Keynesian models of credit rationing, the New Keynesian point of view is briefly presented. Ritthaler (1994) and, in particular, Hillier (1997), among others, have shown using a New Keynesian model based on the assumption of Stiglitz and Weiss (1981), that equilibrium credit rationing is possible in the loan market. Their assumption of an exogenous credit volume and neglecting time in the analysis does not conflict with the general argumentation outlined in this chapter. Figure 5.2 shows such a possible outcome. The demand curve is a gradual function for loans. Debtors are split into two groups of entrepreneurs according to their expected profits from implementing a specific project. The expected profits are derived from the probability of the project to succeed multiplied by the potential profits, which can be accumulated in case of success, minus the amount payable due to the loan, which varies according to the risk of the project (Hillier 1997: 13). It is assumed here that debtors know their specific credit risk; this assumption is relaxed in the Post Keynesian model later.

In the model described in Figure 5.2 it is assumed that entrepreneurs do not borrow money at a specific interest rate when their expected profits are zero. Therefore, the interest rate (i) works as a selection mechanisms for entrepreneurs. The horizontal axis in Figure 5.2 represents the volume of loans. The point (N1+N2) represents the total volume of loans requested. Both groups will ask for loans, in case that interest rates are ib. In the event that the interest rate is increased, entrepreneurs with projects in Group 1 (N1) drop out, as their expected profits are less than zero. Entrepreneurs with projects in Group 2 (N2) still demand loans. Therefore, the demand for loans function is vertical at the volume of loans demanded by entrepreneurs of Group 2. The supply function for loans (Sloans) reflects the bank's uncertainty of the success of the investment projects. The interest rate level for loans has to be multiplied with the expected return for the bank. When there are two groups of investment projects (N1 and N2), the supply function

*Figure 5.2* Asymmetric information and credit rationing: New Keynesian version

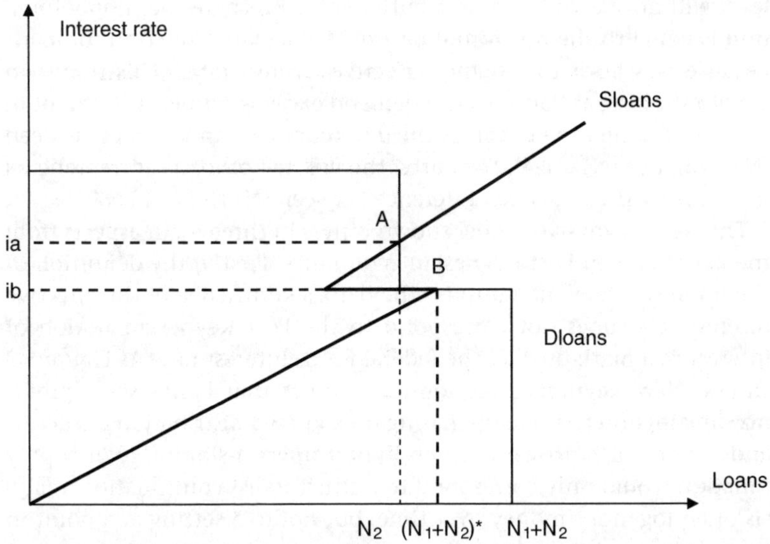


*Source*: Hillier (1997: 25).

for loans first increases constantly and then diverges when a certain level of interest rate is reached which makes the entrepreneurs with lower expected profits drop out. This jump discontinuity arises out of the assumption that banks charge an effective interest rate for the amount of loans given which equals, on average, the deposit interest rate. Banks calculate the effective interest rate by multiplying the interest rate charged for certain investment projects by a probability of default. Therefore, as it is assumed in Figure 5.2 that projects with lower expected profits and lower probability of default are shelved as interest rates increase, which in turn reduces the average interest return for the bank at the point where one group of entrepreneurs drops out, and then rises again continuously. This discontinuity in average effective interest rates is reflected in the shape of the loan supply function as the effective interest rate is assumed to be equal to the deposit interest rate, which is connected to a certain level of deposits supplied. Based on this volume of deposits, the New Keynesian framework derives the volume of loans supplied. Connecting supply and demand for loans, Figure 5.2 shows the possible outcome of a New Keynesian model that leads to credit rationing arising from asymmetric information. An intersection between supply and demand for loans exists at Point A which would be combined with an interest rate of ia. The interest rate level will not be set at Point A but at Point B, where the supply function is equal to the horizontal part of the demand function for loans because this leads to a higher effective interest rate.[9] This results in credit rationing at Point B since demand exceeds supply. The extent of credit rationing can be seen as the difference in loan volumes between (N1+N2) and (N1+N2)*. Similarly, the volume of loans entrepreneurs in group N1 request is the difference between (N1+N2) and N2.

The New Keynesian model shown differs in three main aspects from the paradigms in Post Keynesian economics. Firstly, the definition of the interest rate, which implies the bank's knowledge of the effective interest rate, does not correspond to the Post Keynesian notion of interest as a mark-up over the federal funds interest rate. As Figure 5.2 shows, New Keynesian economics assumes that banks set a profit-maximizing interest rate (ib) basing on a known distribution of success and default of borrowers. Secondly, an upward-sloping loan supply function would only correspond to a structuralist continuation analysis of endogenous money over time, but not to a setting at a point in time. Thirdly, also the loan demand function does not apply for a Post Keynesian framework, as a known probability distribution is assumed and therefore leads to a loan demand function, which consists of a horizontal part.

The knowledge of a true probability distribution of credit risk is not in line with the concept of fundamental uncertainty – see Wolfson (1996) for details – but claims the measurement of risk by probabilistic methods. Taking the above-presented critiques of the New Keynesian framework from a Post Keynesian point of view into account, Wolfson (1996) shows a graphical integration of asymmetric information into a Post Keynesian framework that can be used for a structuralist model of endogenous money. Contrary to the New Keynesian notion of credit rationing, the definition used in this chapter 'refers to any situation in which the bank refuses to lend to a particular borrower, despite the borrower's willingness to pay a higher interest rate' (Wolfson 1996: 463). Credit rationing rises since a bank, due to its estimate of the probability of repayment, accommodates a lower volume of loans compared to the requested volume of borrowers by following an, as Wolfson (1996: 466) puts it, effective loan demand curve. As a result, Figure 5.3 presents an endogenous money model in a structuralist tradition which has been adapted to the assumption of asymmetric information. The main differences between this model and a common

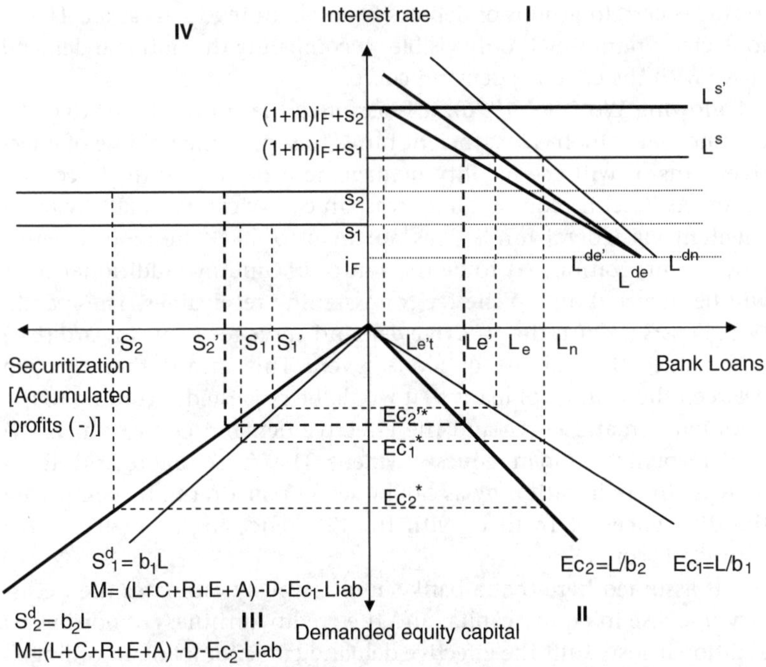


*Figure 5.3* Asymmetric information in an adapted endogenous money model

structuralist view are highlighted in the shape of the loan demand function in quadrant I and also the consequences arising from the effects of changing capital adequacy ratios on bank's balance sheets, as shown in quadrant II.

Starting from the upper-right quadrant, Figure 5.3 shows the demand for loans ($L^d$) and the supply for loans ($L^s$) in a structuralist view, adding asymmetric information. This leads to a splitting of the loan demand function. As Wolfson (1996) argues in depth, the demand for loans from borrowers is a notional one, which means that according to the level of loan demand the bank immediately sets an effective demand function, which excludes the borrowers the bank expects to be less creditworthy. Therefore quadrant I in shows the notional demand curve $L^{dn}$ and the effective demand curve $L^{de}$. The intersection of endogenous loan supply and effective loan demand leads to the credit volume $L_e'$, which implies credit rationing between $L_n$ and $L_e'$. This means that credit rationing in a Post Keynesian framework does not occur due to rationing within some groups of debtors but explicitly excludes certain groups of debtors from obtaining loans at all. Therefore, credit rationing is only visible by comparing the notional demand curve with the effective demand curve.

Following Wolfson (1996), it is assumed that in the event that the commercial bank has insufficient funds to supply the volume of effective loans, it will use liability management to borrow the necessary funds. As Basel II requires an increase in equity capital, liability management via federal funds does not help to meet the requirements. Since securitization has to be the source of funding, additional costs will be incurred due to the fees of assigning receivables. These additional costs (s) turn the effective demand curve for loans inward ($L^{de'}$) and reduce the volume of loans given. This means that the gap between the volume of loans that would be requested according to the notional demand curve and the effective demand curve, which the bank recognizes as loan requests, widens. That furthermore leads to an increase in credit rationing as can be seen in quadrant I by comparing the differences of $L_n$ to $L_e'$ with the difference in the loan volume between $L_n$ and $L_e'$.

It is assumed here that a bank simultaneously estimates the necessary increase in equity capital and the creditworthiness of borrowers; additional costs shift the effective demand curve for loans accordingly. The effects of combining the new effective demand curve with capital requirements of Basel II are indicated by the bold line in quadrant II. Similar to Figure 5.1, the equity capital function is turned inward, but combined with a lower level of demanded equity capital. $Ec_1$* reflects the new volume of demanded equity capital compared to the volume of $Ec_2$* in the event of introducing Basel II requirements without taking credit rationing into account. When integrating Basel II requirements into the model, the volume of securitization is also lower – compare $S_2$ with $S_2'$ in quadrant III – yet the requested level of securitization is nevertheless higher compared to a situation without the introduction of new capital requirements – with and without taking credit rationing into account. Compare in this case the volume of requested securitization $S_2'$ with $S_1$ as a scenario without Basel II and neglecting credit rationing and $S_1'$ when integrating credit rationing without accounting for the new capital requirements. Therefore, interest rates will increase in quadrant IV from $s_1$ to $s_2$.

In general, it should be noted that, converse to the effects described in Figure 5.1, the implementation of the new capital adequacy standards not only shifts the demand for equity capital curve, which lowers the volume of loans given due to an increase in the interest rate, but also lowers the volume of loans even before an increase in interest rates occurs. An increase in the interest rate, as represented in Figure 5.1 by the shift in the loan supply function ($L^{s\prime}$), increases credit rationing further. The intersection of $L^{s\prime}$ with $L^{de\prime}$ and the resulting volume of loans demanded ($L_e{}'_t$) indicates a dynamic process, which is beyond the scope of this chapter.

## Conclusions

This theoretical assessment shows that imposing methods of banking regulation has an impact on capital requirements and appears to be of major significance for macroeconomic development in terms of lending volume in insider financial systems. As the analysis conducted in this chapter does not concentrate on specific groups of debtors, the overall impact on the investment decisions of companies cannot be derived. Nevertheless, a decrease in the loan volume can be assumed. It can be concluded that, contrary to what was intended by the introduction of these new means of banking regulation, central banks' power over commercial banks' lending activities will not increase, but will in fact be reduced further as commercial banks move towards refinancing via securitization. Therefore, stability has increased by reducing credit risk, but seems to be decreasing by rising market risk when banks assign receivables. Palley (2006) has shown that asset-based reserve requirements would enable central banks to increase the influence on commercial banks despite their increasing potential for liability management. Evidence in this chapter supports Palley's (2006) analysis. Depending on the ability of banks to secure funds via liability management, total loan volume will be affected by the introduction of Basel II.

Moving towards a microeconomic investigation of bank lending, it becomes evident that credit rationing due to asymmetric information increases in an endogenous money model when introducing the new capital requirements and simultaneously results in further decreases in the volume of loans. It can therefore be concluded from a theoretical point of view that neither the regulatory power of the central bank is enhanced by the new capital adequacy framework nor that loan decisions for companies are simplified. In fact, credit rationing simply increases. This, in turn, might lead to a negative overall effect on macroeconomic development in countries in which companies are particularly dependent on bank loans when making investment decisions – economies with insider financial systems.

## Notes

1. In contrast to the distinction between market- and bank-based financial systems, which relies heavily on the flow of financial funds and consist of quantitative methods to investigate the activity, size and efficiency of banks and stock exchanges in relation to each other (see among others Demirgüc-Kunt and Levine 1999), this refers here to the distinction between insider and outsider financial systems that traces back to the works of Hirschman (1970), to the relation between debtor and creditor, and to the behaviour of the players involved in the two different concepts of financial systems.
2. Self-regulation mechanisms comprise all measures that are put into place by pure market forces and do not involve any direct action on the part of a supervisory authority. Corporate Governance Codes, for example, aim to increase trust and transparency in a market system. In this case, the aim is to reduce the negative effects of asymmetric information and to increase transparency in the relationship between investors and companies.
3. Numerous developed and less developed countries – in terms of financial sector development – suffered financial crises after liberalization. Finland, for example, faced a banking crisis from 1991 to 1994, Italy from 1990 to 1994, Norway from 1987 to 1993 and Portugal from 1986 to 1989 (Demirgüc-Kunt and Detragiache 1998).
4. Although McKinnon (1973) focused on emerging financial markets and their fragmented economies when discussing negative credit distortions arising from banking regulation, (orthodox) economists believe in similar effects for more developed economies.
5. The effects Basel II in particular might have on the national financial systems via changes in the institutional structure of banking regulation have to be taken into account. As Wolfson (1993) points out, the mechanisms of Pillar II in Basel II consist basically of preventive measures to ensure banking stability, whereas a direct institutional influence has a minor role. Therefore shifts in national financial systems towards a more market-based system, which do not put the same emphasis on institutional settings as bank-based countries do, cannot be neglected.
6. Since both internal-based approaches require sophisticated computer-based risk assessment strategies, which banks are supposed to create themselves, only larger banks will be able to use one of these very costly approaches. Although the standardized approach also requires additional investment for implementation, it is less costly since additional research costs are not required.
7. Economic schools of thought that try to incorporate endogenous money models into their theoretical framework include, among others, New Keynesian Approaches, Post Keynesian Economics, Economics in Marxian Tradition as well as Neo-Austrian Economics. (Flanders 1997; Lapavitsas 2003)
8. A similar possibility to integrate the concepts of fundamental uncertainty and asymmetric information traces back to Dymski (1993) and Bossone (1999).
9. See Hillier (1997: 12, 23) for a detailed discussion.

## References

Akyüz, Y. (2000) *The Debate on the International Finance Architecture: Reforming the Reformers*, UNCTAD Discussion Paper, No. 148.

Arestis, P. and Howells, P. (1996) 'Theoretical Reflections on Endogenous Money: the Problem with "Convenience Lending"', *Cambridge Journal of Economics*, 20: 539–51.

Bank for International Settlements (eds) (2003) *The New Basel Capital Accord. BIS Third Consultative Document* (Basel: Bank of International Settlements).

Bossone, B. (1999) *The Role of Trust in Financial Sector Development*, World Bank Working Paper No. 2200.

Brown, C. (2003) 'Toward a Reconcilement of Endogenous Money and Liquidity Preference', *Journal of Post Keynesian Economics*, 26(2): 325–39.

Chick, V. and Dow, S. (1996) 'Regulation and Differences in Financial Institutions', *Journal of Economic Issues*, 30(2): 517–23.

Chick, V. and Dow, S. (2002) 'Monetary Policy with Endogenous Money and Liquidity Preference: A Nondualistic Treatment', *Journal of Post Keynesian Economics*, 24(4): 587–607.

Chorafas, D. (2004) *Economic Capital Allocation with Basel II: Cost, Benefit and Implementation Procedures* (Oxford: Elsevier Butterworth-Heinemann).

Clinton, K. (1997) *Implementation of Monetary Policy in a Regime with Zero Reserve Requirements*, Bank of Canada Working Paper, No. 8.

Cottrell, A. (1994) 'Endogenous Money and the Multiplier', *Journal of Post Keynesian Economics*, 17: 111–20.

Crotty, J. (1996) 'Is New Keynesian Investment Theory Really "Keynesian"? Reflections on Fazzari, Steven and Anna Variato', *Journal of Post-Keynesian Economics*, 18(3): 333–57.

Davidson P. (1991) 'Is probability Theory Relevant for Uncertainty? A Post Keynesian Perspective', *Journal of Economic Perspectives*, 5(1): 129–43.

Demirgüc-Kunt, A. and Detragiache, E. (1998) *Financial Liberalization and Financial Fragility*, IMF Working Paper No. 98/83.

Demirgüc-Kunt, A. and Levine, R. (1999) *Bank-based and Market-Based Financial Systems: Cross County Comparison*, World Bank Working paper, http://www.worldbank.org/research/projects/finstructure/pdf_files/structures3.pdf#search=%22Demirguc%20%22Bank-based%20and%20market%20based%22%22.

Dymski, G. (1988) 'A Keynesian Theory of Bank Behaviour', *Journal of Post-Keynesian Economics*, 10(4): 499–526.

Dymski, G. (1993) 'Keynesian Uncertainty and Asymmetric Information: Complementary or Contradictory?', *Journal of Post-Keynesian Economics*, 16(1): 49–54.

Dymski, G. (1996) 'Basic Choices in Keynesian Models of Credit', in G. Deleplace and E. Nell (eds), *Money in Motion* (London: Macmillan).

Eatwell, J. and Taylor, L. (2000) *Global Finance at Risk* (New York: New Press).

Fazzari, S.M. and. Variato, A.M. (1994) 'Asymmetric Information and Keynesian Theories of Investment', *Journal of Post-Keynesian Economics*, 16(3): 351–69.

Fazzari, S.M. and Variato, A.M. (1996) 'Varieties of Keynesian Investment Theories: Further Reflections', *Journal of Post-Keynesian Economics*, 18(3): 359–68.

Flanders, M.J. (1997) *Left- and Right-Endogenous Money: A Tale of Two Books*, Tel Aviv University, Working Paper No. 15.

Fontana, G. (2003) 'Post Keynesian Approaches to Endogenous Money: A Time Framework Explanation', *Review of Political Economy*, 15(3): 291–314.

Fontana, G. and Venturino, E. (2003) 'Endogenous Money: An Analytical Approach', *Scottish Journal of Political Economy*, 50(4): 398–416.

Frenkel, M. and Menkhoff, L. (2000) *Stabile Weltfinanzen?* (Berlin: Springer).

Hillier, B. (1997) *The Economics of Asymmetric Information* (Basingstoke: Macmillan – now Palgrave Macmillan).

Hirschman, A. (1970) *Exit, Voice, and Loyalt:. Responses to Decline in Firms, Organizations, and States* (Cambridge MA: Harvard University Press).

Lapavitsas, C. (2003) *Money as 'Universal Equivalent' and Its Origin in Commodity Exchange*, University of London, Working Paper.

McKinnon, R. I. (1973) *Money and Capital in Economic Development* (Washington: Brookings Institute).

Moore, B. (1988) *Horizontalists and Verticalists: The Macroeconomics of Credit Money* (New York: Cambridge University Press).

Moore, B. (1994) 'The Demise of the Keynesian Multiplier: A Reply to Cottrell', *Journal of Post-Keynesian Economics*, 17(1): 121–33.

Moore, B. (1997) 'Reconciliation of the Supply and Demand for Endogenous Money', *Journal of Post Keynesian Economics*, 19(3): 423–28.

Niggle, C.J. (1991) 'The Endogenous Money Supply Theory: An Institutionalist Appraisal', *Journal of Economic Issues*, 30(1): 137–51.

Palley, T. (1994) 'Competing views of the Money Supply Process: Theory and Evidence', *Metroeconomica*, 45(1): 76–88.

Palley, T. (1996) 'Accommodationism versus Structuralism: Time for an Accommodation', *Journal of Post Keynesian Economics*, 18(4): 585–94.

Palley, T. (2006) 'A Post-Keynesian Framework for Monetary Policy: Why Interest Rate Operating Procedures are Not Enough', in C. Gnos and L.-P. Rochon (eds), *Post-Keynesian Principles of Economic Policy* (Cheltham: Edward Elgar).

Pollin, R. (1991) 'Two Theories of Money Supply Endogeneity: Some Empirical Evidence', *Journal of Post-Keynesian Economics*, 13(3): 366–96.

Ritthaler, M. (1994) *Kreditrationierung* (Weiden and Regensburg: eurotrans).

Rochon, L.-P. (1999) *Credit, Money and production: An Alternative Post-Keynesian Approach* (Northampton, MA: Edward Elgar).

Rousseas, S. (1986) *Post-Keynesian Monetary Economics* (Basingstoke: Macmillan – now Palgrave Macmillan).

Sellon, G.H. and Weiner S.E. (1997) 'Monetary Policy without Reserve Requirements: Case Studies and Options for the United States', *Federal Reserve Bank of Kansas City Economic Review*, 2: 5–30.

Shaw, E.S. (1973) *Financial Deepening in Economic Development* (New York: Oxford University Press).

Stiglitz, J. and Weiss, A. (1981) 'Credit Rationing in Markets with Imperfect Information', *American Economic Review*, 71: 393–410.

Strulik, T. (2000) *Risikomanagement globaler Finanzmärkte. Herausforderungen und Initiativen im Kontext der Bankenregulierung* (Frankfurt am Main: Campus-Verlag).

Van Ees, H. and Garretsen, H. (1993) 'Financial Markets and the Complementarity of Asymmetric Information and Fundamental Uncertainty', *Journal of Post-Keynesian Economics*, 16(1): 37–48.

Wolfson, M.H. (1993) 'The Evolution of the Financial System and the Possibilities for Reform', in G. Dymski, G. Epstein and R. Pollin (eds), *Transforming the US Financial System* (New York: M.E. Sharpe).
Wolfson, M.H. (1996) 'A Post Keynesian Theory of Credit Rationing', *Journal of Post Keynesian Economics*, 18(3): 443–70.

# 6

# Monetary and Budgetary-Fiscal Policy Interactions in a Keynesian Context: Revisiting Macroeconomic Governance

*Angel Asensio*

## Introduction

According to the New Consensus Macroeconomics (NCM), economic policy deals with different problems depending on the length of the period considered. If the period is long enough, competitive forces drive the rate of unemployment to the 'natural level'. Theoretically, a succession of such periods should not exhibit statistical evidence of unemployment pressure on wages or consumer prices; the Phillips relation should look vertical. In each of these 'long periods', expected prices variations equal the effective values, and contracts are negotiated in accordance with the right expectations. That is the reason why systematic (hence expected) stimulations of aggregate demand[1] do not reduce real wages and unemployment; they only strengthen inflation.

By contrast, in Keynesian effective-demand-led systems, it is doubtful that market forces spontaneously guide the system towards a natural equilibrium in the long run. Equilibrium is embedded in a changing and uncertain context which makes expectations a poor device for decision making because there is no predictable trend or trajectory. Keynesian analysis breaks with the idea that expectations tend to be right when the length of the periods is extended. It breaks also with the idea that, over the defined 'long periods', contracts are negotiated on the basis of right expectations. The 'long run' which is required for the Phillips curve to be vertical simply makes no sense in such a context.

The difference between the two approaches is less evident in the short run since they agree on the positive impact of aggregate demand policies. Let us summarize the NCM argument. Because the adjustment of wages to the state of affairs takes more time, an inverse relation between the rate of variation in wages and the magnitude of the deviation from the natural rate of unemployment can be observed. Inflation plays a decisive role here (provided it has not been expected) because it reduces the real wages, and makes it acceptable for firms to respond to an increase in demand for goods and services.

In a recent Post Keynesian perspective, Kriesler and Lavoie (2005), following Freedman, Harcourt and Kriesler (2004) and Palacio-Vera (2005), suggested that capacity utilization only influences inflation when its level is very low or when there is full capacity utilization. Making such an assumption within a standard NCM model, which encompasses an IS demand function and a monetary reaction function *à la* Taylor, implies that for a large range of capacity utilization, monetary policy influences the rate of capacity utilization, not inflation. In this case, excess of productive capacity makes it possible for firms to increase production and employment in response to an increasing effective demand without having to pay more attractive nominal wages, and without need for lowering the real cost of labour through inflation. Notice that the contrast with the NCM fades if one makes the reasonable assumption that inflationary pressures begin before full capacity utilization is reached.[2]

Following these considerations one could think that Keynesians agree with the New Consensus as far as short-run economic behaviour is considered. But this idea is wrong, since the 'short period' makes no sense except with reference to the 'long period' of the NCM. 'Short periods' only reveal deviations from the 'long run' equilibrium path. They are accidents that markets forces will correct even without the help of economic policy. On the contrary, in a Keynesian world, equilibrium never is a temporary anomaly; it is a stable solution of the economic system, which is more or less distant from full employment depending on the level of effective demand, and which moves according to it.

Such a disagreement about the nature of the economic equilibrium had to deliver diverging assessments of economic policy. While some see a simple smoothing device devoted to stabilize the system around a natural trend,[3] others deal with a wandering system whose evolution, never known in advance, depends on the support given by public policies. For some, inflation is the consequence of abusive stabilization policies, especially monetary policy;[4] they recommend strong restrictions to the instruments. For others, inflation results from distribution conflict with respect to national income. To tighten monetary policy in such a context would be inaccurate and could provoke a depression, or make it more serious. In addition, the supremacy the

NCM grants to monetary over fiscal policy contrasts with the pitfalls that Keynes identified with respect to the control of the rates of interest, and their influence on effective demand and inflation. It contrasts also with the role of budgetary and fiscal policy in the Keynesian literature.[5]

This chapter aims to extend the reflection on Keynesian alternatives for macroeconomic governance. It focuses on the connection between monetary and fiscal policy facing the triple problem of controlling inflation, public finance and employment. It sheds a new light on monetary policy through analysing complementarities with respect to budgetary and fiscal policy, and through the study of interactions between the policy mix and distribution conflict. The next section compares the equilibrium main properties of the two theoretical frameworks. The functional interdependencies among the different markets are examined methodically (goods, labour, bonds, money). We show that, despite the formal similarity of the system-behaviour around equilibrium, there are strong differences in the conclusions which can be drawn from the two approaches. The reason is of course that the definitions of variables and parameters differ, as well as the adjustment process and properties of the equilibrium. The third section focuses on the implications of such differences for the study of monetary and budgetary-fiscal policies interactions and complementarities in a Keynesian context.

## General equilibrium: alternative theories

We start with a simple linear model which aims to study the effects of the two types of governance in the short run.[6] Variables are expressed in terms of relative variations from their initial value, excepting the rate of interest and the tax rate, which are expressed as variations. First the NCM will be analyzed in terms of general equilibrium. Then, the main Keynesian differences will be put forward from the same general equilibrium perspective.

### Macroeconomics in Walrasian terms

The usual Walrasian macroeconomics is modelled at first in order to extend the framework towards NCM. We consider for the moment a three-market structure (goods, labour and bonds) with two relative prices (the real wage and the rate of interest).[7] However, because of Walras's Law, the equilibrium condition for the market of bonds will remain implicit.

*Labour market*

At equilibrium, variations in real wages and employment compensate for the marginal disutility of labour (supply side) and furthermore insure profit maximization (demand side). The marginal productivity equalization to the real cost of labour induces a decreasing relation between employment and real wage:

$$n = -\rho\omega + d \tag{6.1}$$

$n$ is the relative variation in employment

$\omega$ is the relative variation in the real wage (that is the quantity of goods paid in exchange for the labour unit)

On the other hand, equalization of the marginal disutility of labour to the real wage means an increasing relation. It will be useful to reverse this relation in order to express the real wage as a function of the level of employment given by equation (6.1):

$$\omega = \theta n \tag{6.2}$$

In a monetary economy, equation (6.2) would suppose the nominal wage variation ($w$) to depend on both the price index variation over the period ($p$, see below about the nominal price index determination in the model with money), and the additional labour employed if necessary:

$$w = p + \theta n \tag{6.2'}$$

These two equations insure that firms remain on their demand for labour curve, and that workers remain on their supply curve at equilibrium.

*Goods market*

The supply of goods depends on the quantity of inputs, especially labour in the short run, and therefore technology will be represented as:

$$y = \alpha n + c \tag{6.3}$$

$y$ is the relative variation in the quantity of output and $c$ represents other exogenous technological factors. We assume $\alpha < 1$ (diminishing marginal product of labour).

Equations (6.1) to (6.3) give relative variations in production, employment and real wages as functions of the structural parameters and exogenous variables of the model:

$$n = \frac{d}{1 + \rho\theta}$$

$$y = \alpha \frac{d}{1 + \rho\theta} + c$$

$$\omega = \theta \frac{d}{1 + \rho\theta}$$

Hence, economic activity depends only on technology and labour market conditions. The rate of interest insures aggregate demand for any additional production. Since the market equilibrium requires equal supply and demand:[8]

$$y = -\sigma\hat{i} + \lambda(\varphi g + a) - \gamma\hat{t} \tag{6.4}$$

$g$: relative variation in the government demand for goods
$\hat{t}$: variation in the tax rate
$a$: relative variation in the exogenous part of aggregate private demand
$\hat{i}$: variation in the rate of interest
$\varphi$: the initial tax rate

We get:

$$\hat{i} = -\frac{1}{\sigma}c - \frac{\gamma}{\sigma}\hat{t} + \frac{\lambda}{\sigma}(\varphi g + a) - \frac{\alpha}{\sigma(1 + \rho\theta)}d$$

This rate of interest is both the market-clearing condition for bonds and, through equalization of saving and investment, the condition for aggregate demand of goods to be equal to aggregate supply. Notice that the tax rate, government expenditures and other aggregate demand components do not influence production and employment levels at equilibrium; their variations only produce crowding-out effects through the adjustment of the interest rate.

*Money market*

In this theoretical framework, money is only a transaction device, and demand for money varies following the volume and price of transactions. Assuming a constant money circulation velocity, the equilibrium condition requires any variation in the quantity of money ($m$, exogenous for the moment) to be offset by an equivalent variation in the demand for money:

$$m = y + p \tag{6.5}$$

As far as the demand for real money balances depends on real income, it depends on technology and labour market conditions; hence inflation results from excessive real money balances relative to the need for real money balances (at the previous prices):

$$p = m - c - \alpha \frac{d}{1 + \rho\theta}$$

Other things being equal ($c=d=0$), prices vary in proportion to the money supply, without any effect on real variables and relative prices (including the rate of interest).

*Macroeconomic policy*

For the reason we have just mentioned, the sole valid goal that monetary policy may target concerns inflation control. On the other hand, budgetary and fiscal policy is not necessary for stabilization purposes as far as markets are supposed to work 'perfectly'. It may, however, produce temporary or permanent effects on relative prices and real variables because of distortions on the resources allocation process. This view traditionally puts economic efficiency in conflict with fiscal redistributive laws on which the social order is based.

## The new synthesis

After Keynes had demonstrated the decisive importance of expectations for macroeconomic analysis, the rational expectation hypothesis gave a new impulse to (neo)classical economics during the 1970s. It was shown that in stochastic stationary regimes, the main properties of the classical system continued to work provided that market efficiency was postulated. 'New Keynesian Economics' share most of this revitalized New Classical framework, even though it put forward nominal and real rigidities, which prevent the competitive process to work perfectly in the 'short run'. If nominal wages, for example, are imperfectly flexible, inflationary shocks temporarily move real wages and employment from their natural level. Demand policies may be useful in this case, but only to the extent that they use the surprise-inflation channel. Yet, if money can influence relative prices and other real variables temporary, it plays a limited role in New Keynesian

Macroeconomics because rational expectations make it possible to predict future values of variables without systematic errors. Hence, as far as stochastic shocks only produce temporary deviations in stationary regimes,[9] the 'long-run' behaviour of the system is basically the same as the neoclassical one.

*Labour market*

Using monetary prices and wages, the demand for labour may be rewritten:

$$n = \rho(p - w) + d$$

It is possible to introduce fiscal distortion effects by supposing that in the short run they work through the price of the variable input: replacing the nominal cost of labour ($W$) by $W(1+\xi\, t)$, where $0 \leq \xi < 1$ measures the (weakened) impact of the tax rate on the labour cost, profit maximization requires $\partial Y/\partial N = W(1+\xi t)/P$. The demand for labour relative variation ($n$) then takes the form of a function of the fiscally-corrected labour cost, which relative variation can be approximated by $(p - w - \xi\hat{t})$ for small values of $\hat{t}$:

$$n = \rho(p - w - \xi\hat{t}) + d \qquad (6.1')$$

We will suppose that labour contracts have been negotiated, at the starting point of the period, on the basis of the expected rate of inflation for the current period ($p^a$):

$$w - p^a = \theta n \qquad (6.2'')$$

From (6.1′) we get:

$$w = p + \frac{\theta d - (p - p^a) - \rho\theta\xi\hat{t}}{1 + \rho\theta}$$

$$n = \frac{d + \rho(p - p^a) - \rho\xi\hat{t}}{1 + \rho\theta}$$

Hence, if $p^a = p$ (which is assumed to be true in the 'long run', as a result of rational expectations in stationary regimes), employment and production are the same as in the previous model (forgetting the fiscal distortion effect), but in case of inflationary surprise ($p \neq p^a$), demand shocks influence the level of employment through the prediction error ($p - p^a$).

*Goods market*

Equations (6.3) and (6.4) being unchanged, we obtain from the expression of $n$ above:

$$y = \frac{\alpha\rho(p - p^a) + \alpha\, d - \alpha\rho\xi\hat{t}}{1 + \rho\theta} + c$$

$$\hat{i} = -\frac{\alpha(\rho(p - p^a) + d}{\sigma(1 + \rho\theta)} + \frac{\lambda}{\sigma}(\varphi g + a) + \left(\frac{\alpha\rho\xi}{\sigma(1 + \rho\theta)}\right) - \frac{\gamma}{\sigma}\hat{t} - \frac{1}{\sigma}c$$

Once more, the results diverge from those of the previous model only in the case of inflationary surprise. Providing it is not expected, monetary policy recovers its stabilization power.

*Money market*

Using equation (6.5) in order to determine the behaviour of the price index, we get from the expression of $y$ above:

$$p = \frac{1 + \rho\theta}{1 + \rho\theta + \alpha\rho}(m - c) + \frac{\alpha(\rho\, p^a - d)}{1 + \rho\theta + \alpha\rho} + \frac{\alpha\rho\xi}{1 + \rho\theta + \alpha\rho}\hat{t},$$

for $p \neq p^a$.

But in the long run, for $p = p^a$ and we get:

$$p = m - c - \frac{\alpha}{1 + \rho\theta}d + \frac{\alpha\rho\xi}{1 + \rho\theta}\hat{t}$$

Hence, as far as there are inflation surprises, money quantity variations no more transmit totally to the price index. Since variations in $y$, $w$, $n$ and $\hat{i}$ depend on the price index and therefore on the quantity of money, the classical dichotomy seems to have disappeared. In addition, money does not work through the channel of interest ($\sigma$, which measures the sensibility of aggregate demand to changes in the rate of interest, does not appear in $n$, neither does it in $y$ after having replaced $p$). Indeed, it is through unpredicted variations in the price index that variations in the quantity of money can have real effects, including the rate of interest.

A more sophisticated demand for money can be preferred so as to take risk into account:[10]

$$m = y + p - \eta\hat{i} \tag{6.5'}$$

It can easily be shown that globally the model has similar properties in this case, with the exception that the interest channel works and government expenditures have real effects in equilibrium (provided that $p \neq p^a$, otherwise the dichotomy reappears since employment and production are completely determined by the supply-side equations (6.1′) (6.2″) and (6.3)). The system therefore looks like an extended IS-LM framework (equations 6.4 and 6.5′), which contains a supply set of equations for endogenous determination of wages and prices (see Appendix 6.2).

As Lavoie (2002) pointed out, in recent versions of the new consensus monetary policies consist in controlling the rate of interest rather than the quantity of money, which has to be considered as an endogenous variable. When the central bank controls $\hat{i}$, the LM function only determines the quantity of money that is equal to the demand for money, and therefore it is possible to solve the model for real magnitudes without it (Romer 2000).[11]

## General equilibrium modelling in a Keynesian world

Equation (6.5′) admits different interpretations depending upon the definition of uncertainty. In stochastic stationary regimes, risk makes money a useful portfolio diversification device, as we have just mentioned. This is a step towards the Keynesian monetary theory, but it does not capture its essential features. Indeed, there is a fundamental difference in the way to manage uncertainty when dynamic stability is not ensured, compared with a system where agents may predict the future without making systematic errors. The Keynesian concept of liquidity preference is not captured in equation (6.5′); the liquidity preference does not result from any optimal decision concerning risk and return, which could make sense in stationary regimes, but does not ensure that it is 'the best' solution in a Keynesian world. According to *The General Theory* (chapter 12), its magnitude results from the confidence level that people give to their expectations (whatever the distribution of probabilities they may make use of).

This Keynesian specificity will be formally underlined through considering $\eta_k$ as an exogenous variable which is subject to the kind of volatility that usually affects expectations:

$$m = y + p - \eta_k \hat{i} \qquad (6.5_K')$$

When aggregate demand and prices decrease, the need for transaction-money falls, and the rate of interest decreases, raising the demand and the price of goods and moving the real wages towards their full employment level.[12] But, in Keynesian contexts, the magnitude of the decrease in interest rate (the so-called 'Keynes effect') and of any positive real balance effect (people do not want to hold idle cash balances and therefore increase the demand for goods) depends on speculative decisions concerning the demand for money, with the result that income and employment finally depends on the degree of confidence of the moment and its impact on the demand for money. At equilibrium, there are no competitive mechanisms which could move the economy towards any predetermined 'long-run' solution.

*Labour market*

Contrary to the case in which firms are ensured to sell their production whatever the level, demand for labour will not be determined here by equation (6.1′), but by equation (6.3), which gives the variation in labour that makes the better use of the technology for a given level of the demand for goods.

Since the level of labour is fixed by the demand of firms, the supply-side equation of the labour market must determine the equilibrium wage. In the Classical world, as well as in the NCM 'long run', nominal wages adjustment, together with the real-balance effect, drives the real wages so as to ensure equality between labour supply and demand. The 'invisible hand' simultaneously drives the rate of interest so as to ensure that aggregate demand absorbs the full-employment supply of good. In such a world, money only can induce short-run 'noises', but in a Keynesian world, shifts of the speculative demand for money may keep the 'invisible hand' away from full employment. Hence, as far as nothing in these conditions ensures the equalization of equilibrium real wages and marginal disutility of labour attached to a given level of effective demand, equation (6.2″), which represents the 'Second Classical postulate', must be abandoned.

How, then, has the equilibrium nominal wage to be determined? The *General Theory* discussion of the labour market pointed out that a decrease in wages does not systematically increase employment, because of the negative demand effects it may provoke through the expected return on capital. The existence of an equilibrium with under-employment means that the self-regulatory process failed, either the wages decrease have not been able to stimulate the effective demand or have amplified the depression (but in this case wages should continue to fall),[13] or workers have been able to stop the decrease in wages. We will therefore suppose that nominal wages are anchored in an exogenous (but variable) threshold ($\overline{w}$). The current wage, however, may deviate from this threshold when certain events occur, such as a change in unemployment rate or exogenous disturbances:

$$w = \bar{w} - \theta_k(n_f - n) \qquad (6.2_k)$$

where $n_f$ is the rate of change of the labour force.

*Goods market*

Since the market equilibrium requires that firms adjust production ($y$) to effective demand (equation 6.4), the supply for goods is not unconditionally consistent with the employment level which results from equation (6.1′). This does not mean that firms cannot adjust the marginal productivity of labour to the factor real cost, but only that it is not through the choice of the employment level that they can do it. Equation (6.1′) actually gives the price index variation that makes firms able to remain on their demand for labour curve. When demand increases, it is through inflation that the real wage variation is made equal to the marginal productivity decline, prompting firms to raise their production in order to respond to the increasing demand.

Without changing the formal condition expressed in equation (6.1′), we can rewrite it in accordance with the Keynesian approach to inflation:

$$p = w + n - y - \dot{\alpha} + \xi\hat{t} \qquad (6.1'')$$

where $-\dot{\alpha} + \xi\hat{t}$ is the rate of variation of the mark-up on unit labour cost.[14]

Inflation may be caused by interest rate variations through their impact on aggregate demand and output, but in contrast to the NCM model, this does not require inflation surprises. In addition, inflation reveals its connection with labour costs, including taxes, and with the mark-up. Equation (6.1″) also indicates that a positive shift in output, which reduces the productivity of labour,[15] does not necessarily imply a decline of real wages; it depends on the mark-up behaviour. Thus real wages may vary pro-cyclically.

*Money market*

Following the Post Keynesian approach to endogenous money, we will suppose that banks deliver the quantity of money that is demanded at the current rate of interest, which is influenced by the central bank decisions. However, despite the formal resemblance, the functioning of the market differs from that of the NCM, notably because of the speculative demand instability. Hence, the transmission of short-term interest rate variations, through which the central bank may influence the long-term interest rates, is made uncertain. For example, lower short-term rates (increases in high-powered money) aiming to extend credit do not produce the same decline in long-term rates depending on whether the liquidity preference changes or not. When it rises, banks may be able to sell more credit without having to reduce their interest rates, for non-bank loans rates in this case tend to rise in order to compensate the increasing liquidity preference. Moreover, speculative behaviours also may block the transmission process when the current rates are considered as very low (liquidity trap). Thus automatic monetary rules *à la* Taylor turn out to be excessively optimistic in a Keynesian context.

**Formal similarities and fundamental discrepancies**

From a formal point of view, the differences between the two models concern equations ($6.2_k$) and (6.2″), as long as LM is not explicitly represented. If, as usually supposed, the labour force is constant in the short run ($n_f$=0), differences restrict to wages determinants ($\bar{w}$ or $p^a$) and parameters ($\theta$ or $\theta_k$) which have different definitions in the two models.

Thus, apart from the postulate that shocks ($c$, $\dot{\alpha}$, $p^a$, $a$) are temporary deviations from a stationary regime in the NCM model, the short-run behaviour modelling of non-ergodic systems seems very similar to the modelling of stationary regimes with rational expectations. However, this formal similarity hides fundamental differences about the general equilibrium properties. First, the volatility of the demand for money (equation $6.5'_k$) threatens the ability of interest rates to push aggregate demand up to full employment (whatever way it might take, spontaneous competitive forces or monetary policy). Second, Keynesian equilibrium is driven by effective demand; there is no force of attraction towards any predetermined 'long-run' or 'natural' position; hence the Keynesian unemployment level does not tend to reduce wages beyond some exogenous limit (but a shift in unemployment may however weaken the workers resistance, as in equation $6.2_k$).

Other fundamental discrepancies concern the significance of inflation and the role of monetary policy. We have mentioned the connection between cost-push inflation and demand-led inflation. Indeed, inflationary effects associated with wages, mark-up and/or tax pressures ($\bar{w}$ >0, $\dot{\alpha}$<0, $\hat{t}$>0) in equation (6.1″), depend on the way monetary authorities will pass them on effective demand. For cost pressures come with higher demand for transaction money, inflation can develop only if the central bank satisfies the additional demand of money, in order for example to stabilize the rate of interest. If, on the contrary, monetary authorities aim to stabilize the price index, they do not prevent the rise of interest rates, so as to offset the inflationary effects of increasing costs through a depressive impact on effective demand. Hence, recurrent distributive conflicts, whatever the reason (wage-profit sharing, fiscal pressures), force monetary policy into dilemma: to accept the inflationary consequences and preserve economic activities, or to depress economic activity in order to stabilize the real value of money through a permanent pressure of unemployment on wages. In the Keynesian context, monetary policy is involved in the determination of equilibrium and income distribution; it is not a simple stabilization device for self regulated systems.

## Alternative macro-governance approaches

According to the NCM, debt monetization and willingness to secure extra output are the primary causes of inflation. Solutions stem from governance principles like central bank independence and public deficit limitation, which aim to prevent central banks to create more money than is needed for making transactions at current prices. Whereas such principles seem suitable in a stationary system, they can deteriorate the situation in the presence of Keynesian unemployment. This section compares the main implications of the NCM governance in both stationary and Keynesian regimes.

### NCM governance

The type of governance that is suggested by the NCM is based on targets that are defined in relation to the expected trajectory of the economy. Temporary deviations of the rate of interest may be decided for stabilization purposes, in such a way that the quantity of money evolves in concert with the demand induced by the economic growth, without inflation pressures. Conversely, policies that aim systematically to get extra output through inflation surprise or debt monetization are fully predictable and therefore inefficient; they only feed into inflation. Consequently, the New Consensus pleads in favour of central bank political independence and low inflation targeting. In addition, according to the 'unpleasant monetarist arithmetic' that Sargent and Wallace (1981) pointed out, public deficit limitations are necessary for the credibility and efficiency of monetary policy.

*Modelling macroeconomic governance within the new synthesis vision of the world*

In order to draw some analytical conclusions from the model, let us assume that credible institutions ensure there is no inflation bias, so that active monetary policy only aims to stabilize the system by means of (non-systematic) inflation surprise ($p \neq p^a$).[16] Since the central bank is credible, private agents anchor their expectation on the announced inflation target. However, in front of a shock, authorities deviate from the target in order to stabilize employment, with a magnitude which depends on their degree of 'conservatism' about inflation.

Fiscal authorities for their part have a budget balance target related to their financial policy and debt management constraints. As well as monetary authorities, they concede temporary deviations according to their degree of 'orthodoxy'.

Appendix 6.2 (case b) shows that in the model of endogenous money, monetary, budgetary and fiscal instruments ($\hat{i},g,\hat{t}$) influence the equilibrium value of output, employment and prices. Hence they influence also the budget balance ($b$, see Appendix 6.3):

$$b = \varphi(y - g) + \hat{t} \tag{6.6}$$

We suppose that the deviations of instruments are decided with respect to employment deviations. The short run objectives will be:

$$b = \psi n \tag{6.7}$$

$$p = -\beta n \tag{6.8}$$

Equation (6.8), for example, means that, in order to stabilize the economic activity, a positive (negative) temporary deviation of the price index is accepted in case of a negative (positive) deviation from the natural rate of employment. Parameters $\beta \geq 0$ and $\psi \geq 0$ represent respectively the monetary 'Conservatism' and the fiscal 'Orthodoxy'. $\beta = 0$ means that there are no short-run deviations from the inflation target (full 'Conservatism'). $\psi = 0$ means that the budget deficit (or surplus) depends only on financial long-run considerations, and do not participate in stabilization operations.

This way of modelling policy rules simplifies algebra, but it is consistent with the usual loss-function minimization procedure.[17] Starting from equations (6.1″) (6.2″) (6.3) and (6.4), and provided that the government changes expenditures for example, rather than taxes, in order to reach its objective, we get:

$$g = \frac{\psi - \varphi\alpha}{\varphi(\beta + \theta + 1 - \alpha)}(p^a - \dot{\alpha}) + \frac{\varphi(\beta + \theta + 1) - \psi}{\varphi(\beta + \theta + 1 - \alpha)} c +$$

$$\frac{\beta + \theta + 1 - \alpha + (\psi - \varphi\alpha)\xi}{\varphi(\beta + \theta + 1 - \alpha)} \hat{t}$$

$$b = -\psi \frac{p^a - \dot{\alpha} - c + \xi\hat{t}}{\beta + \theta + 1 - \alpha}$$

$$\hat{i} = \frac{\lambda}{\sigma} a - \frac{\lambda\psi + (1 - \lambda\varphi)(\beta + \theta + 1)}{\sigma(\beta + \theta + 1 - \alpha)} c + \frac{\lambda\psi - \lambda\varphi\alpha + \alpha}{\sigma(\beta + \theta + 1 - \alpha)} (p^a - \dot{\alpha})$$

$$+ \frac{(\lambda - \gamma)(\beta + \theta + 1 - \alpha) + (\lambda\psi - \lambda\varphi\alpha + \alpha)\xi}{\sigma(\beta + \theta + 1 - \alpha)} \hat{t}$$

Public expenditures only respond to supply shocks and, if necessary, to fiscal changes. The reason is that monetary policy neutralizes the effects of demand shocks on output and prices, as the solutions attest:

$$n = -\frac{p^a - \dot{\alpha} - c + \xi\hat{t}}{\beta + \theta + 1 - \alpha}$$

$$y = \frac{(\beta + \theta + 1)c - \alpha(p^a - \dot{\alpha} + \xi\hat{t})}{\beta + \theta + 1 - \alpha}$$

$$p = \beta \frac{p^a - \dot{\alpha} - c + \xi\hat{t}}{\beta + \theta + 1 - \alpha}$$

with the result that government reaches its objective without having to move its instrument, since employment and fiscal revenues remain unchanged.

Finally, because they work through aggregate demand channels, public expenditures and interest rate reactions protect the economy against demand shocks, but only yield imperfect management of supply shocks. It is of interest to note that temporary changes of the fiscal distortion level can usefully improve the policy mix, since they make possible to cancel the effects of the shocks on prices and employment without budget balance deterioration:

$$\hat{t} = \frac{c + \dot{\alpha} - p^a}{\xi} \Rightarrow p = n = b = 0$$

That is the reason why deficit limitations are not really considered by the NCM as obstacles to stabilization.

*New governance in a Keynesian world*

What kind of consequences may have such governance principles in a Keynesian situation of unemployment? In order to answer the question, let the exogenous variable $q$ represent the variation in employment that is initially required for full employment. Since $n$ is the variation in employment for the current period, $q$-$n$ measures the level of unemployment at the end of the period. As authorities think that $q$ reflects the natural rate of unemployment ($\bar{w}$, $c$, $\dot{\alpha}$, and $a$ are supposed to provoke temporary deviations from the trend), they do not take it as a stabilization matter, and follow the policy discussed in the previous section.

The formal results of the previous section can be easily adapted to the present configuration when the labour force remains unchanged during the current period ($n_f = 0$), provided we replace equation (6.2″) by equation ($6.2_k$), which only supposes that $\bar{w}$ and $\theta_k$ replace $p^a$ and $\theta$). It follows that, in the most favourable case where authorities can completely stabilize the price index and the activity level without budget balance deterioration, unemployment remains blocked at its initial level ($q$–$n$=$q$). Thus, as long as the actual level of unemployment is the target level, the policy mix tends to perpetuate unemployment.

In less favourable cases, authorities have insufficient room for manoeuvre in terms of taxes-expenditures capacity of adjustment and interest rate control, with the result that effective demand depressions can not be offset totally. The problem is all the more serious since Keynesian unemployment does not tend spontaneously towards any long-run value, contrary to what authorities think, with the result that they take the new rate of unemployment as the new natural one. That suggests a different explanation of what New Keynesians have referred to as unemployment hysteresis:[18] restricted policy-mix reactions to effective demand depressions only weaken the rise of unemployment, but subsequently neither market forces nor economic policy tends to restore the initial level. Actually, as far as wages respond to the variations in unemployment, not to its level, the NCM concludes real wage rigidity, hiding by the way what in fact is a lack of policy mix flexibility (remember that wage flexibility does not ensure better results in the Keynesian thought).

Things may even be made worse when recurrent distributive tensions exist, because the central bank tends to raise the rate of interest according to the conflict intensity. Indeed, as long as persistent inflationary pressures are interpreted as the result of a 'natural' lower demand for money (provided the supply did not rise), monetary policy takes a harder line and becomes a depressive force. Thus, despite the fact that the two theoretical approaches share the same objectives in the field of macroeconomic governance (that is full employment, price stability and sound public finance), stationary-regime designed governance may be inappropriate in a Keynesian world.

## Keynesian macroeconomic governance

### *Controlling inflation*

Even though inflation always comes from a gap between the money supply and the demand for money expressed at current prices, it is instructive to consider the causes of the gap. For example, according to the real balance effect, a decrease in effective demand may produce inflation insofar as it reduces the demand for money. This is quite different from surprise inflation or seigniorage; it takes part in the adjustment process towards equilibrium. It develops especially when wage rigidity impedes the adjustment of real wages. It would be strange if monetary policy aimed to fight inflation after a demand depression when wages are rigid. Central banks rather tend to decrease interest rates in such cases, so as to facilitate the adjustment. New and old Keynesians could agree on this, despite the former considering effective demand failures as temporary shocks.

Another source of inflation is the conflict about income distribution. Mainstream economics minimizes this recurrent problem because it interprets it in terms of stochastic shock, or in terms of structural change, never as a moving compromise, which interacts with other economic decisions. If the central bank aimed principally to stabilize output, it could be driven to create excessive amounts of money, especially when distributive tensions feed the need for transaction money. Hence, because they have to preserve the public trust in money, monetary authorities may have to take part in the distributive process in such a way that distributive tensions effects on inflation are more or less offset through higher unemployment pressures on wages.

The inflation–unemployment dilemma is considerably more problematic in Keynesian economics. First, the section on similarities and fundamental discrepancies above has shown that, in the presence of recurrent distributive tensions, low inflation targeting may introduce a deflationary bias into monetary policy, with permanently higher unemployment, which contrasts with the neutrality of money in the

NCM 'long run'. Second, when strong tensions compel the central bank to restrict monetary policy, high unemployment may drive the government to accept high deficits in a context of high interest rates. On the contrary, stable distributive conditions help monetary policy to contain interest rates and to contribute to the policy mix efficiency (see below).

Hence, monetary policy is not necessarily the unique way, nor is it the best, to control inflation; legal and institutional rules concerning income distribution play a crucial role as well. Actually, the two aspects should not be considered separately. Furthermore, interactions between monetary and budgetary-fiscal instruments raise additional problems as far as macroeconomic governance is concerned. The following section discusses this point.

*Governing according to the context*

In non-ergodic systems, macroeconomic governance should not hinge on mechanic rules whose consequences are supposed to be well known and able to reach predefined targets. It is always possible to have ideal objectives, but it is not always reasonable to make them the short-run targets of a policy mix because economic policy may spark changes in expectations and private economic decisions, which may in turn make the policy inappropriate (as popularized in the Lucas critique).[19] The Keynesian context requires pragmatic governance, which goes through intermediate targets in order to avoid jolts that could destabilize private expectations and decisions.

Formally, such an approach suggests replacing equation (6.7), which fixed the government objective in the NCM model, by a condition of the type:

$$n = \mu q \qquad (6.9)$$
$$0 < \mu \leq 1$$

where $\mu$ is a parameter that the government chooses depending on the confidence it has in the success of operations. It is important to bear in mind that this equation, like most equations in Keynesian models, does not obey to the stability that is usually assumed. Indeed, $\mu$ is subject to various changing factors. Some of them concern the expected effective demand sensitivity to the policy instruments; others depend on financial constraints which may limit the government room for manoeuvre; others may add political considerations (e.g. public opinion). In this perspective, economic-policy design hinges as much on the selection of the objective (value of $\mu$) as on the adjustment of instruments (value of $g$ or $\hat{t}$ which solves equation (6.9), given equations (6.1″) ($6.2_k$) (6.3) and (6.4)).

Nevertheless, since the budget balance depends on the short-run employment objective, the government may have to limit the increase in public expenditures, unless it is able to adjust taxes. Consequently, employment and budget balance objectives, as well as the concerned instruments, turn out to be interdependent, and therefore must be simultaneously chosen. Hence, let us suppose that the budget-balance target depends more or less on the magnitude of unemployment (according to the room for manoeuvre of the period and to the relative importance the government gives to employment...):

$$b = -\psi_k(q - n) + z \tag{6.10}$$

where $\psi_k \geq 0$ represents the 'fiscal flexibility' (the higher $\psi_k$ is, the less the government adjusts taxes, and the higher is the deficit), and $z$ represents other factors which may interfere in the short run, like deliberate structural deficit due to long-run public investments or debt management considerations. Once again, the problem is as concerned with the selection of the objective (value of $\psi_k$) as it is with the adjustment of instrument (value of $\hat{t}$ or $g$ which solves equation (6.10)).

It is then possible to determine the pair $(g,\hat{t})$ which solves conditions (6.9) and (6.10), given equations (6.1″) ($6.2_k$) (6.3) and (6.4):

$$g = \frac{\alpha\mu(1 - \gamma\varphi) - \gamma\psi_k(1 - \mu)}{\varphi(\lambda - \gamma)} q + \frac{\gamma}{\varphi(\lambda - \gamma)} z - \frac{\lambda}{\varphi(\lambda - \gamma)} a + \frac{1 - \gamma\varphi}{\varphi(\lambda - \gamma)} c + \frac{\sigma}{\varphi(\lambda - \gamma)} \hat{i}$$

$$\hat{t} = \frac{\alpha\mu(1 - \lambda\varphi) - \lambda\psi_k(1 - \mu)}{\lambda - \gamma} q + \frac{\lambda}{\lambda - \gamma}(z - a) + \frac{1 - \lambda\varphi}{\lambda - \gamma} c + \frac{\sigma}{\lambda - \gamma} \hat{i}$$

Within this framework, budgetary and fiscal policy works as a flexible anchor around full employment (since $\mu$ may vary). Actually, because of effective demand and employment sensitivity to the interest rate, the move of instruments required by conditions (6.9) and (6.10) depends upon the monetary policy. Of course, interest rates also matter for the choice of objectives $(\mu, \psi_k)$. For example, if the government thinks that the central bank will accommodate, it can adopt a more ambitious plan. Thus, the central bank can make it more or less difficult for the government to reach the objectives. Notice that central bank participation to economic recovery does not absolutely necessitate lower interest rates. Remember that $\hat{i} = 0$, for example, means that banks adjust the supply of money to the demand expressed at the unchanged rate of interest. Thus, even when the central bank cannot significantly reduce the interest rates (if, for example, they are already very low), it can help in a decisive way by controlling the monetary tensions that economic recovery usually provokes.

## Conclusions

Modelling the NCM and Keynesian approaches of competitive economies within the usual four-macro-markets representation reveals some key sources of divergence. In particular, Keynesian uncertainty plays a crucial role through speculative money demand instability and interest rate adjustment, and through the dominance of effective demand. Hence market interactions differ, with the result that the optimum-oriented competitive forces work in ergodic regimes, not in the Keynesian representation of the world.

Because the NCM governance was designed for efficient stationary systems, it has several drawbacks when implemented in Keynesian non-ergodic systems. In the presence of Keynesian unemployment, as long as actual unemployment and interest rates are interpreted as 'natural' rates, they serve as macroeconomic policy targets, in such a way that the policy mix may anchor the system away from full employment. The situation persists for it seems to be the consequence of real wage rigidity. Our argument suggests a Keynesian explanation (which involves inappropriate economic policy) of what New Keynesians have referred to as unemployment hysteresis. Things may even be made worse by distributive tensions, because the rate of interest tends to rise according to the conflict intensity. Indeed, since inflationary pressures are interpreted as the result of a 'natural' lower demand for money (provided the supply did not rise), monetary policy takes a harder line and becomes a depressive force.

Unfortunately, difficulties do not vanish when authorities adopt the Keynesian vision of the world. For example, as regards inflation control, recurrent distributive tensions force monetary policy into dilemma: to accept the inflationary consequences and preserve economic activities, or to depress economic activity in order to preserve the real value of money through permanent unemployment pressure on wages. From this point of view, legal and institutional rules concerning the distribution of income are revealed to be of primary importance, which corroborates the idea that economic efficiency at the macro level, far from being the automatic outcome of free competitive forces, should not be considered independently of the political and social context.

Governance principles in accordance with the non-ergodic approach have been explored in the final part of the chapter. In contrast with the automatic policy rules of the NCM, we put forward a pragmatic and progressive approach to macroeconomic policy that avoids destabilizing expectations and private decisions. In such a framework, authorities fix intermediate reasonable targets with respect to the confidence they have in the chance of success, which depends on the actual context and moves with it. In our simplified modelling, the taxes–expenditures combination that is required to reach employment and budgetary targets depends upon a set of variables and parameters that represent the macroeconomic changing context and the confidence of authorities. This set of variables, of course, contains the rate of interest, which expresses the monetary influences on the policy mix. Monetary policy modelling is very sensitive in a Keynesian world because the control of the long-term rate of interest is uncertain, at least as far as reductions are concerned; but even when its positive influence on effective demand is doubtful, it matters indirectly through avoiding increases in interest rates when fiscal and budgetary policy aims to stimulate effective demand.

## Appendix 6.1

Starting from the aggregate demand function $\upsilon\,(Y - tY) - \beta\,(i - p^a_{+1}) + G + A$ where $Y$ represents the output volume, $i$ the rate of interest, $p^a_{+1}$ the expected inflation rate till the next period, $t$ the tax rate (taxes/output), $\upsilon$ the propensity to consume, $G$ the governments expenditures, $A$ an autonomous component, the market for goods equilibrium requires: $Y = \upsilon\,(Y - tY) - \beta\,(i - p^a_{+1}) + G + A$.

Differentiating around a solution indexed by 0 (with $d\upsilon$=0 and $dp^a_{+1}$=0), and dividing by $Y_0$, we get:

$$\frac{dY}{Y_0} = \upsilon\frac{dY}{Y_0} - \upsilon t_0\frac{dY}{Y_0} - \upsilon dt - \frac{\beta}{Y_0}\mathrm{di} + \frac{dG}{Y_0} + \frac{dA}{Y_0}$$

Since $t_0=T_0/Y_0$, the equality $dG/Y_0=t_0dG/G_0$ holds when the budget is balanced ($T_0=G_0$). Writing relative deviation rates with small letters ($x=dX/X_0$), except $a=dA/Y_0$, we have:

$$y = \upsilon(1 - t_0)y - \upsilon dt - \frac{\beta}{Y_0}\,di + t_0 g + a$$

hence:

$$y = -\sigma\hat{i} + \lambda(\varphi g + a) - \gamma\hat{t}$$

where

$$\hat{i} = di,$$

$$\hat{t} = dt,$$

$$\varphi = t_0,$$

$$\gamma = \frac{\upsilon}{1 - \upsilon(1 - t_0)},$$

$$\lambda = \frac{1}{1 - \upsilon(1 - t_0)},$$

$$\sigma = \frac{1}{1 - \upsilon(1 - t_0)}\frac{\beta}{Y_0}$$

## Appendix 6.2

(a) The model lends itself to an analysis in terms of aggregate supply and aggregate demand. Equations (6.4) and (6.5′) give the demand equation $y(p)$, which may be written as $p(y)$:

$$p = \frac{-(\eta + \sigma)y + \eta\lambda(\varphi g + a) - \eta\gamma\hat{t}}{\sigma} + m$$

Equations (6.1′) (6.2″), and (6.3) give the supply equation:

$$y = \frac{\alpha\rho(p - p^a) + \alpha d - \alpha\rho\xi\hat{t}}{1 + \rho\theta} + c$$

Resolution yields $y$ and $p$, which permits to solve for $n$ by (6.3), then $w$ by (6.2″), and finally $\hat{i}$ by (6.5′). It should not be forgotten that output variations do not really depend on current price index variations, but on the current price index error of prediction, as the supply equation shows.

(b) When monetary authorities control the rate of interest and adjust the quantity of money to the demand, output ($y$) is determined by the sole aggregate demand components (equation 6.4). We get $n$ by (6.3), then $w$ by (6.2″) and finally $p$ by (6.1′):

$$y = -\sigma\hat{i} + \lambda(\varphi g + a) - \gamma\hat{t}$$

$$n = \frac{\lambda(\varphi g + a) - c - \sigma\hat{i} - \gamma\hat{t}}{\alpha}$$

$$w = p^a + \frac{\lambda\theta(\varphi g + a) - \theta c - \sigma\theta\hat{i} - \gamma\theta\hat{t}}{\alpha}$$

$$p = p^a + \frac{\lambda(1+\rho\theta)}{\alpha\rho}a - \frac{\gamma(1+\rho\theta) - \alpha\rho\xi}{\alpha\rho}\hat{t} - \frac{1+\rho\theta}{\alpha\rho}c + \frac{\lambda\varphi(1+\rho\theta)}{\alpha\rho}g$$

$$- \frac{\sigma(1+\rho\theta)}{\alpha\rho}\hat{i} - \frac{d}{\rho}$$

Output variations here depend on the rate of interest, but it can easily be shown that if it is set so as to avoid any price index error of prediction ($p{=}p^a$), then the results are the same as in the case of exogenous money supply where $m$ is set so as to avoid errors of prediction.

## Appendix 6.3

The budget balance ($B$) is defined as:

$$B = tPY - PG$$

Differentiating around a solution indexed by 0 yields:

$$dB = t_0P_0dY + P_0Y_0dt + t_0Y_0dP - P_0dG - G_0dP$$

and dividing by the initial value of output:

$$dB/(P_0Y_0) = t_0dY/Y_0 + dt + t_0dP/P_0 - dG/Y_0 - (G_0/Y_0)(dP/P_0)$$

Hence, around a situation of balanced budget where $t_0 = G_0/Y_0$ (remember $g = dG/G_0$):

$$b = t_0(y - g) + dt$$

and, with the same notation as in Appendix 6.1:

$$b = \varphi(y - g) + \hat{t}$$

## Notes

1. This kind of policy aims to maintain the rate of unemployment below the natural rate. It differs from occasional (not expected) policies, which may have temporary impact on economic activities because of inertia of wages (see below).
2. This may occur because of bottlenecks in installed capacity and the lack of some skills of labor and goods (including capital goods) in some industries.
3. The system may jump from a trend to another, when the regime changes.
4. See the discussion of the relation between inflation targeting and the NCM in Arestis and Sawyer (2003a).
5. See Arestis and Sawyer (2003b).
6. The short run we are discussing now is the one for which capital stock and productive capacity may approximately be considered as constants. It is different from the 'short run' mentioned in the introduction.
7. Had the model an additional market for money, there would have been a third relative price (the price of money in terms of goods: $1/p$). As we know, in such a system real prices and other real variables are independent of money (which only accounts for nominal variables and prices; see below).
8. See Appendix 6.1.
9. This point supposes that competitive mechanisms anchor the system in a predetermined trajectory. It has been identified as the dynamic stability of a stochastic process (ergodicity). See Vercelli (1991: 40, 154) and Davidson (2002: 39, 69).
10. Following Tobin (1958), money helps to diversify portfolios in order to optimize the return/risk ratio (the higher the rate of interest, the more one is encouraged to increase the proportion of risked assets, and to reduce the proportion of money).
11. See the case (b) of Appendix 6.2. As stated in Palley (2006), this assessment of endogenous money substantially differs from the Post Keynesian one.
12. Theoretically, it is possible that flexible nominal wages reach this solution without any variation in the rate of interest (but it is not certain; see *The General Theory*, ch. 19): through positive effects on the marginal efficiency of capital and effective demand, wage flexibility may produce inflation, reduce real wage and rise production. If on the other hand nominal wages are sticky, the role of interest rate becomes crucial.
13. See Tobin (1975) and Palley (2005) about this kind of instability.
14. It is not essential to make imperfect competition assumptions in order to obtain a mark-up relation. For example, starting with the production function $Y=CN^{\alpha}$, $\alpha < 1$, competitive pricing requires the marginal productivity to be equal to the real cost of labour: $\partial Y/\partial N=W(1+\xi t)/P \Rightarrow P=W(1+\xi t)/(C\alpha N^{\alpha-1})=(WN(1+\xi t)/Y)/\alpha$; hence, by differentiation of the associated logarithmic expression (for small values of $\hat{t}$), we have $p = w + n - y - \dot{\alpha} + \xi\hat{t}$, where $\dot{\alpha}$ is the rate of variation in α (exogenous). Notice that an increasing mark-up on unit labour cost expresses in this case a declining wages-output ratio ($\dot{\alpha} < 0$) and/or increasing fiscal taxes ($\hat{t} = dt > 0$).
15. From equation (6.3), we have: $y-n=(\alpha-1)n+c$. Hence, an increase in effective demand and employment reduces the productivity of labour and raises the unit cost of production. This shows that cost pushed inflation and demand

led inflation may express the same reality. In fact, whatever apparent causes it has, inflation always requires an increase in demand (see below).

16. According to the 'no-inflation-bias' hypothesis we should have in general $p^a = 0$, but it may be useful to conserve this variable as an exogenous temporary shocks on expected inflation.
17. For example, the first-order condition that $g$ must verify in order to minimize $L=(1/2)(\zeta n^2+b^2)$ is $\zeta n(\partial n/\partial g)+b(\partial b/\partial g)=0$, which is equivalent to $b=\psi n$ provided that $\psi=-\zeta(\partial n/\partial g)/(\partial b/\partial g)$. This approach sometimes raises difficulties that will not be discussed here.
18. On hysteresis, ergodic and non-ergodic regimes, see the Minisymposium in the *Journal of Post Keynesian Economics*, 15(3), Spring 1993.
19. Keynes raised the question in *The General Theory* (Ch. 15, see the last third of Section II). Of course, the meaning and implications considerably differ owing to the methodological opposition (see Vercelli 1991).

## References

Arestis, P. and Sawyer, M. (2003a) *Inflation Targeting: a Critical Appraisal,* The Levy Economics Institute Working Papers, No. 388.

Arestis, P. and Sawyer, M. (2003b) 'Reinventing Fiscal Policy', *Journal of Post-Keynesian Economics*, 26 (1): 3–26.

Davidson, P. (2002) *Financial Markets, Money and the Real World* (Cheltenham: Edward Elgar).

Freedman, C., Harcourt, G.C. and Kriesler, P. (2004) 'Has the Long-run Phillips Curve Turned Horizontal?', in G. Argyrous, M. Forstater and G. Mongiovi (eds), *Growth, Distribution and Effective Demand: Alternatives to Economic Orthodoxy* (Armonk: M.E. Sharpe).

Kriesler, P. and Lavoie, M. (2005) *The New View on Monetary Policy: The New Consensus and its Post-Keynesian Critique,* unpublished paper, http://aix1.uottawa.ca/~robinson/ english/wp/2005/dal-rope.pdf.

Lavoie, M. (2002) *A Post-Keynesian Alternative to the New Consensus in Monetary Policy,* paper presented at the ADEK conference, CEMF, Université de Bourgogne, Dijon, 14–16 November.

Palacio-Vera, A. (2005) 'The "Modern" View of Macroeconomics: Some Critical Reflections', *Cambridge Journal of Economics*, 29(5): 747–67.

Palley, T.I. (2005) *Keynesian Models of Recession and Depression,* unpublished manuscript, November 2005, http://www.thomaspalley.com/docs/research/KeynesianModelsRevisited2.pdf.

Palley, T.I. (2006) 'A Post Keynesian Framework for Monetary Policy: Why Interest Rate Operating Procedures are not Enough', in C. Gnos and L.-P. Rochon (eds), *Post Keynesian Principles of Economic Policy* (Cheltenham: Edward Elgar).

Romer, D. (2000) 'Keynesian Macroeconomics without the LM Curve', *Journal of Economic Perspectives*, 14 (2): 149–69.

Sargent, T. and Wallace, N. (1981) 'Some Unpleasant Monetarist Arithmetic', *Federal Reserve Bank of Minneapolis Quarterly Review*, 5: 1–17.

Tobin, J. (1958) 'Liquidity Preference as Behaviour Towards Risk', *Review of Economic Studies*, 25: 65–86.

Tobin, J. (1975) 'Keynesian Models of Recession and Depression', *American Economic Review*, 65: 195–202.
Vercelli, A. (1991) *Methodological Foundations of Macroeconomics: Keynes and Lucas* (Cambridge: Cambridge University Press).

# 7
# Monetary Policy from a Circuitist Perspective

*Claude Gnos*

## Introduction

As Arestis says, circuit theory is 'a strong component of the endogenous money thesis' (1996: 113). This notably means that circuitists endorse the original Post Keynesian dismissal of the orthodox Monetarist approach to monetary policy by which the quantity of money in the economy should be regulated so as to stifle inflationary pressures. From the endogenous view, money creation is, in Moore's words (1988), 'credit-driven', meaning that money is demanded by the general public and firms to finance spending which is dependent upon prices and money wages. Hence it is prices and money wages that are factors determining the amount of money created and not the contrary. This led Post Keynesian writers to relate inflation to distributional conflicts which should be addressed by means of institutional measures designed to regulate income distribution. Paraphrasing a famous formula by Friedman, Davidson (1991: 100) concluded that 'inflation is always and everywhere a distribution phenomenon'. Weintraub (1979) proposed a tax-based income policy that would charge those firms which let wages rise more than productivity. Circuitists too have pointed out the distributional aspects of inflation (Parguez 1991: 61–89, and Bradley, Friboulet and Gnos 1996: 107–34). Another well-known divergence between orthodox and heterodox approaches concerns the interest rate, which is considered as an endogenous variable in the monetarist tradition while Post Keynesians and circuitists argue for its exogeneity. However, none of the approaches mentioned stopped there.

Besides the distributional approach they initially favoured, which may be labelled a cost-push perspective, Post Keynesians consider that they are entitled to 'reclaim the demand-pull approach to inflation', too (Palley 1996: 166). Accordingly, they focus on the growth of aggregate nominal demand, which Palley (1996: 167) links to the 'growth of supplies across the entire spectrum of financial liabilities'.

The orthodox view has also evolved. Since the early 1980s a new approach to monetary policy has emerged which consists in manipulating the central bank interest rate in order to exert direct control over the inflation rate instead of the money supply. Inflation targeting has thus replaced money-supply targeting. Post Keynesians consider that this development reinforces their own analysis because, in this way, both the actual practice of central banks and the 'New Consensus Macroeconomics' that ensued on the theoretical level acknowledge the exogeneity of the interest rate and 'at least implicitly admit the endogeneity of money' (Rochon and Rossi 2006: 5). This does not mean, however, that the orthodox and Post Keynesian views are converging. Inflation targeting is seen by its neoclassical proponents as part of the traditional scheme by which fighting inflation is a sufficient condition for ensuring the efficient allocation of resources and boosting investment and growth, a claim which Post Keynesians reject out of hand. For Post Keynesians, fighting inflation does not exempt governments from implementing fiscal policies (Arestis and Sawyer 2003a, 2003b). Even more radically, Sawyer argues that 'the use of interest rates to control inflation may be counterproductive as far as inflation is concerned' (Sawyer 2002: 42). This is so, he emphasizes, because a rise in interest rates has an effect on costs, which translates into higher prices.

In what follows, my purpose is to investigate the contribution of circuit theory to the current debates on monetary policy. I aim to show that circuit theory may contribute to the search for criteria by which to decide whether or not there is excess credit and therefore excess nominal demand (the Post Keynesian criteria being inadequate in my view) and that in so doing it leads to a renewed approach to monetary policy. The structure of the chapter is the following. The second section will provide a critical appraisal of the current Post Keynesian attempt to define demand inflation and to provide a means of fighting it. The third section will turn to the circuitist contribution to the search for identifying demand inflation. The fourth section will set out the positive contribution of circuit theory to defining monetary policy. The final section will conclude.

## A critical appraisal of the Post Keynesian reference to excess nominal demand in explaining and fighting inflation

### The Post Keynesian approach to demand inflation

To identify the possible inflationary effect of credit expansion feeding demand, Palley (1996: 170) refers essentially to unemployment: 'positive nominal demand shocks increase output and employment, and if a sector is pushed beyond full employment, they also raise prices'. He then develops a model for considering multisectoral economies where the effects of demand growth on employment are diversified depending on the specific situation of each sector. From the model he concludes that 'there exists a systematic and exploitable trade-off between the rate of unemployment and the rate of inflation' (Palley 1996: 166). He also allows for the effect of expectations about inflation which, he argues, may impair any positive effect on output of an increase in nominal demand by raising wages and thence production costs.

It should be observed that Palley's reference to employment is consistent with Keynes's own views in chapter 21 of the *General Theory* that the quantity theory may be reformulated as follows: 'So long as there is unemployment, employment will change in the same proportion as the quantity of money; and when there is full employment, prices will change in the same proportion as the quantity of money' (Keynes 1936: 296).

Although he does not explicitly mention workers' expectations, Keynes also acknowledges that an increase in the quantity of money may raise wages before full employment has been achieved. This is so, he argues, because entrepreneurs are more likely to satisfy workers' claims when demand for their output is rising (Keynes 1936: 301). Keynes emphasizes too that the way in which demand increases matters. A sudden large increase in demand will create temporary bottlenecks and translate into price increases, while a smoother change will favour employment.

It should also be observed that reference to chapter 21 of the *General Theory* does not guarantee the relevance of the argument. As mentioned, Keynes suggests that he has only to reformulate the quantity theory, and this is just what he does. To refer to unemployment in the way he does is a refinement of the quantity theory, not a dismissal of it. It means that instead of comparing the quantity of money in the economy with the quantity of goods available, as monetarists used to do, Keynes and Palley after him compare the quantity of money with the quantity of goods that can be produced if employment is extended accordingly. In the same way Moore (1988: 351) argues that '[d]emand inflation is caused by too rapid an increase in credit money, which enables aggregate demand to grow more rapidly than the growth rate of potential output with stable prices'. I will argue that the logic of the neoclassical approach is thus maintained, which is in contradistinction to the way Keynes actually analyzed a monetary economy of production.

**Lessons from Keynes's principle of effective demand**

To make my point, I propose to refer to the principle of effective demand which Keynes considered 'the essence of the General Theory of Employment' (Keynes 1936: 29). This principle, as we know, is based on entrepreneurs successively paying out factor cost and then recouping that cost from proceeds for a given volume of employment they hire. As Keynes (1936: 24–5) puts it, 'entrepreneurs endeavour to fix the amount of employment at the level at which they expect to maximize the excess of the proceeds over the factor cost'. Circuitists who endorse this approach observe that Keynes on this occasion outlines a theory of distribution by which profits are a redistributed share of wages, which is transferred from purchasers to firms (Gnos 1998, 2004). In effect, he makes a sharp distinction between wages that form the factor cost met by entrepreneurs and simultaneously the factors' income, and profits, which constitute the entrepreneurs' income, and are derived from the excess of the proceeds of sales over factor cost, paid by consumers. In this view, profits are not additional to wages but part of them. Just as value-added taxes currently allow governments to capture some part of consumers' incomes, profits are an excess of proceeds over factor cost, but do not form an additional income for the economy as a whole. From this we may draw two main propositions that help to show the ambiguity of Keynes's and the Post Keynesians' approach to demand inflation.

A first proposition is that demand is identical to supply, just as Keynes argues in the *General Theory*, when he defines income as being identical to the value of current output (Keynes 1936: 63–5). It is true that this conclusion has often been disputed in the literature. The dispute, I would suggest (Gnos 2004), arose because of a misunderstanding of the distribution theory involved in the principle of effective demand. On my view, arguing that demand is identical to supply does not mean that aggregate demand is necessarily equal to aggregate supply. The identity in fact relates to the formation and spending of wages, which entails the formation and spending of the income of the economy as a whole, while the equilibrium condition relates to aggregate demand (*D*) and supply (*Z*) as measured in terms of prices (in Keynes's own words *D* is the 'expectation of proceeds' and *Z* is 'the aggregate supply price of the output' (Keynes 1936: 24–5)). As mentioned, profit results from the excess of proceeds over factor cost, and thus it is dependent on the amount of their income wage-earners (and we should add profit-earners and those who derive their incomes from firms' profits) are prepared to spend in buying the various goods available. Accordingly, firms may earn more or less profits, depending on the kind and the quantity of the goods they produce. Of course, they may even make losses.[1] This grounds the role of entrepreneurs' expectations as described by the principle of effective demand. It might be emphasized that all of the elements of this interpretation are to be found in the *General Theory*. In addition to the definition of profit as an excess of proceeds from sales over factor cost, it should be noted that Keynes (1936: 25) defines *D* as a function of employment: $D = f(N)$. We thus have confirmation that the income which is expected to fuel the purchases of goods produced is dependent on the volume of employment. Is it not clear, then, that, in the logic of Keynes's theory, the income of the economy as a whole amounts to the wage bills *E*, with $E = N \times W$ where *W* stands for the wage-unit? This is precisely what Keynes (1936: 43) suggests when he chooses to measure quantities in wage-units. It is also in accordance with the way he refutes the traditional argument by which cutting wages would allow firms to lower prices and so stimulate demand for goods: 'if the wage-unit changes, the expenditure on consumption corresponding to a given level of employment will, like prices, change in the same proportion' (Keynes 1936: 92).

A second proposition is that the payment of factor cost relies on credit, and results in a net addition to the stock of saving. This is actually a proposition that Keynes set out after the publication of the *General Theory*, in papers on the 'finance motive' (Keynes 1937a, 1937b). To start production, he argues, firms have to secure 'a provision of cash' provided by banks or the market, which 'does not absorb or exhaust any resources' but generates new net saving when spent on factor cost (Keynes 1937a: 208–9). Since they are paid in money, wages are deposited with banks and thus constitute a net addition to the stock of saving until they are spent in the purchase of goods. As a counterpart, firms are indebted to banks or the general public.

The two propositions we have just clarified allow us to consider with a critical eye the way Post Keynesians, and to some extent Keynes himself, deal with demand inflation. On the one hand, it can be seen that the view according to which monetary policy should stimulate demand in order to ensure full employment is flawed. Production generates wages (and incomes derived from wages) that are sufficient to pay for the output, which will occur provided that firms produce goods which meet demand and have correctly anticipated it. This is an inference that Post Keynesians should be aware of, because it is entirely consistent with Keynes's theory of employment. Namely, what is the fundamental cause of unemployment for Keynes? It is in no way a lack of income, but a demand deficiency resulting from a deficiency of spending both on consumption and investment goods relative to current income, which is dependent on consumers' propensity to consume and entrepreneurs' inducement to invest (Keynes 1936: 27–8). Accordingly, the solution lies not in an increase in credit that would allow demand to expand, but, by Keynes's analysis, in various measures designed to increase the general public's propensity to consume and entrepreneurs' inducement to invest, as well as in the intervention of the state which should commit itself to spend any excess of saving over private investment. Keynes expanded on this in his concluding notes to the *General Theory* (Keynes 1936: 372–84). On the other hand, however, the reference to employment or to the so-called 'potential output' is not entirely irrelevant because firms need credit to implement production and hire workers, which allows them to pay wages corresponding to a set of newly produced goods. To be fair, we have to acknowledge that, among Post Keynesians, Davidson appears to be well aware of this. Criticizing the Monetarist view that the possible inflationary effect of an increase in the quantity of money in the economy is to be evaluated with reference to the goods produced and available, he explains that it may be that the increased quantity of money is spent on the wages of workers employed for producing a new set of goods, in which case money creation is not inflationary (Davidson 1991: 100).

All in all, we may conclude that what is to be done is to discriminate between increases in the quantity of money according to whether they are used to finance demand or to finance production. The former generates inflation, not the latter. However, things may be not so simple, because bank credit, which is the source of money creation, may equally well meet the needs of firms and households. This is so when banks provide funding to households corresponding to liquidity that some households choose to hold. Without the intermediation of banks, resources would remain idle and thus act negatively on entrepreneurs' proceeds and thence on employment. How, then, are we to discriminate between credit operations with respect to their inflationary impact? In the next section, I propose to examine in some detail the way circuit theory deals with this issue.

## The circuitist renewed attempt to identify demand inflation

The analysis of demand inflation and of the ways and means to fight it has long been of great concern to circuitists, especially for the members of the so-called Dijon–Fribourg School. Under the guidance of Schmitt (1966, 1984), they have focused on the way the banking system functions, and their conclusion is that avoiding inflation is not just a matter of quantitative regulation but, so to say, of qualitative regulation, too (see Cencini 1996; Rossi 2001). To set out this point of view, we will first deepen the analysis of the criteria for deciding whether an increase in credit money is inflationary and secondly (next section) focus on the ensuing monetary policy recommendations.

The distinction between the formation and the spending of wages, which lies at the core of circuit theory, rules out any monetary policy aimed at regulating credit and money creation regardless of what it is used for. When firms ask for credit to pay wages, any inflation is due to higher wages rather than to an excess of credit money. Just as the endogenous view of money insists, the causal relation is then from wages to money: inflation in this case is cost-pushed. Monetary policies aimed at restricting credit, then, are not only ineffective but also counterproductive because they prevent firms from expanding employment. It is true, however, that the accommodative behaviour of banks with regard to firms' demand for money may be an incentive for firms to increase wages. But even in this latter case a distribution policy would be more appropriate. By contrast, when funding demand in excess of current income, there is no doubt that credit generates inflation. We namely have checked that the income of the economy as a whole is sufficient to pay for its whole output. This is not the entire story, though.

As briefly mentioned in the previous section, it can be observed that credit granted to households is not necessarily a source of inflation. This is the case because credit has a well-known role in allowing people who are willing to save current incomes in order to spend them in the future to lend them to people willing to spend their future incomes in advance. By providing credit, banks in this case allow the general public to act in accordance with its wishes and, moreover, they act in the interest of the economy as a whole in allowing the spending of incomes that would otherwise be left idle. This confirms that any blind quantitative regulation of credit would be misguided, even if it were to be applied to households as opposed to firms. In fact, credit should be controlled with regard to the way it finances spending, whether increasing nominal demand relative to the incomes available or allowing transfers of income among members of the general public.

By the same line of reasoning we may take a closer look at credit when it is granted to firms. It has been observed that the financing of wages from credit does not generate inflation. But, of course, firms do not only finance wages alone from credit. They also buy raw materials and capital goods from credit. What happens then? In fact, this case is similar to the case of household spending financed by credit. We still have to determine whether credit leads to an increase in nominal demand relative to available incomes or to a financial operation by which savers lend incomes to borrowers.

It should be noticed that firms do not necessarily fund wages by means of bank credit. They may use the cash available to them as a consequence of the formation of profits or cash provided by their owners or lenders in financial markets. In other words, savings may be used to pay for wages. This procedure is not inflationary but deflationary rather. When borrowed to fund spending on goods, savings are spent on goods by borrowers in the place of their holders. This is consistent with the circuit of the successive formation and spending of wages. But when savings are borrowed to pay wage-bills, a deflationary gap opens in the sense that, to the cash lent to and spent by firms, there correspond two sets of goods: goods produced earlier when this cash was first paid to wage-earners, and the goods newly produced in the current period when the same cash is paid again to wage-earners. It should be observed, too, that this deflationary gap may well coexist with an inflationary gap, because both are formed in transactions that coexist daily.

All in all, circuit theory denies the relevance of mere reference to the quantity of money in order to identify demand inflation. It is a renewed approach that is proposed, based on a straightforward distinction between money operations according to whether they pertain to the formation, the spending or the transfer of wages. In this view, the source of inflation and deflation is to be found in interferences and mismatches between these diverse operations. This criterion is very acute: as just said, it can account for the simultaneous occurrence of inflation and deflation, which is a feature that Keynesians failed to account for in the 1970s, when what was termed 'stagflation' held centre stage. It also allows us to re-examine Keynes's view that demand deficiency, which generates unemployment, is essentially the result of excessive savings. In Keynes's view, excessive saving is the result of income holders' and entrepreneurs' behaviour. Circuit theory does not dismiss this explanation, especially with regard to the way uncertainty may influence economic agents' behaviour, just as Post Keynesian writers, notably Davidson (2002), may argue. But, in addition to this, it argues that excessive savings may be the result of interferences between the formation of new incomes and existing savings. In this case, excessive saving is not a matter of behaviour. It might be added that this circumstance makes it very difficult to interpret actual data, because when pre-existing deposits are used to pay new wages, they literally vanish in the act, as if through a trapdoor, and so are no longer recorded in the statistics as savings.

## Policy recommendations

At first sight, the analysis developed above does not provide a simple way to regulate money. Before deciding to restrict money creation, monetary authorities should discriminate between the operations involved. Moreover, how could a quantitative control of money deal with deflation which is not primarily a quantitative issue, as has been shown, but is more likely to be due to the misuse of pre-existing incomes in the payment of wages, while inflation is due to banks granting credit in excess of pre-existing incomes?

The nature of the issues involved prompted Schmitt (1984) to revive an approach to monetary policy that had been initiated by Ricardo (1810) and had inspired the Bank Act passed in England in 1844. At that time, it was decided to separate the Bank of England's activities into two departments, dealing, respectively, with the issuance of notes and with discounting operations. The main aim was to avoid any mismanagement of the issuing notes and, more specifically, any uncontrolled expansion of such issues that would result in price inflation. Schmitt similarly endorses the idea that the management of money and credit may be a matter for structural features of the banking system. However, his proposals are fundamentally different from the 1844 experiment (Bradley 2001). The Bank Act was mainly inspired by the 'Currency Principle', which was defined in accordance with the traditional exogenous view of money and consisted of a recommendation that the circulation of notes should comply with convertibility rules.

Schmitt's proposals are on the contrary in line with the endogenous thesis. They are grounded in the distinction between money creation, financial intermediation and the formation of 'fixed' capital in firms, and result in a threefold division of banking activities. Let us consider in turn the separation of monetary and financial entries, and the recording of fixed capital.

**Segregating banks' monetary and financial activities**

To set out Schmitt's views, it may first be observed that banks usually provide two functions: they simultaneously issue money and are financial intermediaries between lenders and borrowers. As actual practice confirms, these functions may well be separated: as financial intermediaries, for example, banks compete with a wide range of non-bank institutions. Schmitt proposes that banks' monetary and financial activities be separated with reference to both functions. Money creation would be carried out by banks' issuing departments, while their financial departments would collect and lend savings. As a first approximation, it may be surmised that this distinction, which relates essentially to the way entries are recorded in banks' books, would help to prevent interferences and mismatches between money creation and lending operations, which is the aim to be achieved as shown above.

Let us consider the simple case of the payment of wage-bills to workers (W1) by firm F1 which benefits from money created (£1,000) by the issuing department of a bank. This operation would be recorded as shown in Table 7.1.

The payment of wages thus has a twofold consequence. On the one hand, firm F1 has become indebted to the issuing department of the bank. As a counterpart F1 has temporarily at its disposal the goods which are being produced, until the goods are made available in the market and are sold to wage-earners (or, more generally, to income-holders if we allow for the fact that wages will be partially distributed). When the goods are sold, F1 is able to reimburse the bank and its debt with ID is cancelled accordingly. On the other hand, workers obtain

*Table 7.1* The separation of banks' activities into two departments

| | *Issuing department (ID)* | | *Financial department (FD)* | |
|---|---|---|---|---|
| | *Assets* | *Liabilities* | *Assets* | *Liabilities* |
| Firm F1 | £1,000 | FD £1,000 | ID £1,000 | W1 £1,000 |

wages in the form of deposits with the financial department of the bank, which they will hold until they spend them on goods or on assets in the financial markets.

The above entries have the merit of making it possible to compute the savings available and which the bank may lend. The amount of these loanable funds is denoted by the amount of the financial department's claims on the issuing department. As soon as the FD pays £*x* on behalf of depositors who thus spend their savings on goods, or lends £*x* to borrowers who spend the amount on goods, both deposits and claims are cancelled accordingly. Of course, this also means that F1 has sold goods and its debt is reduced. The present-day structure of banks' books allows them to lend regardless of the amount of savings they hold insofar as they capture the deposits that result from loans. In this regard, they just meet a liquidity constraint defined *vis-à-vis* the other banks and the central bank.

In addition to the dissociation of the two departments in their books, the banks would have to meet a further requirement consisting in inquiring about the use – the payment of wage-bills or the purchase of goods – their customers are to make of the money they wish to borrow. They would have to charge the payment of wage-bills to the issuing department and the purchase of goods to the financial department. However, this enquiry would not impose any additional constraint on banks compared with present practice insofar as such an enquiry is already part of the procedure by which they examine their customers' applications for credit. One may wonder, however, what happens when firms have at their disposal deposits they have earned in the form of profits or have borrowed in the financial market, and want to spend them on wage-bills. Should banks refuse to pay wages out of pre-existing deposits? Fortunately, such restrictive behaviour is not required. Actually, the reform essentially concerns the way banks record monetary and financial flows in their books. There is no question of preventing firms from using savings in whatever way they wish. Again, the only constraint on banks, would consist in enquiring about the use of the money they are going to debit firms, which is easy to do. To illustrate our point, let us suppose that a second firm, F2, has deposits (£*x*) at its disposal in the place of workers in the above accounts, corresponding to goods produced by F1, and for which F2 asks the bank in order to pay its own workers.

As we see (Table 7.2), in the bank's books F2 appears both on the assets side of ID and on the liabilities side of FD. The entry on the liabilities side of FD shows that £*x* have been saved by F2, and the bank

*Table 7.2* The payment of wages by firm 2 holding pre-existent deposits

| | *Issuing department (ID)* | | *Financial department (FD)* | |
|---|---|---|---|---|
| | *Assets* | *Liabilities* | *Assets* | *Liabilities* |
| Firm F1 | £1,000 | FD £1,000 | ID £1,000 | W1 £1,000 – £ *x*<br>F2 £ *x* |
| Firm F2 | £ *x* | FD £ *x* | ID £ *x* | W2 £ *x* |

is thus aware that it may lend £*x* without any danger of creating excess demand: goods exist as a counterpart to £*x* which are stored by firm F1. The payment of W2's wage-bill generated new savings held by W2, and simultaneously a debt of F2 with ID. The logic of the circuit of incomes is upheld. Of course, the two entries for F2 offset one another so that F2 has no net debt with the bank, which would not be the case if it had to borrow money from the bank. From F2's viewpoint, the payment of the wage-bill was funded from the deposit held with the bank. This case is quite emblematic of the proposed reform. The dissociation of banks' activities into two departments allows banks to manage monetary and financial flows in such a way that inflation and deflation are avoided, without imposing any specific constraint on the economic agent's behaviour.

## The implementation of a fixed capital department in banks

In extending the analysis of the use firms make of savings, Schmitt (1966, 1996) came to further conclusions. His attention was drawn to the investment of retained profits. Capital goods bought out of retained profits are a net asset for firms, they are literally 'fixed' in firms, which is not the case when firms buy goods out of savings they borrow. This has crucial consequences, which become obvious when we consider the amortization of capital goods.

To make the point, let us first consider the amortization of capital goods financed out of borrowed savings. In this case, from one period of time to another, firms sell goods the price of which includes the amortization of the price paid for capital goods the firms bought earlier. This means that, as regards their value passed on in the price of goods that have been newly produced and sold, capital goods are on the same footing as raw materials that income-holders buy as component parts of the newly produced goods. They belong to the category of intermediate goods. As a counterpart, income-holders leave new capital goods available that firms buy out of the sums of money obtained from amortization. The whole process is consistent with the successive formation and spending of incomes as described by circuit theory, which means that it does not generate any inflationary or deflationary gap.

By contrast, when firms spend retained profits on capital goods, an inflationary gap is generated. To understand this, we have first to observe that the replacement of capital goods is ultimately the payment of the wage-bills of the workers producing the capital goods; it namely amounts to inter-firms purchases. When firms borrow money to pay wages, they become indebted to banks or to savings-holders, and, simultaneously, when paying wage-bills, they temporarily have at their disposal the goods which have been produced, but do not appropriate them in the sense that the goods are subject to a debt that will have to be repaid by selling the goods produced. This constraint applies to the amortization process analysed in the preceding paragraph: firms have to buy replacement capital goods out of incomes they obtain from workers who have to pay prices for consumption goods that include the amortization of the price of such capital goods. The analysis runs differently when firms do not borrow money but pay wages out of funds obtained in amortizing capital goods originally funded by retained profits. New capital goods are produced that are outside the purchasing power of wages: from period to period firms immediately appropriate these capital goods in paying wage-bills. As mentioned above, capital goods are then, from the outset, a net asset to firms; they are 'fixed' in them. In Schmitt's words, the wages paid in the production of such goods are 'empty': 'from the moment they are handed out by firms, [they] are completely empty of all purchasing power, that is, devoided of any output' (Schmitt 1996: 102). An inflationary gap is generated, which will be repeated from one period to another through the amortization process, and which consists in these 'empty' wages. The spending of 'empty' wages by workers reconstitutes the retained profits that firms initially spent on capital goods.

Paradoxically, this inflation gap is also a cause of persistent deflation and unemployment. This is because the purchase of capital goods out of retained profits is a process of accumulation which cannot be adapted to the ups and downs of the economy. I cannot expand much on this topic here, but to give an idea of the argument let us consider the following case. Suppose that in an economy suffering from underemployment, the government attempts to stimulate demand for consumption goods, for instance, as is the case now (2006) in France, by facilitating the general public's access to bank credit. Are firms then in a position to benefit from such an impetus while reducing their production of capital goods and producing consumption goods instead? If they had previously invested out of borrowed savings, there would be no obstacle. They would just need to employ more workers in the production of consumption goods and fewer workers in the production of capital goods. This is not possible, however, where firms have invested retained profits. This is so because, in the latter case, when spending amounts of money provided by the amortization of fixed capital on wages, firms appropriate the goods produced which workers then cannot buy. As emphasized already, in spending their 'empty' wages, workers merely reconstitute the retained profits that firms initially spent on equipment. They cannot, in addition, buy newly produced goods, be they consumption goods. This situation is not harmful when investment goods are produced: they are fixed in firms and will vanish with their value when the equipment is depreciated or obsolete. When producing consumption goods instead, firms accumulate inventories they cannot sell, which prompts them to restrict their production instead of expanding it.

To face the problems raised by the formation of fixed capital, Schmitt proposes supplementing the segregation of banks' activities into two departments with the implementation of a third department (CD for 'capital department') in charge of firms' fixed capital. The idea is to record firms' deposits (profits) both in the FD and in the CD. The separation of the ID and FD would guarantee that the profits saved by firms are not spent in the payment of wages. And the recording of profits in the CD's books would fix them in banks as a counterpart to the capital goods fixed in firms, and thus deter them from being available in the FD for loans that would fuel demand in excess of the goods for sale. Where firms would be willing not to maintain the whole amount of their fixed capital and produce consumption goods instead, the payment of wages would be funded by the ID as mentioned in Table 7.1, while firms' deposits would be cancelled in the CD's books and so become available for loans in the FD.

## Conclusion

Circuit theory relates to a methodology propounded by Keynes both in *A Treatise on Money* (1930: in particular 120–1) and in the *General Theory* (1936), by which the complexity of economic transactions derives significance from a restricted number of operations, namely the formation, spending and transfer of incomes which, as the principle of effective demand and Keynes's developments on the choice of units of measurement make obvious, may be identified with wages. The aim of this chapter was to show that, in this way, circuit theory may contribute to current debates on economic policy, especially monetary policy, which is a *raison d'être* of any economic theory grounded in the real world. Actually, its contribution is twofold.

First, circuit theory helps to clarify the usual reference made both by orthodox and heterodox theories to excess nominal demand when they come to define inflation. We have concluded that the source of inflation is to be found in interferences and mismatches between the formation, spending and transfer of money incomes. On this view, inflation and deflation may, and indeed do, coexist. Secondly, circuit theory dismisses the traditional approaches of money regulation that amount to quantitative rules, and favours a reform of the structural features of banking, in proposing a twofold division of banks' monetary and financial activities, along with the implementation of a specific department recording the retained profits that firms devote to the accumulation of capital.

The circuitist approach to monetary policy has not been widely known to date, which is why the focus here has been on its general features. There is still much to be done, both to propose a detailed presentation of the workings of the reform of the banking system propounded and to formulate recommendations for the management of interest rates, which would then be free from any considerations about inflation.

## Note

1. Keynes already analysed firms' losses in the way suggested here, in his *A Treatise on Money* (1930: 159–60), wherein he emphasizes that losses mean 'a transfer of wealth from the pockets of the entrepreneurs into the pockets of the general public' (1930: 159).

## References

Arestis, P. (1996) 'Post-Keynesian Economics: Towards Coherence', *Cambridge Journal of Economics*, 20: 111–35.

Arestis, P. and Sawyer, M. (2003a) *On the Effectiveness of Monetary Policy and of Fiscal Policy*, Working Paper No. 369 Levy Economics Institute of Bard College, Annandale-on-Hudson.

Arestis, P. and Sawyer, M. (2003b) 'Reinventing Fiscal Policy', *Journal of Post Keynesian Economics*, 26(1): 3–25.

Bradley, X. (2001) *An Experience in Banking Departmentalisation: The Bank Act of 1844*, Working Paper No. 14, Research Laboratory of Monetary Economics at the Centre for Banking Studies, Lugano.

Bradley, X., Friboulet, J.-J. and Gnos, C. (1996) 'From Keynes's to the Modern Analysis of Inflation', in A. Cencini and M. Baranzini (eds), *Inflation and Unemployment: Contributions to a New Macroeconomic Approach* (London: Routledge).

Cencini, A. (1996) 'Inflation and Deflation: The Two Faces of the Same Reality', in A. Cencini and M. Baranzini (eds), *Inflation and Unemployment: Contributions to a New Macroeconomic Approach* (London: Routledge).

Davidson, P. (1991) *Controversies in Post Keynesian Economics* (Aldershot: Edward Elgar).

Davidson, P. (2002) *Financial Markets, Money and the Real World* (Cheltenham, UK and Northampton, USA: Edward Elgar).

Gnos, C. (1998) 'The Keynesian Identity of Income and Output', in P. Fontaine and A. Jolink (eds), *Historical Perspectives on Macroeconomics: 60 Years After the General Theory* (London: Routledge).

Gnos, C. (2004) 'Is *Ex-ante Ex-post* Analysis Irrelevant to Keynes's Theory of Employment?', *Review of Political Economy*, 16(3): 335–45.

Keynes, J.M. (1930) *A Treatise on Money*, 2 vols (London: MacMillan).

Keynes, J.M. (1936) *The General Theory of Employment, Interest and Money* (London: Macmillan).

Keynes, J.M. (1937a) [1973] 'Ex Post and Ex Ante', in *The Collected Writings of John Maynard Keynes*, vol. XIV (London: Macmillan), pp. 179–83.

Keynes, J.M. (1937b) [1973] 'The "Ex Ante" Theory of the Rate of Interest', The Economic Journal, reprinted in The Collected Writings of John Maynard Keynes, vol. XIV (London: Macmillan).

Moore, B. (1988) *Horizontalists and Verticalists: The Macroeconomics of Credit Money* (New York: Cambridge University Press).

Palley, T. (1996) *Post Keynesian Economics* (New York: St Martin's Press).

Parguez, A. (1991) 'L'inflation zero: un état ideal ou l'objectif impossible', *Economies et Sociétés*, 11–12: 61–89.

Ricardo, D. (1810) *The High Price of Bullion. A Proof of the Depreciation of Bank Notes* (London: John Murray). Reprinted in P. Sraffa and M. Dobb (eds) (1951), *The Works and Correspondence of David Ricardo*, vol. 3, Pamphlets and Papers 1809–11 (Cambridge: Cambridge University Press).

Rochon L.-P. and Rossi, S. (2006) 'Endogenous Money: The Evolutionary Versus Revolutionary View', *Quaderni di ricerca*, Working Paper No. 14 (Lugano: Research Laboratory of Monetary Economics at the Centre for Banking Studies).

Rossi, S. (2001) *Money and Inflation: A New Macroeconomic Analysis* (Aldershot: Edward Elgar).

Sawyer, M. (2002) 'Economic Policy with Endogenous Money', in P. Arestis, M. Desai and S. Dow (eds), *Money, Macroeconomics and Keynes* (London: Routledge).

Schmitt, B. (1966) *Monnaie, Salaires et Profits* (Paris: Presses Universitaires de France).

Schmitt, B. (1984) *Inflation, chômage et malformations du capital* (Albeuve, Switzerland and Paris: Castella and Economica).

Schmitt, B. (1996) 'Unemployment: Is There a Principal Cause?', in A. Cencini and M. Baranzini (eds), *Inflation and Unemployment: Contributions to a New Macroeconomic Approach* (London and New York: Routledge).

Weintraub, S. (1979) 'A TIP for MAP', in J.H. Gapinski and C.E. Rockwood (eds), *Essays in Post-Keynesian Inflation* (Cambridge, MA: Ballinger).

# 8
# A Policy-Game Framework for the Dollar–Euro Exchange Rate

*Philip Arestis and Elias Karakitsos*

## Introduction

Most dollar-euro models are unstable in the sense that the influence of variables such as (short- or long-term) interest rate differentials, change through time from, statistically significant, positive to negative, and sometimes to being insignificant. This instability inherent in all currency models based on the small open paradigm or the two-country model is due to a policy-game framework, in which the equilibrium shifts from Stackelberg-leader to Stackelberg-follower.[1] Once account is taken of this game framework, and the shift of the equilibrium between Stackelberg-leader and Stackelberg-follower, the resulting dollar-euro model is stable. The US has a clear preference for the Stackelberg-leader equilibrium when the economy is overheated or cools down, but inflation continues to rise because of inertia. The US has a clear preference for the Stackelberg-follower equilibrium when the economy is in recession or on the recovery phase of the business cycle. In each case markets impose the relevant equilibrium because it is stable for the world economy and global financial markets, based on the premise that 'what is good for the US is also good for the rest of the world'. The question of stability/instability issue can only be answered when the business cycles of the US and euro area can be investigated in terms of them being synchronized or de-synchronized. Under synchronized circumstances, there is a conflict of interest in that both players want either a strong or weak currency, and the resulting equilibrium is unstable. When the business cycles are de-synchronized the equilibrium is always stable because one player wants a strong currency while the other a weak one. We utilize such a framework in this chapter in an attempt to study the dollar–euro exchange rate at the theoretical level without forgetting at the same time the realities of the wider real world.

In the next section we pose the question of the relevance of the chronic US external current account imbalance. Then we examine the relationship between the dollar and the current account imbalance at the theoretical level, and a new way of looking at the determinants of the exchange rate is discussed; in doing so we make extensive use of the game-theoretic approach as this is applied in the foreign exchange market. The final section summarizes and concludes.

## The relevance of the chronic US current account deficit

The deficit in the US current account, which records transactions in goods and services, has progressively widened since the recession in the early 1990s. In the 1980s it was also in deficit, but it narrowed with the dollar depreciation following the Plaza Accord in 1985. Under free floating, the capital account, which records transactions in assets and Foreign Direct Investment (FDI), is the mirror image of the current account and represents the financing of the current account deficit. The discrepancy, if any, between the current account and the capital account reflects changes in foreign exchange reserves, which on occasions may arise from central bank intervention in the foreign exchange market. The current account deficit (the external imbalance) stood at the historical record of 7.0 per cent of nominal GDP in December 2005. It is, thus, bigger than the 3.3 per cent recorded in the early 1990s, which was the previous record deficit in the last fifty years. The financing of the current account deficit, so far, has not been a problem since the surplus in the capital account has exceeded the deficit in the current account. For example, in the second quarter of 2003 the surplus in the capital account was 6.2 per cent of GDP, outstripping the deficit in the current account by 1 per cent.

The financing of the huge US current account deficit has so far been met very easily, as the residents in the Rest of the World (ROW) have been willing to lend the US the necessary funds to cover this deficit. This process has turned the US into a serious net debtor to the ROW in the last twenty years. However, the debt is in US dollars and there are no immediate good reasons why residents in the ROW should lose their confidence in the ability of the US to service this debt. There is a risk, however, that ROW residents may lose their appetite to hold US assets, if they continue to suffer huge losses on their holdings of US assets. During September and October 2003 there was a temporary drop in the desire of foreign investors to accumulate US assets, but that was restored subsequently. The risk that foreigners may, at some point in time, lose their appetite implies that it would be better that the US should balance or, at least, reduce its current account deficit. The dollar has been on declining trend in the second quarter of 2006 (the timing of revising this chapter) and this should help the current account deficit.

An interesting aspect of the chronic US current account deficit is that the dollar is a reserve currency, and the US debt is simply domestic rather than foreign. This means that any crisis in the US must come from lack of confidence in its ability to service its domestic debt. Although foreign residents hold more than half of the US general government debt, this is smaller than any other G7 economy. Moreover, although the US corporate debt is large (46 per cent of US GDP), foreign residents hold only one quarter. Hence, there are no compelling reasons why foreign residents should lose their confidence in the ability of the US to service its debt. However, foreign residents may lose their appetite to lend the US, if they continuously suffer losses from their holdings of US assets. One factor that has contributed to such losses is the falling dollar exchange rate and the other is the bad timing of foreign residents in buying US assets. From this point of view the huge current account deficit (the external imbalance) is one of the problems that face the US economy. Figure 8.1 shows that as a percentage of GDP direct holdings of equities by the personal sector increased from 44 per cent in 1952 to 87 per cent in 1968, but then declined to just 20 per cent in 1982 and then recovered to a peak of 101 per cent in March 2000. Since then direct holdings fell to 44 per cent, but have recovered recently and stood at 48 per cent of GDP in December 2005. However, such large swings reflect changes in the value of equities, which can be seen if direct holdings are expressed as a percentage of the total. The proportion of equities held directly by the personal sector has been on long-term downtrend from 91 per cent in 1952 to 34 per cent lately (see Figure 8.1). This reflects a portfolio shift by the personal sector from direct to indirect holding through life insurance companies, pension funds and mutual funds. The proportion of total holdings of equities by the personal sector (both direct and indirect) declined by merely 5 per cent – from 98 per cent in 1952 to 93 per cent in the mid-1990s (see Figure 8.2). However, since the burst of the bubble in March 2000 the proportion of total holdings by the personal sector has fallen by 7 per cent, which was almost entirely bought by foreign residents.

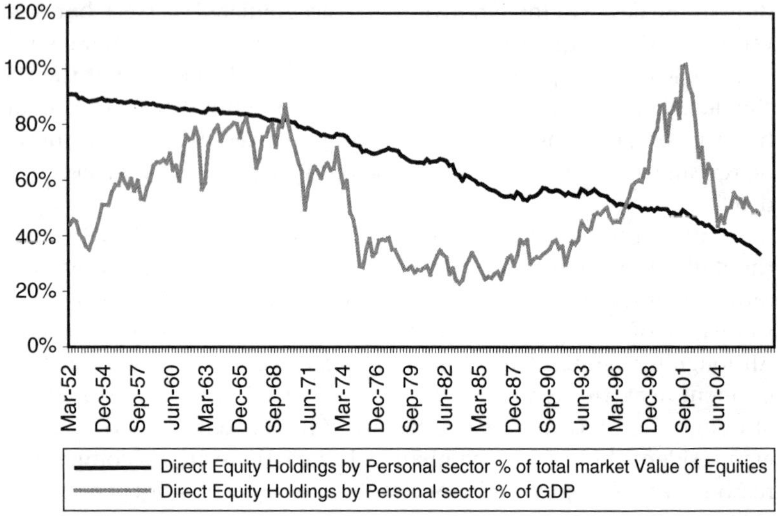


*Figure 8.1* Direct holdings of equities by personal sector

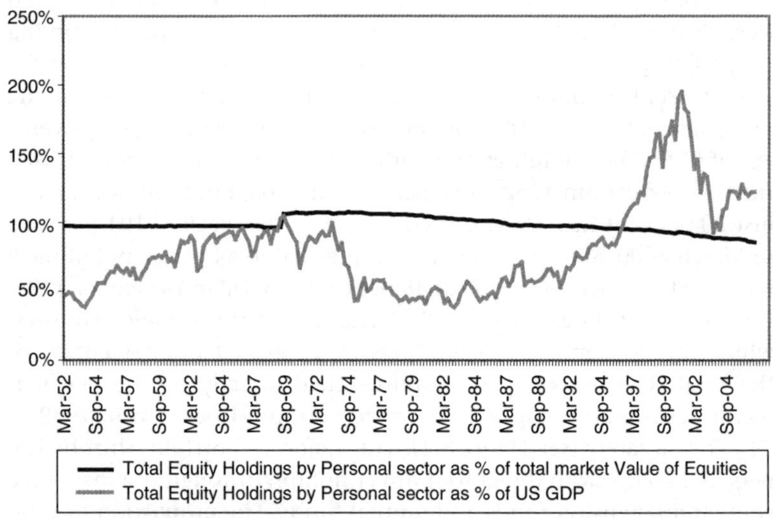


*Figure 8.2* Total holding of equities by personal sector

Figure 8.3 shows that the proportion of ROW holdings of US equities has increased from just 2 per cent of US GDP in 1952 to just over 8 per cent in September 1990, but it remained low throughout the major bull market of the 1990s. The proportion of ROW holdings of US

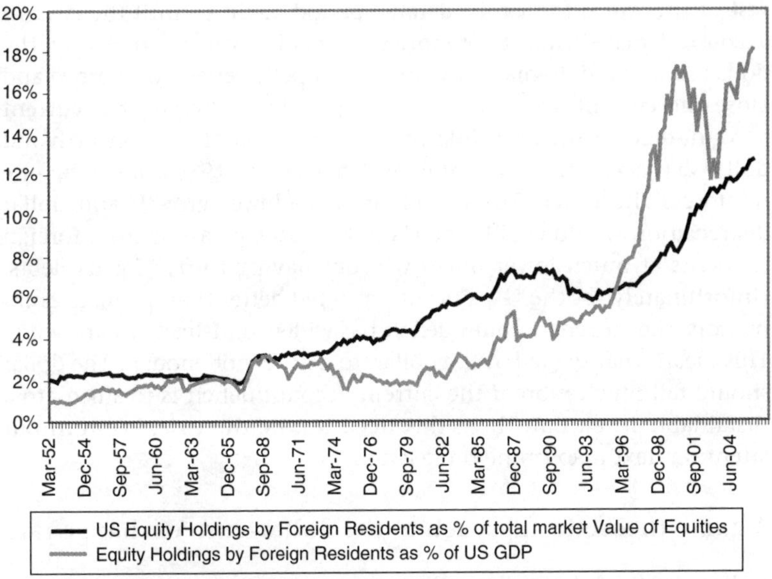


*Figure 8.3* US stock equity holdings by foreign residents

equities increased during the bear market by 4 per cent from March 2000 till September 2002. This means that foreign residents not only missed the major bull market of the 1990s, but also were net buyers during the bear market. During the bear market of 2000–03 the US personal sector sold its stock holdings to ROW residents who foolishly believed that this was simply an opportunity to buy US shares. Nonetheless, ROW residents have increased their holdings of US equities in the bull market from 2003 to 2006. In the second quarter of 2003 foreign residents bought aggressively the US bond market, which started one of its biggest collapses. Therefore, foreign residents have suffered capital losses in the past from holding US assets and the dollar current decline (May 2006) may aggravate such losses. Sustained losses in US assets may reduce the appetite of ROW to hold such assets. Hence, from this point of view the huge current account deficit is one of the problems that face the US economy. The current account deficit has persisted for far too long. This means that the US lacks the foundations for a sustainable new business cycle, since the current account deficit is bound to grow even bigger in case growth continues unabated.

In theory, the current account can be corrected in one of two ways. The US economy should expand at a smaller rate of growth than the rest of the world for a considerable period of time, until the current account deficit shrinks to at more sustainable level. Alternatively, the dollar should fall dramatically for US competitiveness to improve and close the current account deficit. In practice, however, the current account deficit usually shrinks by a combination of lower growth and dollar depreciation, as with the US deficit in the 1980s, since the one reinforces the other. The combination of lower growth and dollar depreciation would enable the US to buy back its assets from foreign residents at much lower prices without having to pay for its debts. Unfortunately for the US, since it has fared better than its main competitors, the current account deficit has widened instead of narrowing. This means that the fall in the dollar, to date, is not enough. The dollar should fall much more if the current account deficit is to shrink to a sustainable level. But, then, this need not be the case. We turn our attention next to examine these issues.

## A game-theoretic approach to the dollar–euro exchange rate

Although the dollar fall would help to correct the current account deficit, there is no presumption that the ballooning current account deficit should lead to further dollar falls. If this were the case, then the dollar should have fallen any time in the previous 13 years. Unfortunately, and in spite of such a popular belief, the current account is not a dollar determinant. Neither for that matter is the capital account. Most dollar forecasts are systematically wrong because they are based on variables that are not the main determinants of the dollar exchange rate that they purport to be. Neither the small open economy paradigm nor the two-country model (see, for example, Dornbusch 1976; Dornbusch and Fisher 1980; Fleming 1962; Mundell 1960, 1963) have had much success in explaining dollar movements. In an attempt to offer an alternative to existing approaches, we put forward a game-theoretic framework to currency determination (see also Frowen and Karakitsos 1998).

### Exchange rate determination

The value of a currency depends on the policy actions of the two countries involved, which affect other economic fundamentals. This entails that a game-theoretic framework is appropriate in which the equilibrium outcome depends on the policy decisions of both players and where the interactions of such decisions are explicitly modelled. In game theory there is the non-cooperative game, in which each player pursues its own objectives without caring for the objectives of the other, but where the decision of one player adversely affects the other. When the players agree to compromise in the pursuit of their objectives by taking into account also the objectives of the other player, we then have the co-operative game. In exchange rate analysis these considerations are paramount. This is so since policy makers in each country pursue policies that attempt to bring the best possible outcome (optimum) in terms of such target variables as inflation, growth and unemployment, through manipulating the level of interest rates, tax rates or discretionary government spending (in other words, monetary and fiscal policy). The exchange rate is a very important variable in the transmission of these policy actions on the target variables. For example, tight monetary policy with the objective of curbing inflation would be more effective if the currency appreciates, since it is expected to reduce imported inflation. On the other hand, easy monetary policy with the objective of promoting growth would be more effective if the currency depreciates because gains in competitiveness would boost exports and reduce imports. However, such policy decisions, to the extent that they are successful in affecting the value of the currency, would affect economic magnitudes in the other country involved. The policy decisions of one country may favourably or adversely affect economic magnitudes in the other country, where the outcome depends on the state of each economy in the business cycle. If the business cycles are synchronized then the policy decisions of one country will adversely affect the targets of the other. On the other hand, if the business cycles are not synchronized, then the policy decisions of one country will favourably affect the other country.

These considerations imply that a game-theoretic framework is appropriate for foreign exchange rate analysis, where the interactions of the two players are explicitly modelled. Normally, the game is played non-cooperatively because each policy maker decides on monetary and fiscal policy with the objective of achieving the targets of its own country without consideration for the effect on the growth or inflation of the other country. When the business cycles of the two countries are not synchronized it does not really matter whether the game is played cooperatively or not. But it does matter, when the business cycles are synchronized, because in such a case both countries need a strong currency if they wish to beat inflation or a weak currency if they opt to promote growth. If both players are of equal weight (symmetric game) and they do not cooperate, in the sense that each country pursues policies that maximize its own targets without due consideration for the targets of the other country, then the relevant equilibrium is Nash. The Nash equilibrium is always worse than a cooperative equilibrium, which is called Pareto, but it is stable, whereas the latter is unstable. Stability in this context means that once the equilibrium is achieved there is no incentive by either player to deviate from it. A simple example makes the difference between Nash and Pareto obvious. In a stadium with seats for all spectators, they prefer to stand up so that they can see better (Nash equilibrium). Once one person stands up to see better, there is an incentive for everyone to stand up. In the Nash equilibrium all spectators stand up, whereas in Pareto equilibrium they all sit down. Clearly, the Nash equilibrium is worse than Pareto because all spectators are better off sitting than standing and, collectively, they see equally well whether sitting or standing. The Pareto equilibrium, however, is unstable, because a single (short) spectator has the incentive to stand up to see better, but its actions would trigger a process that would result in all spectators standing up. In the currency market there are few instances when the game is played cooperatively, such as the Plaza Accord of 1985 and the Louvre Accord of 1987. But most of the time the game is played non-cooperatively.

If one of the players is more powerful than the other (asymmetric game) then the relevant non-cooperative equilibrium is Stackelberg, whereas the Nash equilibrium is relevant if both players carry equal weight. The strong player is called the 'leader', while the other the 'follower'. In the context of the dollar–euro rate two characteristics suggest the asymmetric nature of the game and the prevalence of the Stackelberg-equilibrium. The euro area is more vulnerable than the US to supply shocks, such as the price of oil. Hence, the US can be considered as the leader, while the euro area as the follower. The leader can exploit its advantage over the follower to achieve an even better outcome. This is accomplished by taking into account the possible reaction of the follower in deciding about its own strategy. In this asymmetric game there are two possible equilibria: Stackelberg-leader and Stackelberg-follower. The first is achieved when the leader exercises its leadership role, while the second is achieved when the 'leader' deliberately lets the 'follower' lead the game. In what follows we show that the US has a clear preference for the Stackelberg-leader equilibrium, when the economy is either overheated or cools down, but inflation continues to rise because of inertia. On the other hand, the US has a clear preference for the Stackelberg-follower equilibrium when the economy is either in recession or in the recovery phase of the business cycle, when there is spare capacity.

## A policy choice model

This framework is a Stackelberg game with two players: the US as the leader and the euro area as the follower. Such a framework is more appropriate because of the US dominance in the world economy, and the US preference for a stable equilibrium for the world economy and global financial markets. The implication of this Stackelberg game is that what matters for the dollar is the US and not its relative position against its main trading partners. Hence, popular variables, such as (short or long) interest rate differentials, growth differentials, money supply differentials, inflation differentials, which emanate from the small open economy or the two-country model, may lead to erroneous conclusions about dollar movements. The models that involve such variables are usually unstable, in the sense that the impact of these variables on the dollar–euro exchange rate changes through time from, statistically significant, to statistically insignificant and sometimes from positive to negative. The model instability is due to a shift in the equilibrium from Stackelberg-leader to Stackelberg-follower. Once account is taken of this game framework and the shift of the equilibrium between Stackelberg-leader and Stackelberg-follower the resulting dollar–euro model is stable. Moreover, the Stackelberg game framework does not imply that the traditional variables should be used for the US only. Instead, what is important is that the dollar should move in such a way so that the US economy can benefit under all circumstances. If this is not so, then not only is the US, but also the rest of the world, at risk, as the economic and financial system would be unstable. Within this framework, the value of the currency is an equilibrium outcome within a policy game. In this game-theoretic framework there are two equilibria, but only one of them is stable and most of the time investors enforce the stable equilibrium. The stable equilibrium reflects the best possible outcome from the US point of view, given the state of the economy in the business cycle and the time-varying priorities of the US policy makers, among the main targets of economic policy. We explore this theoretical premise, in the case of the dollar–euro exchange rate, in what follows.[2]

We begin by assuming that each policy maker chooses its monetary policy by optimizing an objective function that is penalizing deviations of actual inflation from its desired level and deviations of actual growth from its desired level. The utility function $U$ for each country may be specified as follows:

$$U_i = \tfrac{1}{2}[q_{ip}\,(p_i - p_i^d)^2 + q_{iy}\,(y_i - y_i^d)^2] \qquad (8.1)$$

where $q_{ip}$ is the penalty weight that the policy makers in country $i = 1,2$ are attaching to inflation and $q_{iy}$ is the penalty weight on growth; $p_i$ and $y_i$ are actual inflation and growth respectively, and $p_i^d$ and $y_i^d$ are desired inflation and growth respectively. Country 1 is the US and country 2 is the euro area. The bliss point is taken as the rate of growth of desired output and as inflation the rate that corresponds to desired output.

The US central bank is assumed to adopt a 'balanced' approach to monetary policy between the two conflicting targets of inflation and growth. It is, thus, assumed that the US central bank pursues monetary policy in a more 'symmetrical' manner than the ECB, and attaches equal degree of importance to the two conflicting targets of inflation and growth. On the other hand, the ECB is assumed to attach greater weight on inflation than on growth. This implies that while for the US it is assumed that $q_{1p} = q_{1y}$, for the euro area it is assumed that $q_{2p} > q_{2y}$, that is for the US the degree of priority on growth is equal to that on inflation, while for the euro area it is assumed that the priority on inflation exceeds that on growth. Each policy maker optimizes its own objective function subject to the economic model that defines the feasible combinations of inflation and growth, given the choice of the monetary policy instrument. The model allows for the spill-over effects of monetary policy from one country to the other. Thus, growth in each country is affected by the monetary policy of the two countries. Inflation depends on the output gap and imported inflation. The latter is influenced by monetary policy as a rise/fall in the domestic interest rate appreciates/depreciates the domestic currency and depreciates/appreciates the foreign currency. We may, therefore, describe the US model by equations (8.2) and (8.3), while that of the euro area by equations (8.4) and (8.5):

$$\Delta p_1 = p_1 - \bar{p}_1 = \alpha_1 \Delta y_1 + \beta_1(\Delta r_2 - \Delta r_1) + \beta_1 \Delta pm \tag{8.2}$$

$$\Delta y_1 = y_1 - \bar{y}_1 = \lambda_1 \Delta r_1 + \mu_1 \Delta r_2 \tag{8.3}$$

$$\Delta p_2 = p_2 - \bar{p}_2 = \alpha_2 \Delta y_2 + \beta_2(\Delta r_1 - \Delta r_2) + \beta_2 \Delta pm \tag{8.4}$$

$$\Delta y_2 = y_2 - \bar{y}_2 = \lambda_2 \Delta r_2 + \mu_2 \Delta r_1 \tag{8.5}$$

The symbols are as above, with the exception of $r_i$ which is the short-term interest rate (i.e. the instrument of monetary policy), and $pm$ which is the price of imported raw materials (e.g. oil) expressed in foreign currency and where $\bar{y}$, $\bar{p}$ denote the rate of growth of potential output and the inflation rate that corresponds to it and subscript *i* denotes each of the two players. In each model the following restrictions apply:

$$\alpha_i > 0,\ \beta_i > 0,\ \lambda_i < 0,\ \mu_i < 0,\ |\mu_1| < |\mu_2|,\ |\lambda_i| > |\mu_i| \qquad (8.6)$$

A number of characteristics are embedded in the model, which differentiate the US from the euro area. The coefficient $\beta$, which measures the degree of supply-side openness, assumes that the euro area is more open than the US, i.e. $\beta_2 > \beta_1$. Consequently, the euro area relies much more than the US on imported raw materials. The penultimate inequality in (8.6) implies that the spill-over effect of US monetary policy on the euro area is bigger than the spill-over effect of the euro area on the US. Thus, the euro area is both more susceptible to imported inflation and it is also more vulnerable to 'a beggar-thy-neighbour' policy than the US. The last inequality in (8.6) implies that domestic monetary policy has a bigger effect on domestic growth than the foreign one (see Karakitsos 1988a, 1988b). The US is 'stronger' than the euro area in the sense elaborated above. Therefore, in a game framework the US can be considered as the leader, while the euro area is the follower. The indifference curves drawn in Figures 8.4, 8.5 and 8.6 reflect these assumptions.

Using these assumptions, in Figure 8.4 we draw the indifference curves for both the US and the euro area, which take the form of ellipses. Ellipses further away from the bliss point represent lower utility and are therefore less desirable. The US indifference curves have as their centre the bliss point $A_u$. The US ellipses are very flat. By contrast, the indifference curves for the euro area are very steep. The US bliss point lies in the second quadrant of Figure 8.4. On the other hand, the bliss point for the euro area, denoted by $A_e$, lies in the fourth quadrant in the same figure. The optimal policy for each country is obtained by minimizing the objective function (8.1) above, subject to the economic model as summarized in equations (8.2) and (8.3) for the US and equations (8.4) and (8.5) for the euro area. Each central bank is choosing its monetary policy by taking as given the monetary policy of the other. The optimal monetary policy for each country is described by its reaction function. In Figure 8.4 the US reaction function is denoted by U, while that of the euro area is denoted by E. These two reaction functions take this shape in view of the two assumptions that the euro area is more vulnerable to imported inflation and to 'beggar-thy-neighbour' policies than the US, and that the euro area cares more about inflation than the US. The US reaction function is almost flat and the reaction function of the euro area is very steep.

*Figure 8.4* Three possible equilibria in a non-cooperative game

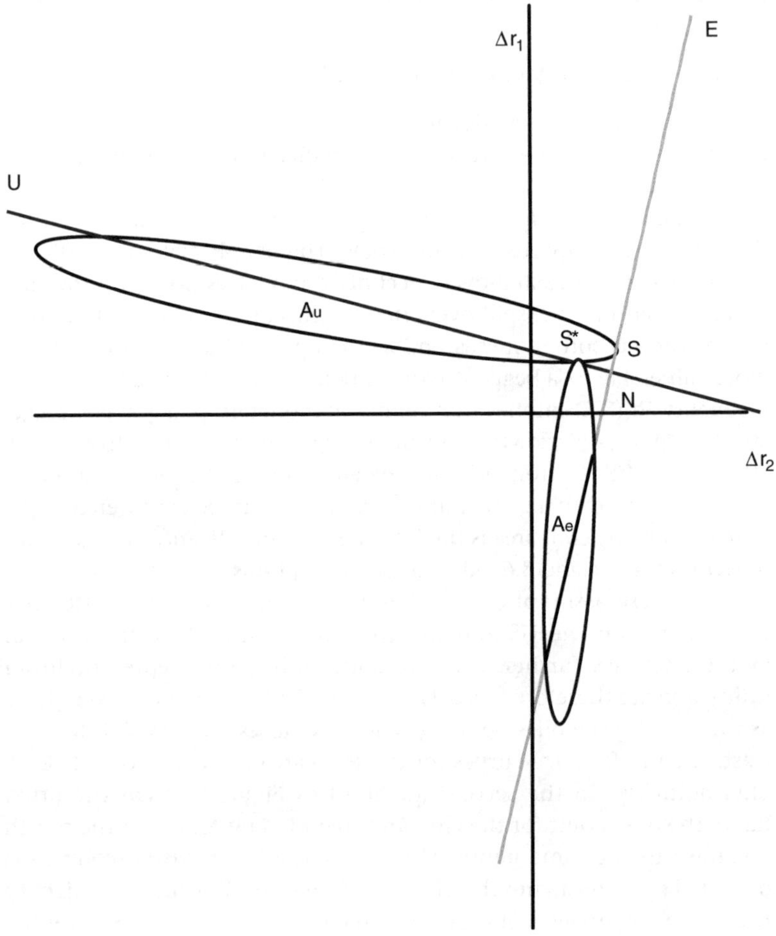


*Notes*: N = Nash equilibrium, S* = Stackelberg-follower, S = Stackelberg-leader, E = Euro area's reaction function, US = US's reaction function, Au and Ae refer to the US and Euro area points respectively $r_1$ = US interest rate, $r_2$ = Euro area interest rate.

The intersection of the two reaction functions determines the Nash equilibrium, denoted by N, which is attained in quadrant 1 under the assumptions made earlier. This implies that as a result of a surge, say, in imported raw material prices the euro area is forced into tighter

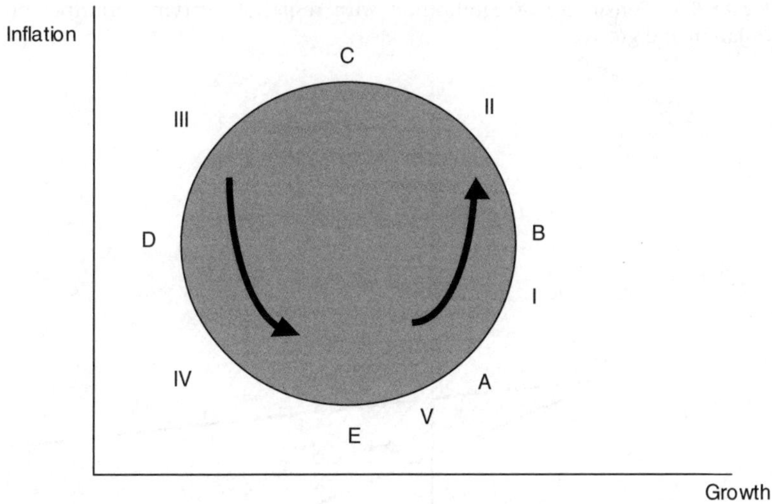


*Figure 8.5* Central bank objection function

monetary policy than the US. This appreciates the euro against the dollar and introduces a deflationary effect in the euro area with higher unemployment than in the US. The Stackelberg-leader equilibrium with the US as the leader is defined as that point on the reaction function of the euro area that is tangential on the US indifference curves. In Figure 8.4 the Stackelberg equilibrium is attained at point S. Clearly, this is a better solution for the US because it lies on a lower indifference curve than the one that passes through point N. This implies that the Stackelberg equilibrium with the US as the leader is Pareto efficient for the US, but not for the euro area, since its equilibrium lies on a higher indifference curve for the euro area. The Stackelberg-follower equilibrium in which the US lets the euro area act as a leader is defined as a point on the US reaction function that is tangential to the euro area's indifference curves. In Figure 8.4 the Stackelberg equilibrium with the euro area, as the leader, is attained at point S*. This is a better outcome for the euro area, since it lies on a lower indifference curve. But it is also optimal for the US. Hence, the Stackelberg-follower equilibrium is Pareto-efficient for both the US and the euro area.

## The choice of equilibrium

Figure 8.5 illustrates the way in which the objective function of a central bank changes in the course of the business cycle. Point A repre-

*Figure 8.6* Sensitivity of equilibrium with respect to varying priorities on inflation and growth

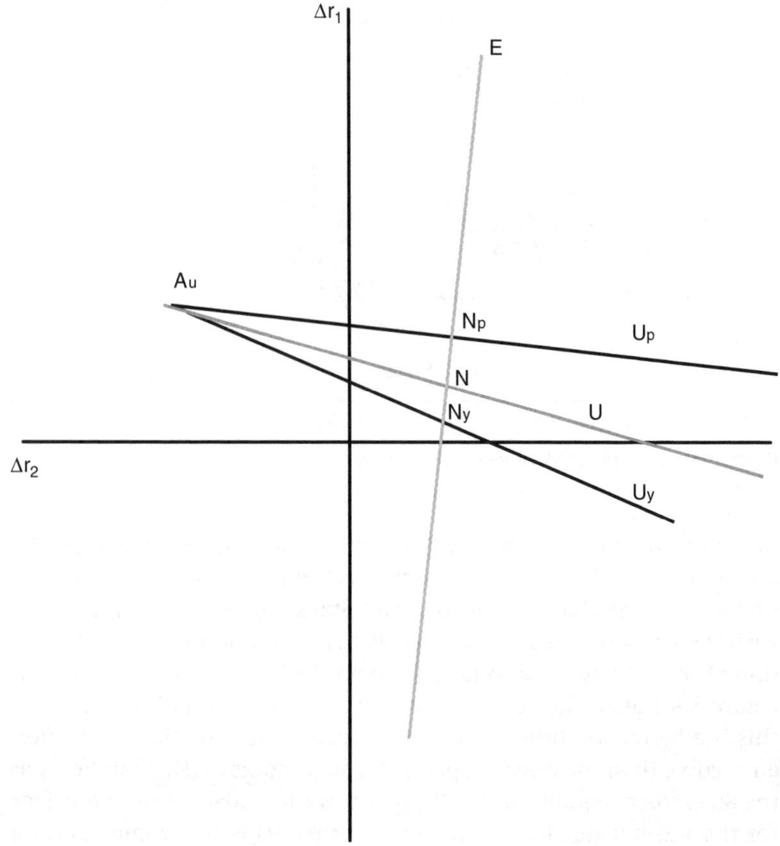


*Notes:* The symbols are as defined in Figure 8.4, and the subscripts have the following meaning: y-subscript = priority on growth, p-subscript = priority on inflation, No-subscript = neutral position.

sents the bliss point, defined as the rate of growth of potential output. The inflation rate that corresponds to the rate of growth of potential output is the steady-state rate of inflation. Points B and D represent the peak and the trough of the business cycle in terms of growth rates, respectively. Points C and E represent the maximum and minimum rates of inflation in the business cycle, respectively. These points divide the business cycle into five phases.

In Phase I growth is rising above potential, with inflation increasing – usually with a lag. In Phase II the economy decelerates, but inflation continues to rise in view of unit labour cost increasing for two reasons. The first is due to wage-inflation rising, and the second to labour productivity growth falling. In the initial part of phase II wages are increasing as fast as inflation as employees try to protect the purchasing power of their wages. Immediately after point B is reached, employees are in a position to protect their real wages since their bargaining power is strong (unemployment is low and few jobs are lost). However, as the economy moves towards point C the bargaining power of employees weakens (unemployment is rising and the number of jobs lost increases). Consequently, employees find it more and more difficult to protect the purchasing power of their wages; the real wage rate declines. Labour productivity growth declines as firms lag behind in adjusting their labour force to declining demand for their products, for two reasons. The first is due to uncertainty as to whether the drop in the demand for goods is temporary or permanent. The second reason is that costs of adjustment in hiring and firing and training costs are forcing firms to cope with reduced working hours and fewer temporary staff before they start making permanent staff redundant. However, as the fall in demand gathers pace, and the economy approaches point C, falling profitability is forcing firms to absorb into their profit margins the higher cost and decrease their labour force. In Phase III the economy moves into recession and inflation falls fast, as unit labour cost declines rapidly. Unemployment rises fast, with the number of jobs lost increasing rapidly. Productivity rises as firms shed their labour force faster than the drop in demand. Profit margins are squeezed further as demand is extremely weak in the recession. In Phase IV the economy recovers, but inflation continues to fall, as unit labour cost rises at a decreasing rate. This is the inverse of phase II; the correlation between inflation and growth is negative in this phase.

It is now possible to show how a central bank changes its priorities in the course of the business cycle. In phases I and II, where priority on inflation increases, central banks follow tight monetary policy. In phases III and IV where priority on growth increases and that on inflation recedes, central banks follow easy monetary policy. Hence, in general, interest rates rise from E to C and fall from C to E. Central banks are given certain characteristics, depending on the values they attach to the penalty weights on inflation and growth at the steady state, i.e. point A. A central bank can be characterized as balanced, when the penalty weight on inflation is equal to the penalty weight on growth. A central bank is wet (or a dove) when the penalty weight on growth exceeds that on inflation. A central bank is tough (or anti-inflation hawk) when the penalty weight on inflation exceeds that on growth. It is, therefore, evident that when a central bank is balanced, interest rates would start falling at point C and rising at point E. When a central bank is wet or dove, interest rates would start falling just before point C and rising after point E. When a central bank is anti-inflation hawk, interest rates would start falling after point C and rising before point E. Now when central banks change their priorities in terms of their targets, reaction functions inevitably rotate. This is shown in Figure 8.6. The US reaction function rotates anti-clockwise when the priority on inflation increases, i.e. when the economy is in phase I or II. When the priority on growth increases, i.e. when the economy is in phase III or IV, the US reaction function rotates clockwise. Nonetheless, the rotation of the US reaction function in the course of the business cycle is small, and in what follows we assume that the US reaction function is fixed in the course of the business cycle. The reaction function of the euro area, on the other hand, rotates clockwise when the priority on inflation increases, i.e. when the economy is in phase I or II. The reaction function rotates anti-clockwise when the priority on growth increases, i.e. when the economy is in phase III or IV. The euro area reaction function is much more sensitive than the US in the course of the business cycle, and it takes three positions. It is neutral when the economy is growing at the rate of potential output (i.e. in the steady state), steeper when the economy is in recession or in recovery (i.e. in phase III or IV) and flatter when inflation is rising (i.e. in phase I or II). In Figure 8.7, E denotes the euro area's reaction function in the neutral position; $E_y$ denotes the euro area's reaction function when the ECB attaches high priority in promoting growth. $E_p$ denotes the euro area's reaction function when the ECB attaches high priority in beating inflation.

We may now consider the equilibrium positions that both the US and the euro area would prefer. When both the US and the euro area are in phase I or II, then the reaction function of the euro area would be flatter and point N would be further to the right to $N_p$ in Figure 8.7. Both the US and the euro area welfare is smaller in the new Nash equilibrium $N_p$, relative to N. If the US chooses the Stackelberg-leader equilibrium $S_p$, its welfare is even worse. Given the anti-inflation bias of the ECB, the euro area is bound to choose the $S_p$ equilibrium, and for the US the choice of the Stackelberg-leader equilibrium is self-enforceable. Inevitably an interest-rate war ensues. This is precisely what happened

*Figure 8.7* Europe and US reaction functions

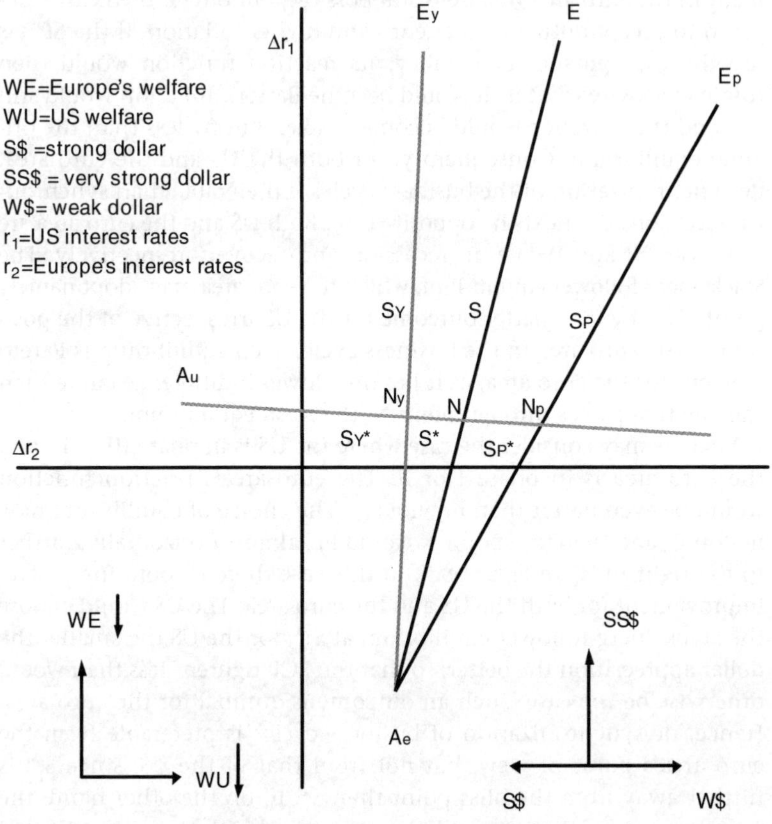


*Notes*: N = Nash equilibrium, S* = Stackelberg-follower, S = Stackelberg-leader, E = Europe's reaction function, A = bliss point, Y-subscript = priority on growth, P-subscript = priority on inflation, No-subscript = neutral position.

in the first half of the 1980s, and also between the Asian–Russian crisis and the burst of the 'new economy' bubble in the late 1990s. We may note the obvious, but pertinent point, that so long as the business cycles are synchronized this would always be the case. The point can be strengthened by assuming that the euro area is in phase III or IV when the US is in phase I or II, in other words, when the business cycles are not synchronized. The euro area reaction function is now at $E_y$, steeper than E and $E_p$ with point N shifting now to $N_y$. The US can improve its welfare by choosing the Stackelberg-leader equilibrium ($S_Y$), while the euro area welfare is somewhat reduced. However, improvement in the euro area welfare is still possible, but only if the ECB is prepared to accept both a weaker euro and higher inflation. If the ECB is unwilling to pursue such policy, its reaction function would then rotate clockwise (that is, it would become flatter). Inflation would still rise and the currency would become weaker, but by less than the original equilibrium. Consequently, for both the US and the euro area, de-synchronization of the business cycles is preferable than synchronization. Consider next the opposite case. Both US and the euro area are in phases III and IV, i.e. in recession and recovery respectively. The Stackelberg-follower equilibrium, which the euro area may adopt namely point S*, is by far a better outcome for the US irrespective of the position of the euro area in the business cycle. Such equilibrium is Pareto efficient for the euro area, as it lies on a lower indifference curve than the one that passes through point N, the Nash equilibrium.

Next we may consider the case where the US is in phase III or IV and the euro area is in phase I or II. The euro area's reaction function would be even flatter than previously. The choice of equilibrium now lies on $E_p$ and therefore point N would lie, almost horizontally, further to the right to $N_p$ in Figure 8.7. In this case there is room for welfare improvement for both the US and the euro area. The US would choose the Stackelberg-follower equilibrium at $S_p$*; for the US the smaller the dollar appreciation the better, so that the ECB tightens less than would otherwise be the case. Such an outcome is optimal for the euro area. Hence, de-synchronization of business cycles is preferable from the euro area's point of view, but not from that of the US, since $S_p$* is further away from the bliss point than S*. If, on the other hand, the business cycle of the euro area is synchronized with that of the US and both are in phase III or IV, the US would still choose the Stackelberg-follower equilibrium. The dollar would appreciate compared to the new Nash equilibrium at $N_y$, since the euro area interest rates rise only slightly. The dollar would be even stronger compared to the original Nash equilibrium N. Synchronization is preferable from the US point of view because the euro area growth is higher at $S_y$* than at $N_y$ and hence US exports are more buoyant, in spite of the stronger dollar. The choice of Stackelberg-follower equilibrium is Pareto efficient also for the euro area as the stronger dollar results in smaller degree of tightening by the ECB.

In summary, the Stackelberg-leader equilibrium is a better outcome for the US when the economy is either overheating or is cooling down (i.e. in phases I and II). The Stackelberg-follower equilibrium is a better outcome for the US when the economy is either in recession or in the recovery phase (i.e. in phases III and IV). The next question is to inquire how the US enforces its choice of equilibrium, whether this is a Stackelberg-leader or a Stackelberg-follower outcome. In each case markets impose such equilibrium because, usually, this is the only stable equilibrium in the absence of foreign exchange intervention. A market economy relies upon market discipline for the stability of the system. Investors, in trying to protect the value of their portfolios, usually enforce a stable equilibrium. Whenever the US business cycle is not synchronized with that of the euro area, the resulting equilibrium is stable, simply because there is no conflict: one player's interest dictates a strong currency, while the other's dictates a weak currency. By contrast, whenever there is synchronization of the business cycles, there is conflict in that it is in both players interest to have either a weak or strong currency. In the latter case, investors impose the equilibrium that enhances US welfare even if that is detrimental to the euro area in the short run, since it is stable. Thus, in phases I and II when the Stackelberg-leader equilibrium is prevalent and the US budget deficit is shrinking, investors buy dollars, as this helps the US to fight inflation and provide finance to a widening current account deficit. The alternative would imply instability for the US and, consequently, for the world economy and its financial system. In phases III and IV, when the Stackelberg-follower equilibrium is prevalent and the US budget deficit is widening, investors sell dollars, as this helps the US economy to recover, which in time will revive the rest of the world, and helps to close the current account deficit. The alternative would again imply instability for the US and the world financial system. One important qualification to this thesis is the possibility of 'irrational exuberance'. Investors in their monolithic pursuit of profit can choose an unstable equilibrium.

The stability issue clarifies why the ECB in some periods is unable to stem either falls or rises in the value of the euro. In the post-bubble environment a rate cut by the ECB does not have the desired effect of restraining the rise in the euro, in view of the euro area's business cycle being synchronized with that of the US. Since the burst of the bubble in 2000 both the US and the euro area are struggling to recover and a weaker currency is desired by both. In the absence of intervention the only stable equilibrium is the one that favours dollar weakness, and this is the one that markets impose. The equilibrium with a weak dollar is stable because it would lead to a US-led world recovery, whereas a dollar rise (and consequently a euro fall) would not help the rest of the world to recover and, perhaps, not even the euro area itself. In this respect, the experience of France in the early 1980s is pertinent. At the time, the rest of G7 pursued deflationary policies in order to fend the inflationary effect of the second oil shock, while the socialist French government pursued expansionary policies to fight the recession. In the event, within a short period of time, France was forced to reverse its policies, since it led to instability through a currency crisis. In the period between the end of the Asian–Russian crisis (1998) and the burst of the equity bubble (2000) the ECB, and prior to it the Bundesbank, was again unable to stem the fall of the euro, in spite of tight monetary policy because its business cycle was again synchronized with that of the US. By contrast, whenever the US business cycle is not synchronized with that of the euro area, the resulting equilibrium is stable, simply because there is no conflict – one player's interest dictates a strong currency, while the other's dictates a weak currency. This was the case between 1994 and 1998, when the US was overheated, but the euro area was operating with spare capacity.

It follows from this analysis that the dollar is strong when the US wants to cap inflationary pressures and it is weak when the US wants to promote growth through exports. Referring to the period mid-2003 to the end of 2004, the dollar was weak because the US wanted to have an export-led recovery. Once the economy became overheated from mid-2004 to early 2006 the dollar appreciated. Now that fears of a slowdown emerge, the dollar has resumed a downhill. In the second half of the 1990s the dollar was strong because the US was growing faster than its potential, thereby creating inflationary pressures. The strong economy helped to reduce the budget deficit and general government debt and bond yields fell, while monetary and fiscal policy was tight. In the last three years the economy has been weak, monetary policy is easy, fiscal policy is also easy and both the budget deficit and general government debt are soaring. The overall effect of these factors has contributed to the dollar fall and would continue to cause a fall in the future.

## Summary and conclusions

The huge US current account deficit (the external imbalance) has persisted for far too long, although, so far, it has been financed very easily. The accumulation of those deficits has turned the US into a net debtor to the ROW of the order of 23 per cent of its GDP. This external debt has been used, for a long time, mainly to sustain the US excess expenditure over its income, but also to buy ROW companies. Compared to other countries the external debt of the US is large, but it is in US dollars. Hence, traditional insolvency problems that are created by debt to ROW in ROW currency do not arise in the case of the US. Although foreign residents hold more than half of US government debt, the debt is smaller than any other G7 country. Moreover, although US corporate debt is 46 per cent of GDP, foreign residents hold only one quarter. Hence, there is no compelling reason why foreign residents should lose confidence in the ability of the US to service its debt.

However, foreign residents may lose their appetite to lend the US, if they continuously suffer losses from their holdings of US assets. Foreign residents have not only missed the major US bull equity market in the 1990s, but they have also suffered losses during the bear equity market of 2000–03. Moreover, foreign residents have recently suffered heavy losses on their holdings of US bonds. The dollar has declined recently, which may have aggravated such losses. From this point of view the external imbalance is one of the problems that face the US economy. Unless the current account deficit is balanced in the long run or at least narrowed down, the US lacks the foundations for a sustainable new business cycle, since the current account deficit is bound to grow even bigger in the case of a recovery.

The US will be able to get rid of its debt not by paying it back, but by buying it back at lower prices once foreign residents have suffered huge losses on their holdings of US assets. During the bear market of the last three years the US sold its stock holdings to the ROW. Slower growth and sharp dollar depreciation would enable the US to buy back its assets from the ROW. Unfortunately for the US, despite the recession and the low growth of the last three years, the US fared better than its main competitors, so the current account deficit widened instead of narrowing. This means that the dollar fall, so far, is not enough. The dollar should fall much more if the current account deficit is to shrink to a sustainable level. But even a bigger current account deficit will not cause a dollar fall, since, despite popular belief, it does not affect it. The opposite is true. The current account deficit is affected by the real value of the dollar.

Our game-theoretic approach to dollar determination reveals that the currency is strong when the economy is growing faster than its potential, fiscal policy is easy and monetary policy is tight, the government debt is falling and bond yields are declining.[3] All these factors point to a stronger dollar in the future. In essence, the dollar would begin to rise because the US economy is becoming overheated and the authorities would be concerned to curb inflation.

## Notes

1. We elaborate on the meaning of these terms below – see the subsection on exchange rate determination; see, also, Arestis and Karakitsos (2004) where we elaborate further on a number of issues dealt with in this chapter.
2. Game theory has been used extensively in microeconomics, but not to the same extent in macroeconomics. In the latter case, applications in the area of macro policies in an interdependent world is probably one exception. The contributions by Cooper (1985) and Hamada (1974, 1976, 1979) and applications by Canzoneri and Gray (1983), and Sachs (1983), utilize game theory and deal with the behaviour of the exchange rate.
3. There seems to be a contradiction between the effects of fiscal policy and government debt, but this is not so. In the short run easy fiscal policy (widening budget deficit) boosts the dollar, but in the long run the higher government debt that results from such policy, weakens the currency.

## References

Arestis, P. and Karakitsos, E. (2004) *The Post-Bubble US Economy: Implications for Financial Markets and the Economy* (Basingstoke: Palgrave Macmillan).

Canzoneri, M. and Gray, J. (1983) *Two Essays on Monetary Policy in an Interdependent World*, Discussion Paper No. 219, Federal Reserve Board International Finance.

Cooper, R.N. (1985) 'Economic Interdependence and Co-ordination of economic Policies', in R.W. Jones and P.B. Kenen (eds), *Handbook of International Economics*, vol. II (London: Elsevier Science Publishers).

Dornbusch, R. (1976) 'Expectations and Exchange Rate Dynamics', *Journal of Political Economy*, 84: 1161–76.

Dornbusch, R. and Fisher, S. (1980) 'Exchange Rates and the Current Account', *American Economic Review*, 70(5): 960–71.

Fleming, J.M. (1962) 'Domestic Financial Policies under Fixed and Under Flexible Exchange Rates', *International Monetary Fund Staff Papers*, 9 (November): 369–9.

Frowen, S.F. and Karakitsos, E. (1998) 'A Strategic Approach to the Euro Prospects', *Public Finance*, 53(1): 1–18.

Hamada, K. (1974) 'Alternative Exchange Rate Systems and the Interdependence of Monetary Policies', in R.Z. Aliber (ed.), *National Monetary Policies and the International Financial System* (Chicago: University of Chicago Press).

Hamada, K. (1976) 'A Strategic Analysis on Monetary Interdependence', *Journal of Political Economy*, 84(4): 677–700.

Hamada, K. (1979) 'Macroeconomic Strategy and Co-ordination under Alternative Exchange Rate Regimes', in R. Dornbusch and J.A. Frankel (eds), *International Economic Policy* (Baltimore: The John Hopkins University Press).

Karakitsos, E. (1988a) 'The Transmission of Monetary Policy in Interdependent Economies: An Empirical Investigation between the US and Europe', in P. Arestis (ed.), *Contemporary Issues in Monetary Economics* (London: Macmillan).

Karakitsos, E. (1988b) 'Asymmetrical Effects of Monetary Policy Between the US and Europe', *Journal of Economic Dynamic and Control*, 12(1): 79–85.

Mundell, R.A. (1960) 'The Monetary Dynamics of Adjustment under Fixed and Flexible Exchange Rates', *Quarterly Journal of Economics*, 74(1): 51–61.

Mundell, R.A. (1963) 'Capital Mobility and Stabilisation Policy under Fixed and Flexible Exchange Rates', *Canadian Journal of Economics and Political Science*, 29: 475–85.

Sachs, J. (1983) *International Policy Co-ordination in a Dynamic Macro-Model*, NBER Working Paper No. 1166 (Washington, DC: National Bureau of Economic Research).

# 9

# The New Governance in Monetary Policy: A Critical Appraisal of the Fed and the ECB

*Edwin Le Heron*

## Introduction

Over the course of the last fifty years, four monetary policy regimes succeeded each other. A particular view of governance corresponds to each monetary policy regime. First, until 1974, for the Keynesian regime founded on the Keynesian synthesis, the government exercised direct management of economic policy. During this time, monetary policy was only one element of the global policy and under the full discretion of the government.

Second, from 1974 to 1982, the Monetarist regime developed the monetary policy rule, called 'monetary targeting'. Monetary policy became self-governing. The rule versus discretion debate shed light on both of these outdated monetary policy regimes. But whereas the rule (quantity theory of money) had to be respected, Friedman said nothing about a specific organization of the central bank. The theoretical framework changed; not the institutional design.

Third, during the 1980s, the basic Friedmanian policy evolved with the rational expectations revolution. Kydland and Prescott (1977), Barro and Gordon (1983) or Rogoff (1985) provided new 'decisive' arguments in favour of rule, and against discretion. These are the famous arguments: dynamic inconsistency, inflation bias, reputational equilibrium, and strategic delegation to a conservative banker. The new classical economics developed the approach by credibility to propound alternatives to the rule issuing from the quantity theory of money. The great novelty was the institutional design: full independence of the central bank had become essential for its credibility. The credibility strategy meant minimal governance, since the central bank was fully independent. Respect of the rule and transparency were enough.

Fourth, at the beginning of the 1990s, the belief in an automatic natural long-term equilibrium disappears with the new Keynesian economics and, consequently, the theoretical foundations of the rule. If the rule no longer existed, the independent central bank needed a new legitimacy. It is the beginning of a new challenge for governance in central banking. A single or predetermined equilibrium does not exist, and strong uncertainty makes the management of expectations necessary, so good co-ordination between the central bank, the government and economic agents is therefore essential. This implies a high level of communication and a definition of the objectives of monetary policy accepted by all. There is 'confidence' when there is a mutual understanding between the central bank and the economic agents.

The generalization of the inflation-targeting regime after 1990 and the 'risk management' of Greenspan at the Fed correspond to the choice of a confidence strategy. The new governance is today the focal point of modern monetary policy. The term 'governance' refers to the relationship between the central bank and the government, the elected representatives and/or the general public and to the decision-making processes in the central bank. Governance comprises the traditions, institutional design, mandate, accountability, communication strategies and processes that determine how power is exercised, how citizens are given a voice, and how decisions are made on issues of public concern.

The debate of rule *versus* discretion is no longer relevant. Credibility versus confidence appears to be much more useful for understanding the changes in modern monetary policy. We have pointed out four conflicts between a credibility strategy and a confidence strategy (Le Heron and Carré 2006): independence versus governance, responsibility versus accountability, common knowledge versus common understanding, transparency versus openness. After a short review of the governance in the successive monetary regimes, we shall develop the new governance within a comparison of the ECB (credibility strategy) and the Fed (confidence strategy).

## A short review of the governance in the successive monetary regimes since 1960

### The Keynesian consensus

During the 1960s, the Keynesian regime[1] was basically applied throughout the 'capitalist world'. The social democratic leadership, politics and statesmen were the centre of attraction of the economic views. The naturalist or 'spontaneous' view of liberalism was rejected.

For Keynesians, the statesman is the only one who can think globally and hence must deal with macroeconomic problems. He is the only one who can make global expectations and envision an optimal situation. Because of the expectations of economic agents, particularly those of entrepreneurs which do not lead spontaneously to social optimal market equilibrium, the statesman must intervene in the market. Money is not neutral either in the short run or in the long run. Monetary policy is part of economic policy and depends on the government. The central bank is under total political control and merely implements the decided policy. To deal with international monetary relations in terms of the Bretton Woods agreement, fixed exchange rates are preferable to the market mechanism. It is believed that sufficient quantities of reserves in foreign currencies and a reasonable exchange rate are enough to maintain the autonomy of monetary policy.

The IS–LM model did not originally integrate a mechanism of price determination and the Phillips curve completed awkwardly. If the Philips curve is accepted, there is a trade-off between inflation and unemployment. The monetary policy of the Keynesian synthesis follows four principles:

1. Monetary policy is only one element of a macroeconomic policy, which tries to fulfil four objectives: the 'magic square'. Monetary policy, fiscal policy, income policy and the management of public debt must be coordinated to fulfil these objectives, along with one that gives priority to employment and production. A lot of emphasis is placed on the short term. Internal and external objectives coexist.
2. Alone, the efficiency of the monetary policy is weak. Monetary policy should be avoided because of its potential negative consequences such as the instability of monetary policy instruments, financial instability, high volatility of money demand with the speculative motive, liquidity traps and impacts on the balance of payments.
3. The instrument is the money supply and the objective is a low and stable interest rate. The impact of monetary policy is exerted through the interest rate channel and the credit channel by changing the liquidity position of financial institutions. This impact, however, is judged weak and slow to manifest itself.
4. Official control of quantity is usually preferred to price control in the credit market and the foreign exchange market. Moreover, selective policies are justified.

So for the Keynesian monetary policy, there is no governance but a *government with full discretion.*

**The Monetarist consensus**

The Monetarist model was imposed progressively during the 1970s and corresponded to a renewal of a naturalist Walrasian economics based on a modified quantity theory of money. The general framework of natural laws leading a real economy to general market equilibrium was again accepted. However, following the dichotomy between monetary and real spheres, money does not depend upon natural laws. The market cannot only manage money. Money is only neutral in the long run and, therefore, it is the role of monetary authorities to neutralize money in the short run. Inflation is only a monetary phenomenon.

Due to institutions like money, the statesman is useful to preserve natural equilibrium. The use of money for short-term objectives must be completely avoided, as it is unnecessary in the long run because of natural equilibrium and would disturb the economy by causing inflation.

1. Since money should not be regulated by the government for a short-term objective and cannot be managed by the market, the central bank and technicians of money are entrusted with the aim of neutralizing money via a simple quantitative rule. The money supply should grow at a rate equal to the natural growth rate of production, which is dependent only on real factors.
2. Monetary policy is effective and useful, but only for one long-term internal objective: the control of inflation. Monetarists want a strict monetary discipline; that is the respect of a rule.
3. The instrument is the short-term interest rate and the objective is the stabilization of the money supply as measured by monetary aggregates. The rate of interest can be changed rapidly and abruptly. The surprise effect may work. The demand for money and the velocity of money are assumed stable in the short run.
4. One has to choose a flexible exchange rate system. The external stability of money (exchange rate) is the result of internal stability (no inflation).

To apply the Monetarist framework, we did not need an independent central bank, but only a monetarist government. There is no governance in the monetarist approach, only a monetary targeting rule.

If Monetarism was rapidly accepted, it was subsequently rapidly rejected at least in its initial form. According to Goodhart (1991: 275–7), the macroeconomic conditions that generated a consensus around Monetarism disappeared after 1982. The demand for money was increasing and unstable. The velocity of money became unpredictable. The main target of money supply could no longer be calculated. As the governor of the Bank of Canada Gerald Bouey remarked in 1983: 'We did not abandon M1, M1 abandoned us.'

**The credibility strategy**

In the 1980s, a new system in monetary policy began to appear: the credibility strategy. Credibility has evolved from new classical economics (NCE) to propound an alternative to the rule issuing from the quantity theory of money. The credibility framework is a synthesis of Monetarism and the NCE, especially with the rational expectations hypothesis. The rational expectations school strengthens the binding commitments to the natural equilibrium. The credibility literature starts with Kydland and Prescott (1977) and their time-inconsistency and inflation bias, continues with Barro and Gordon (1983) – that is, reputation as a solution to time inconsistency, and ends with Rogoff (1985) – strategic delegation to a conservative banker, Walsh (1995) or Svensson (1997).

The fundamental assumption of the monetarist and the NCE framework is the existence of a single long-term natural equilibrium (with exogenous and neutral money). The central bank knows this 'true' model of the economy and its credibility comes from the respect for this. The fixed rule, founded on the belief in the natural equilibrium model, can be interpreted as a commitment to respect this model. As agents are representative and hold rational expectations, everyone knows the same model. They can observe if the central bank is respecting it. Monetary policy is, therefore, a technical and economic problem. The different Taylor rules are the final attempt to find the miraculous solution: an automatic way to determine monetary policy. But these kinds of rules are at best an ex-post analysis, never an ex-ante continuous decision-making process. The times are always changing. A good Taylor rule works when it is useless (stable economic conditions) and it is inefficient when it is useful (exogenous shock for instance).

The central bank and economic agents refer to the same model, which is common knowledge. The model of the economy imposes a rule on the central bank, which takes a commitment to respect it and credibility follows at once. The common economic knowledge and a full transparency are sufficient for expectation co-ordination and anchorage. It builds expectations; it is a benchmark for policy makers and agents. To avoid the inflation bias of governmental policies, the independence of the central bank becomes obviously imperative. Full independence is the enforcement of the natural price stability-oriented and long-term-oriented strategy, and its related culture of stability and neutrality of money. As money is neutral, there is no problem of democracy. Monetary policy is only a technical problem, of respect for the rule. A central bank assumes responsibility only for the respect of a unique mandate: inflation.

By a strategy of 'credibility', we mean that a central bank adopts a model of behaviour and then follows it. It says what it does, and does what it says. The simplified chain of the credibility strategy is: rule–commitment–enforcement–independence–transparency–credibility.

The great novelty was the institutional design: the full independence of the central bank and the delegation of monetary power to a conservative central banker became necessary for credibility. The credibility strategy is only internal governance. Independence, respect of the rule and transparency are enough.

## The new governance of the confidence strategy

### *The beginning of governance in monetary policy*

At the beginning of the 1990s, the belief in an automatic natural long-term equilibrium disappears with the New Keynesian Economics (NKE) and, consequently, the theoretical foundations of the rule. If the rule did not exist anymore, the independent central bank needed a new legitimacy to found its monetary policy. It marks the beginning of the importance of governance in central banking. The generalization of Greenspan's 'inflation targeting' and 'risk management' at the Fed after 1990 corresponds to this evolution.

'Inflation targeting' tries to anchor directly the inflation expectations of the economic agents. Although influenced by the New Keynesians, inflation targeting is not a theory but a policy framework. A single or predetermined equilibrium does not exist, and strong uncertainty makes necessary the management of expectations, so good co-ordination between the central bank, the government and economic agents is therefore essential. This implies a high level of communication and a definition of the objectives of monetary policy accepted by all. There is 'confidence' when there is a mutual understanding between the central bank and the economic agents. The simplified chain of this confidence strategy is: communication–common understanding–governance–

accountability–openness–confidence. With the confidence strategy, governance is today the focal point of the modern monetary policy.

*The New Keynesian counter-revolution*

The confidence paradigm is founded upon the New Keynesian counter-revolution and the importance of uncertainty. 'Uncertainty is not just an important feature of the monetary policy landscape, it is the defining characteristic of that landscape' (Greenspan 2003: 1). With uncertainty, we cannot implement optimal rules or contracts. Because of imperfections and uncertainty, central banks and agents are in constant interaction. Monetary policy is seen as a co-ordination process, which differs from the non co-operative conception defended by the credibility framework.

With the New Keynesians, the explanation of inflation changes from money to expectations and an excess demand.

*The foundations of governance*

Full independence produced a 'democratic deficit' that is eliminated in the governance arrangement. Governance organizes the relation between elected representatives, the government, the economic agents and the central bank. In a 'checks and balances' arrangement, governance balances the subservience of monetary policy to elected representatives, on the one hand, and independence limited to instruments, on the other.

In a democracy, the central bank should be accountable, first of all, to elected representatives. It differs from full independence that pretends to be directly responsible to the general public. Central banks cannot be fully transparent. With openness, central banks simply open a window, because complete transparency could be counterproductive. A central bank practicing openness in a democratic society could be called a communicational central bank – that is to say a central bank that tries to build a consensus with the public on its monetary policy decisions. The common understanding creates the confidence link between the central bank and the agents. This 'common understanding', which implies a high level of communication, should be understood on two levels: in the first place each takes the other into account and, secondly, the strategy and the conventions of the central bank correspond to those of the other economic agents.

*The governance framework*

Confidence introduces a political revival in central banking. The confidence strategy starts from the evidence that the central bank is embedded in a democratic system. It pursues the idea that accountability is a quid pro quo for independence. Independence is balanced by democratic accountability, and we talk about 'governance'.

Accountability is not a purely technical question, but a democratic issue. It is connected to openness because accountability means that the central bank is accountable for its actions to democratic authorities, and has to take into account its democratic mandate in its day-to-day functions. Ultimately, accountability highlights that there is no clear evidence on the benefits of total independence. It is a tough question for members of the Fed, as Meyer (2000: 4) says: 'there is no consistent evidence of a relationship between central bank independence and real economic activity nor consistent evidence that central bank independence lowers the cost of reducing inflation or increases the effectiveness of stabilization policy'.

A central bank is actually an independent institution with unelected officials. Central banks earn legitimacy not by the ballot box, but by procedures of accountability. As Ferguson (2002: 2) points out: 'Such democratic accountability is even more important for central bankers, because the voting populace does not directly elect them'. Democratic accountability reveals a mutual dependency between the government and the central bank (the confidence link).

Governance must take into account four levels:

1. The decision-making processes in the central bank (self-governance):
   - Organization of the monetary policy committee (MPC),
   - Communications strategy: publications, statements, report, minutes of the MPC, speeches of the members the MPC,
   - The internal decision-making process: vote, consensus, advising, timing with the number of scheduled meetings,
   - The decision-making conflict resolution inside the MPC: dissents treatment, dissents mentioned in the minutes, publications of the dissents decision proposal.
2. The relation between the central bank and the elected representatives and/or the government (the politics and the institutional design)
   - The mandate (unique, hierarchical or dual, explicit or implicit) issued from the parliament or from the government,
   - Override procedures in case of exogenous shock, of non-respect of the mandate.
3. The relation between the central bank and the general economic policy

  - Balance of risks (unemployment, inflation),
  - Policy mix; co-ordination
  - Regulation of the financial markets (bubble, crash).
4. The relation between the central bank and the general public
  - How decisions are made on issues of public concern (entrepreneurs, households),
  - Common understanding.

Levels 2, 3 and 4 correspond to accountability (external governance).

The confidence strategy indicates a revival of politics in central banking. Governance is the delegation of authority, not the separation of power as with full independence. Governance aims to balance the independence of instruments and the dependence of goals.

## Independence of the ECB versus governance of the Fed: a critical appraisal

Independence is linked to the credibility strategy since governance is linked to the confidence strategy. The debate of credibility versus confidence appears to be useful for offering an understanding of the changes in monetary policy and the differences between the independence of the ECB and the governance of the Fed.

The ECB is a creature of central bankers and follows an outdated 'credibility strategy', as a 'new Lady in old clothes'. On the other hand, the Fed is a creature of Congress. Its strategy of 'risk management' can be defined as an up-to-date 'confidence strategy'. We shall analyse these two antagonistic central banks to understand the new governance, as defined above.

### ECB: an extraordinarily full independence

The ECB claims that 'full independence' is a condition for implementing and maintaining price stability: 'When exercising their powers and carrying out their tasks and duties, neither the ECB nor any NCB (National Central Bank) nor any member of their decision-making bodies shall seek or take instructions from Community institutions or bodies, from any government of a member state or from any other body' (Article 108 of the Maastricht Treaty, 7 February 1992).

#### *A creature of central bankers: self-governance*

Full independence of the ECB is the institutionalization of a monetary sovereignty. The ECB is far more independent than the German Bundesbank (Buba) ever was. The Bundesbank law could be changed by a simple majority in Parliament. The Buba is accountable to the federal audit agency (Bundesrechnungshof) and the decisions of German law courts. The European Parliament cannot change the ECB's mandate. Moreover, the ECB's statutes are difficult to shift because the modification of the Maastricht Treaty requires a unanimous vote of the European Union members and the ECB is not accountable to the European institutions. The Buba illustrates that central banking is a political question; it could anchor inflation expectations because it had a democratic role to play. The ECB has one leading economic task: to ensure price stability. Full independence is claimed to be a prerequisite for ensuring price stability, which is presented as a public good. The Buba had a social role to play: to safeguard a common good – namely, money. With price stability, the ECB tries to preserve the inheritance of the credibility earned during the 'fight' against high inflation. Price stability is presented as the wisdom of central banking inherited from 'the great experience of the 1960–1970s'. While the Buba was the inheritance of the German hyperinflation crisis of the 1920s that is principally a political and social crisis, the ECB is a consequence of the theoretical dogma of independence that emerged in the 1980s with the credibility literature. Paradoxically, the independence of the ECB is closer to that of the German Reichsbank[2] (1875–1945), the predecessor of the Buba, which 'managed' the hyperinflation crisis.

> Contemporary economists (...) concluded that the Reichsbank had become a 'second government' that acted independently from the elected government. The democratically elected government was the less powerful one. Being independent did not prevent the Reichsbank from adopting the horrific policies of the 1920s and early 1930s. (Werner 2006: 107)

The ECB is not a creature of elected representatives, but rather a creature of the folk wisdom theory of central bankers. From a theoretical point of view, the full independence of the ECB results from time inconsistency, institutional design (Persson and Tabellini 1993) and the 'free lunch' literature. 'This evidence points to a potential free lunch: delegating monetary policy to an independent central bank with a clear price stability mandate leads to lower and less variable inflation without increasing the volatility of output' (Issing *et al.* 2001: 130).

Full independence is a maximum interpretation of Rogoff's solution (1985): delegation to a conservative central banker. The ECB's full independence aims to serve its own interests: namely its reputation and its credibility. The ECB scheme does not organize the delegation, but rather the separation of monetary policy from the democratic order. To avoid short-term political pressures (time inconsistency and inflation bias), monetary policy (a political issue) moves to central banking (a technical issue). 'Only central bankers, neutral and objective technical experts as they are, can take decisions for the benefit of the people' (Werner 2006: 107). There is a democratic deficit.

The monetary policy committee is the governing council with currently 18 members: 12 national central banks' governors (a maximum of 15 after the future enlargement) and only six from the executive board. More, two members of the executive boards were previously governors of a central bank. Such is the case of the governor Trichet, who comes from the Bank of France, and before that with Duisenberg. The monetary policy committee is under the control of the central bankers.

*The discrepancy between full independence and accountability*

Responsibility means that the central bank, rather than elected representatives, has the ultimate responsibility for monetary policy in society. On the other hand, accountability reveals a mutual dependency between politicians and central banks. This link of confidence rests notably on the possibility of sanctioning the central bank (override procedure). In the responsibility approach of the ECB, effective accountability to elected representatives is impossible because it would contradict its independence:

> If any political body – such as parliament or government – were able to intervene or influence directly the policy-making of the central bank, they would actually be taking part in the decision-making process itself and hence would share the responsibility for the policy outcomes. This would not only contradict the independent status of the central bank, but it would also render the concept of accountability meaningless. (Scheller 2004: 126)

Not only is the ECB fully independent, but the Stability and Growth Pact makes it possible to avoid the free rider and chicken game (budgetary expansion with monetary restriction) by enforcing budgetary rules. The European policy mix is dominated by monetary policy without any flexibility. For the ECB, accountability is only judged by the general public on the announced objective of price stability.

*An ineffective parliamentary accountability*

The ECB is accountable to the European Parliament in the procedure of 'quarterly monetary dialogue', but it is not an effective accountability. The Parliament can change neither the ECB's law nor its objectives or targets. It can neither remove the central bankers nor put a sanction on the ECB. There is no override procedure. 'Formal sanction mechanisms would be too blunt and would have potentially negative implications for the efficient fulfilment of the central bank's mandate' (ECB 2002: 47).

The European Parliament has limited powers, which consist in the ability to call the president and other members of the ECB board to discuss EMU monetary policy (Maastricht Treaty, Art. 109b). The candidates for the ECB board must appear before the European Parliament prior to their appointment. The Parliament has the right to give an opinion on their appointment (Art. 11, ECB Charter), with the exception of the president. Yet since the Parliament has only a consultative role, it is accountability without power. As Buiter (1999: 23) puts it, what is required is 'a European Parliament with teeth'.

*A fascinating archetype of responsibility*

The ECB has developed a peculiar way of building its legitimacy. It rests on two pillars: (i) the belief in the neutrality of money in the long run and (ii) technocracy. First of all, money does not really matter. Inflation is a monetary phenomenon, justifying the mandate on price stability. The best gift from monetary policy to the general public is price stability. With neutral money in the long run, full independence does not imply a democratic shortage, while monetary policy becomes only a technical problem. Secondly, central bankers are experts. They are wise people who have to be insulated from the short-sightedness of politicians. This explains its rejection of democratic accountability. The ECB claims to be directly responsible to the general public at large, and not indirectly via elected representatives. Direct responsibility to the public is an elegant way of earning legitimacy without passing through the traditional legitimacy of democratic oversight or subservience to elected representatives. Parliamentary sanctions are replaced by a simple public scrutiny as a way of earning legitimacy.

> The ECB is accountable first and foremost to the citizens of the European Union from whom the Treaty's legitimacy derives and –

> more formally – to the European Parliament, which is the only European institution directly elected by EU citizens. (ECB 2004: 68)

This is not a fair argument, for two reasons. First, it contradicts our representative democracies. Secondly, the public does not have any direct legal or constitutional power over the ECB.

The ECB asserts that democratic accountability is not feasible: the ECB is an unconventional supranational central bank. There is no government of the EU; and the European Parliament has not authorized the Treaty on the ECB. So the Parliament does not have the power to modify its statute. From their own viewpoint, the ECB is only responsible to those who have voted for the Treaty – that is, European citizens.

> Accountability is the legal and political obligation of the ECB to justify and explain its decisions to the citizens of Europe and their electoral representatives. Accountability is enhanced by a high degree of transparency. (ECB 2002: 45)

Using credibility literature, the ECB justifies its full independence cum responsibility through the principal–agent theory. In this delegation approach, the principal is the democratic authority (government or parliament). However, the ECB's approach is based on political authority rejection, the public is the principal in the contract: 'A clearly defined mandate lies at the very heart of the aforementioned "contract" between the people and the independent central bank' (ECB 2002: 50).

The problem arises because the people did not write the statute and did not give the mandate to the ECB. It explains why the ECB has a commitment to transparency and price stability. The people monitor the ECB's performance through the definition of price stability: 'It created a benchmark against which its performance can be assessed' (ECB 2002: 50). But without any public sanction in case of non-fulfilment, the transparency on price stability does not confer a public legitimacy, it only 'imposes self discipline' (ECB 2004: 68).

*The lack of ECB communication*

Communication is only the need for credibility: you are supposed 'to say what you do and do what you say'.

> Price stability is unambiguously assigned overriding importance. This provision reflects a broad consensus existing in the economic

> discipline that the maintenance of price stability is the appropriate objective of monetary policy. The consensus is rooted in the belief that monetary policy makes its best contribution to overall economic welfare by maintaining price stability. (Issing 2001: 7)

We will shed some light on the lack of robustness of such a 'divine coincidence' between inflation stabilization and output stabilization promoted by the price stability strategy. Nevertheless, the ECB (Issing *et al.* 2001: 39) makes a critical appraisal of the Fed's communication. It considers that the Fed has a strategy of secrecy that is counter-productive (and even perilous) for central bank credibility, since it depends on the president's personality. The Fed does not have an explicit nominal anchor, but a personal anchor: the chairman – Greenspan.

*ECB: the pitfalls of 'maximum transparency'*

The ECB defines transparency as

> an environment in which the central bank provides in an open, clear and timely manner all relevant information on its mandate, strategy, assessments and policy decisions as well as its procedures to the general public and the markets. Transparency is ultimately about the genuine understanding by the public of the entire process of monetary policy-making. (ECB 2002: 60)

The ECB associates transparency with efficiency, accountability, predictability and effectiveness. The ECB states frankly: 'We mean what we say... even if we have perhaps not always been entirely successful in saying what we mean' (Issing 1999: 505).

By pretending to be a pragmatic conservative central banker, the ECB attempts to improve its reputation. It is generally agreed that old-fashioned secrecy was a way for non-independent central bankers to free themselves from the government (Mishkin 2004: 1). Transparency is the new means used by the ECB to increase its independence from elected representatives. Transparency is of the first importance for the ECB's legitimacy: A high degree of transparency helps to ensure accountability to the public.

*Transparency does not mean understanding*

In the literature, we find three kinds of criticisms about the ECB's communications. First, its explanations, through the two-pillar strategy, were unclear. Secondly, the ECB only communicates on inflation while at the same time focusing on other objectives, such as growth. This is not transparent. Thirdly, the ECB does not communicate enough with financial markets.

Even Issing (1999) recognizes that full transparency is impossible, and prefers to talk about maximum transparency, which could be viewed as the folk wisdom of central banking: 'do what you do, but talk only about inflation' (Faust and Henderson 2004: 55). Communication is supposed to clarify, not obscure the mandate and the strategy.

Fully independent, not accountable, with a weak communication: there is no true governance at the ECB. The ECB has self-governance. The links are cut with the political power (European Commission, European Council, European Parliament) and with the general economic policy (Ecofin). At the same time the general public is essentially concerned by unemployment, but the ECB speaks only on inflation.

### The Fed: the challenge of central banking in a democratic society[3]

The Fed is embedded in a stronger representative democracy. It benefits from an instrumental independence, but not independence for the objectives, remaining subservient to elected representatives.

#### *A 'creature of the Congress'*

The Fed rejects both time inconsistency and free lunch theories:

> I have never found the literature on time inconsistency particularly relevant to central banks... There is no consistent evidence of a relationship between central bank independence and real economic activity nor consistent evidence that central bank independence lowers the cost of reducing inflation or increases the effectiveness of stabilisation policy. (Meyer 2000: 3–4)

The Fed's independence is the production of elected representatives, not economic theory. It has a limited delegated authority: 'the Fed independence is a product of congressional legislation and can therefore be diminished at the will of the Congress' (Meyer 2000: 16). The Fed represents a political revival in central banking. It is a break with the consensus on independence in the 1980s that led to the full independence of the ECB.

Regarding democracy, the difference between the ECB and the Fed is important. The Fed is a 'creature of the Congress' (Meyer 2000: 6). So it benefits from political legitimacy. This legitimacy process is strengthened by democratic accountability procedures. Central bankers 'are accountable both to the Congress from which we derive our monetary policy mission and, beyond, to the American people' (Greenspan 2001: 1).

The Federal Open Market Committee (FOMC) has 19 members, but only 12 votes: seven from the Board of Governors and only five from the regional central banks' presidents. Moreover, the governor is generally not a president of a regional central bank. It is more often a practician (Greenspan) or a theoretician (Bernanke). For the Fed, independence should be limited by a 'checks and balances' arrangement. Governance insists on the politics of monetary policy and on the democratic founding of the Fed that explains its democratic device for prosperity.

The Fed strategy of 'risks management' can be defined as a 'confidence strategy'. It is now a commonplace that the Fed is no longer 'cryptic' or leading an informal '"just do it" strategy' (McCallum 1995: 207). It has changed since 1994. The Fed's efficiency stems from explanations that allow the building of a common understanding between itself and market participants. In contrast to the ECB, the Fed does not pursue a reputation of providing a culture of stability – that is, credibility for low inflation. People have confidence that the Fed will be aggressive in response to varied shocks – that is, to lead stabilization policies that maintain prosperity. Hence, the Fed has a social role to play, 'regulating public conflict over inflation's redistributive powers' (Faust 1996: 267).

*The Fed: effective democratic accountability*

The Humphrey–Hawkins procedure produces an effective accountability with a double meaning. First, there is the subservience to potential sanctions for the central bank. Presentation of the Fed's president in Congress is an effective testimony because the Congress can abolish or remodel the Fed by a simple majority. Secondly, accountability has an economic effect: it has an impact on market participants' expectations. This communication significantly reduces uncertainty in financial markets (Kohn and Sack 2003). The Humphrey–Hawkins procedure reveals that political pressure on monetary policy is orientated towards more accountability from the central bank, and not towards more over-expansionary policy (time inconsistency): 'Accountability is the critical mechanism for ensuring both that the central bank is operated in a way consistent with democratic ideals and that the central bank operates under incentives to meet its legislative mandate for monetary policy' (Meyer 2000: 10).

The Fed has a democratic and institutional commitment to its mandate. Monetary policy is not rule-based on economic laws; rather, it is founded on democratic principles. However, legitimacy is not obtained by the ballot box, but by procedures of accountability: 'Such democratic accountability is even more important for central bankers, because the voting populace does not directly elect them' (Ferguson 2002: 2). The Humphrey–Hawkins testimonies appear to be a procedural institutionalization of the Fed's legitimacy.

The ECB exercises its direct responsibility to the public by monitoring its performance on the definition of price stability. It is radically different from the Fed, which is democratically accountable to Congress – which verifies the accordance with its mandate with no quantification or prioritization of the objectives.

*The 'quiet revolution' of the Fed in the 1990s: the dual mandate and communication*

For the Fed, monetary policy is a 'deliberative process' (Ferguson 2002: 4) between the central bank and the agents. The Fed's communications strategy intends to influence expectations by 'improving the public's understanding' (Kohn 2005: 1). The Fed demonstrates that the expectations channel and communications strategy are intimately related. But the Fed puts priority on action. Communication is not a goal per se, it is aimed at enhancing action: 'Actions speak louder than words', but 'actions and words likely speak louder than actions alone' (Thornton 2002: 11–12).

Around 1994, the Fed underwent a 'quiet revolution'. First, the Fed began to reveal its actions in real time. Second, it started to implement a fully explicit interest rate policy. Third, there was the 'Jackson Hole incident', when Blinder broke the 'Secret of the Temple'. Blinder simply announced publicly that Greenspan was following the dual mandate, and that he was a hawk not only on inflation, but also on employment. It was necessary to return to the democratic mandate of the Fed: Congress had imposed multiple goals without a hierarchy or quantitative numerical definitions.

Common understanding is a critical issue, since the central bank does not perfectly control inflation. Communication is regarded as a framework and an instrument of monetary policy, as it intervenes in the expectations formation process. Numerous papers from the Fed demonstrate the efficiency of the combination between action and communication, open market and 'open mouth' operations. The central bank cannot achieve its objectives without public support – that is, without convincing inflation expectations: 'We confirm a potentially important role for central bank communications to shape public expectations of future policy actions' (Bernanke *et al.* 2004: 4).

In 1994, the policy decision was announced immediately to the public. In 1999/2000, the announcement of the policy decision was accompanied by the publication of a statement giving an explanation of the current decision, and an explanation of the forward-looking decision through the economic outlook, an assessment of the balance of risks and economic conditions in the 'foreseeable' future. It demonstrates that the timing, number, organization and content of meetings are key components of communication strategy. The Fed communication strategy permits markets to concentrate their attention on eight pre-set dates per year on which it announces its key policy rate. This system is often referred to as the bank's fixed announcement dates, or simply fixed dates. In November 2001 the ECB adopted also a system of 12 pre-set dates per year on which to announce its key policy rate. Before 1999, agents had to guess at future official rates during the inter-meeting periods, via speeches, testimonies, interviews or macroeconomic data. After 1999, agents were advised of future monetary policy at the time of the meeting through the Fed's communications strategy: immediate release, statement, economic outlook, balance of risks, and so on. This new communication framework also enhances the common understanding between the central bank and agents:

> Not only do they have a larger effect on the level of interest rates if they are accompanied by an asymmetric assessment, but also the volatility induced by the FOMC (Federal Open Market Committee) meetings has been significantly lower since 1999. Third, market participants anticipate the next monetary policy decision earlier. (Ehrmann and Fratzscher 2005: 26–7)

Extensive and forward-looking explanations strengthen the transmission of monetary policy, reduce market participants' uncertainty and reduce transmission lags. Forward-looking information favours the common understanding of the path of future interest rates. With the expectations theory of the term structure, the Fed shapes the yield curve, thus enhancing and accelerating the linkage between short and long rates: Therefore, the Fed has a stronger and earlier impact on the economy.

In contrast to the ECB, the Fed uses the expectations channel by giving no explicit nominal anchor, since there is no explicit inflation target. Inflation expectations amplify and accelerate the impact of the nominal interest rate on inflation via the real interest rate. The ECB tries to neutralize the inflation expectations channel. Compared with the Fed, the impact of the nominal interest decision is more certain, but lower and slower. The time frame of transmission is medium- to long-term. It employs an indirect channel of transmission to inflation, passing through on output with a two-year lag. The Fed tries to use the expectations channel. The impact of the nominal interest rate decision is more uncertain but faster and stronger. The time frame of transmission is short- to medium-term. It employs a direct channel of transmission to inflation with a one-year lag.

Communications should contain extensive and clear explanations and convey forward-looking information – that is, the ability to make the central bank comprehensible to the general public. Before I served on the Federal Reserve Board, I believed the Fed could and should offer much more by way of explanation. Now, having been there, I feel absolutely certain. (Blinder 1999: 75). We move from 'Never explain, never excuse' to 'explaining more it is better understood'. The public should be able to understand the short-term tactical change in the central bank's long-term strategy.[4] Forward-looking explanations ('policy inclination', 'economic outlook') participate in the formation of expectations for the market.

*Communications strategy: enhancing both efficiency and flexibility*

Communication improves monetary policy efficiency and the public understanding of monetary policy, enabling the public to anticipate or react in line with the central bank. This common understanding simplifies the link between the Federal funds rate and the market-based long-run interest rate that has a strong effect on the economy. By increasing the speed of transmission, communication reduces one of the major problems of monetary policy – lags:

> Given that one of the limits on the effectiveness of monetary policy are the long lags between policy actions and their effect on aggregate demand, this anticipatory effect on long-term rates potentially speeds the effect of monetary policy and, in principle, can make it more effective. (Meyer 2003: 21)

Uncertainty induces flexibility – that is, tactical deviations from the strategy. This means severe shifts in the direction or in the amplitude of interest rates (from 25 to 50 base points). Flexibility is feasible as soon as market participants understand and validate tactics by following the Fed. Otherwise, agents play a non-cooperative game with the central bank, which inhibits monetary policy efficiency: 'failing to communicate with the public does not create genuine policy flexibility but only reduces the potency and predictability of the effects of given policy actions' (Bernanke 2004b: 8). By ensuring public understanding, communication allows for more flexibility. Open market and 'open mouth' operations are complementary. The Fed needs a common understanding to achieve the inflation expectations management required to link the short-term official interest rate and the long-term market interest rate. The common understanding is that the Fed is a 'statue with feet of clay' (Le Heron 2004: 49) that needs public support.

*Fedspeak's revolution: from cryptic statements to openness*

Reviewing the Fed literature, we note that communication or 'fedspeak' is considered to be the key aspect of its policy framework. It is linked with effectiveness and democratic considerations:

> Openness is more than just useful in shaping better economic performance. Openness is an obligation of a central bank in a free and democratic society. U.S. elected leaders chose to vest the responsibility for setting monetary policy in an independent entity, the Federal Reserve. Transparency of our activities is the means by which we make accountable to our fellows citizens to aid them in judging whether we are worthy of our task. (Greenspan 2001: 3)

Previously, 'Fedspeak' corresponded to the enigmatic and esoteric art of the Fed. Greenspan is famous for his declaration in Congress in 1987: 'Since I have become a central banker, I have learned to mumble with great incoherence. If I seem unduly clear to you, you must have misunderstood what I said' (Matthew 2006: 1). Nowadays, 'fedspeak' means clear and extensive communication.[5]

In the 1990s the novelty of Greenspan's communication is less its accountability or transparency than what he explains: the dual mandate – that is, the respect of its democratic mandate. The appropriate term for the 'risk management paradigm' of Greenspan is 'openness'. This openness about the dual mandate is the cornerstone of Greenspan's Fed.

Bernanke (2004a: 8) exposes the counter-productivity of full transparency:

> Other possibilities for improved transparency may exist. Importantly as we think about these, we should not simply take the view that more information is always better. Indeed, irrelevant or badly communicated information may create more noise than signal; and some types of information provision – an extreme example would be televising FOMC meetings – risk compromising the integrity and quality of the policy-making process itself.

Moreover, the Fed argues for limited transparency towards financial markets.[6] Limited transparency points out the importance of independence towards financial markets, and not on political authority, such as the ECB.

Openness also concerns inflation targets. The Fed considers uncertainty as the key element of monetary policy. Money is no longer neutral. There is no standard rate of inflation. Greenspan considered inflation to be a psychological phenomenon. Price stability is 'when economic agents no longer take account of the prospective change in the general level price level in their economic decision-making... By price stability, however, I do not refer to a single number as measured by a particular price index' (Greenspan 2003: 2). Greenspan preferred an implicit inflation target that gives flexibility to the policy mix. The implicit inflation target can be 2 per cent, 3 per cent or 4 per cent depending on circumstances.

A central bank practicing openness in a democratic society could be defined as 'communicational'; that is to say, a central bank that tries to build a common understanding with the general public of its monetary policy decisions and actions. The 'central bank should be able to reduce uncertainty, focus and stabilize private sector expectations, and with intelligence, luck, and persistence develop support for its approach in policy-making' (Bernanke 2004a: 4). Communications strategy is the keystone anchoring the agents' inflation expectations.

## Conclusions

With the Keynesians, the Monetarist and the credibility regimes of the new classical economics, governance was not important. Governance as a keystone of monetary policy began only in the 1990s, when the independent central banks searched for a new political legitimacy to found their action after the New Keynesian counter-revolution. Inflation targeting and the confidence regime were the starting point of this process.

*Table 9.1* Independence for credibility (ECB) versus governance for confidence (Fed)

| | *Credibility strategy* | *Confidence strategy* |
|---|---|---|
| *Governance* | *European Central Bank: a conservative central bank* | *The Fed: a democratic central bank* |
| *Monetary policy strategy* | • Cross-checking<br>• Stability-orientated strategy<br>• Medium-term orientated strategy | • Risk management paradigm<br>• Balance of risks strategy (since 2000)<br>• Interest rate policy (since 1994) |
| *Independence versus Governance* | • Creature of central bankers<br>• Supranational bank<br>• Goal and instrument independence<br>• Quasi-unique mandate, primacy to price stability<br>• Priority to inflation close to 2% view as the real level of the price stability<br>• Full independence<br>• Transparency and commitment on price stability<br>• Monetary order linked to an independent monetary power | • Creature of Congress (Congress oversight)<br>• Congress sets the goals. Federal Reserve Act (1977), the 'full employment and balanced growth act' (Humphrey–Hawkins Act)<br>• Instrument independence<br>• Dual Mandate: 'goals of maximum employment, stable prices, and moderate long-term interest rates'.<br>• Neither prioritization nor quantification of the objectives<br>• Balancing independence, delegated authority and now governance<br>• Openness and accountability on its dual mandate<br>• Monetary policy as a deliberative process |
| *Responsibility versus Accountability* | Responsible directly to the public (Maastricht Treaty)<br>• Judicial review (Art. 230–233)<br>• Dismissal of members of the executive Board, 'compulsorily retired' by the Court of Justice of the European Community (Art. 11.4)<br>• Annual report to the European Parliament (Art. 113(3)). Monetary dialogue with the European Parliament. Quarterly hearings to the Committee on Economic and Monetary Affairs (Art. 113(3)) | Accountable to elected representatives<br>• Congress has the power to overrule any interest rate decision made by the FOMC by passing a statute that the president will sign.<br>– Congress can threaten to:<br>– Change the structure of the Fed<br>– Remove a governor<br>– Specify particular qualifications for Board members<br>– Alter the composition of the FOMC |

*Table 9.1* Independence for credibility (ECB) versus governance for confidence (Fed) – *continued*

| | *Credibility strategy* | *Confidence strategy* |
|---|---|---|
| | • Quarterly reports on the activities of the euro system<br>• Rule 40a: 'Written questions to the ECB' by all members of European Parliament<br>• Definition of price stability is a yardstick against which the public can hold the ECB accountable<br>• No effective accountability since the European Parliament cannot change central bank law or mandate | • Bi-annual hearings at Congress (Humphrey-Hawkins testimony)<br>• Congressional report<br>• The congress can demand accounting of policy by summoning the chairman, board members and reserve presidents to congressional hearings<br>• Effective accountability since the Congress can change central bank law or mandate |
| *Communication* | • Monthly press conference (12/year) since 11/2001 (previously press releases every 2 weeks)<br>• Annual report, monthly bulletin, real-time information<br>• No publication of the proceedings of the meetings (Art. 10.4)<br>• The Governing Council may decide to make the outcome of its deliberations public (Art. 10.4)<br>• No publication of voting records or verbatim records<br>• No publication of internal inflation forecasts, but publication of staff macroeconomic projections 2/year (since December 2000) | • Immediate statement after each (8/year) scheduled meeting of the FOMC<br>• Bi-annual report and monthly reports<br>• Immediate public announcement of FOMC decision (since 1994)<br>• Minutes of the FOMC published 3 weeks after the meeting since 2004 with votes and naming names (previously a little over 6 weeks)<br>• Publication of detailed verbatim transcripts after 5 years<br>• Regular speeches by the members to outside audiences<br>• Publication of inflation and output forecasts (2/year) |
| *Monetary Policy Committee* | • The Governing Council has 18 members. It is dominated by the central bankers<br>– 6 from the Executive Board<br>– 12 national central banks' governors and maximum 15 votes after the enlargement | • FOMC has 19 members but only 12 votes:<br>– 7 from the Board of Governors<br>– 5 from regional central banks' presidents. Always New York's Fed that has responsibility for implementing decisions |

On the one hand, the ECB adopted the credibility strategy, which reduces governance to self-governance – that is to say, full independence. However, the ECB has evolved since its creation and is slowly getting closer to the regime of inflation targeting. On the other hand, the Fed of Greenspan adopted a confidence regime where governance is the keystone of its policy (Table 9.1). Could we see a modification in the policy of the Fed that will move it closer to flexible inflation targeting? It was Bernanke's wish before his nomination. So a convergence of monetary policy regimes is possible in the near future.

## Notes

1. One can find it in the Radcliff Report for the UK. By Keynesian, one means the Keynesian Synthesis represented by the IS-LM-EE model of Hicks–Hansen–Mundell–Flemming.
2. See Werner (2006).
3. 'A central bank in a democratic society is a magnet for many of the tensions that such a society confronts. Any institution that can affect the purchasing power of the currency is perceived as potentially affecting the level and distribution of wealth among the participants of that society, hardly an inconsequential issue' (Greenspan 1996: 1).
4. Contrary to the credibility framework, the myopia comes rather from the financial participants than from the government.
5. 'The Fed chairman now intends his speeches and testimonies to be understood, not misunderstood.' (Blinder *et al.* 2001: 73).
6. 'This, of course, is not to say that a central bank will never surprise the market. As I mentioned earlier, the most important task of a central bank is to get monetary policy right. At times, getting policy right will involve taking action unexpected by the market – for example, in its timing and magnitude' (Ferguson 2001: 5).

## References

Barro, R. and Gordon, D. (1983) 'Rules, Discretion and Reputation in a Model of Monetary Policy', *Journal of Monetary Economics*, 12(1): 101–21.

Bernanke, B. (2004a) *'Fedspeak'*, Meetings of the AEA, San Diego, January 3, http://www.federalreserve.gov//boarddocs/Speeches/2004/200401032/default.htm.

Bernanke, B. (2004b) *'Central Bank Talk and Monetary Policy'*, Remarks at the Japan Society Corporate Luncheon, New York, October 7, www.federalreserve.gov/Boarddocs/Speeches/2004/200410072/default.htm.

Bernanke, B., Reinhart, V. and Sack, B. (2004) *Monetary Alternatives at the Zero Bound: An Empirical Assessment*, Board of the Governors of the Fed, Finance and Economics Discussion Series, 2004–48.

Blinder, A. (1999) *Central Banking in Theory and Practice* (Cambridge, MA.: MIT Press).

Blinder, A., Goodhart, C., Hildebrandt, P., Lipton, D. and Wyplosz, C. (2001) *How Do Central Banks Talk?*, Geneva Reports on the World Economy, No. 3 (London: Center for Economic Policy Research (CEPR)).

Bouey, G. (1983) *House of Commons Standing Committee on Finance, Trade and Economic Affairs, Canada, Minutes of Proceedings and Evidence*, No. 134, 28 March 1983, p. 12.

Buiter, W. (1999) 'Alice in Euroland', *Journal of Common Market Studies*, 37(2): 181–209.

ECB (European Central Bank) (2002) *Monthly Bulletin*, November, http://www.ecb.int/pub/pdf/mobu/mb200211en.pdf.

ECB (European Central Bank) (2004) *The Monetary Policy of the ECB*, http://www.ecb.int/pub/pdf/other/monetarypolicy2004en.pdf.

Ehrmann, M. and Fratzscher, M. (2005) *Transparency, Disclosure and the Federal Reserve*, ECB Working Paper, No. 457.

Faust, J. (1996) 'Whom Can We Trust to Run the Fed? Theoretical Support for the Founders' View', *Journal of Monetary Economics*, 37: 267–83.

Faust, J. and Henderson, D.W. (2004) 'Is Inflation Targeting Best-Practised Monetary Policy?', *Federal Reserve Bank of St. Louis Review*, July: 51–80.

Ferguson, R. (2001) *Transparency in Central Banking: Rationale and Recent Developments*, Remarks by Governor R. Ferguson, Washington DC, April 19, www.federalreserve.gov/Boarddocs/speeches/2001/20010419/default.htm

Ferguson, R. (2002) *Why Central Banks Should Talk*, Remarks by Vice Chairman R. Ferguson, Geneva, January 8, www.federalreserve.gov/BoardDocs/speeches/2002/20020108/default.htm.

Goodhart, C. (1991) 'The Conduct of Monetary Policy', in C.J. Green and D.T. Llewellyn (eds), *Surveys in Monetary Economics* (Oxford: Basil Blackwell).

Greenspan, A. (1996) *The Challenge of Central Banking in a Democratic Society*, Remarks by Chairman A. Greenspan, at the Annual Dinner and Francis Boyer Lecture of The American Enterprise Institute for Public Policy Research, Washington, D.C, December 5, http://www.federalreserve.gov/boarddocs/speeches/1996/19961205.htm

Greenspan, A. (2001) *Transparency in Monetary Policy*, Remarks by Chairman A. Greenspan, Fed, October 11, http://www.federalreserve.gov/boarddocs/speeches/2001/20011011/default.htm

Greenspan, A. (2003) *Monetary Policy under Uncertainty*, Remarks at a symposium sponsored by the Federal Reserve Bank of Kansas City, 29 August, http://www.federalreserve.gov/boarddocs/speeches/2003/20030829/default.htm.

Issing, O. (1999) 'The Eurosystem: transparent and accountable or Willem in Euroland', *Journal of Common Market Studies*, 37(3): 503–19.

Issing, O. (2001) *The Euro Area and the Single Monetary Policy*, Central Bank of the Republic of Austria, Working Paper No. 44.

Issing, O., Gaspar, V., Angeloni, I. and Tristani, O. (2001) *Monetary Policy in the Euro Area: Strategy and Decision-Making at the European Central Bank* (Cambridge: Cambridge University Press).

Kohn, D. (2005) *Central Bank Communication*, Remarks by Governor Kohn, Washington DC, 7 January, http://www.federalreserve.gov/boarddocs/speeches/2005/200501072/default.htm.

Kohn, D. and Sack, P. (2003) *Central Bank Talk: Does It Matter and Why?*, Federal Reserve System of Washington D.C., Finance and Economics Discussion Series, No. 2003–55, May.

Kydland, F. and Prescott, E. (1977) 'Rules Rather than Discretion: The Inconsistency of Optimal Plans', *Journal of Political Economy*, 85(3): 473–92.

Le Heron, E. (2004) 'From the Canadian Experiment of the 1990's: A New Consensus on Monetary Policy', *Investigaciòn Econòmica*, 63(249): 13–54.

Le Heron, E. and Carré, E. (2006) 'Credibility versus Confidence in Monetary Policy', in R. Wray and M. Forstater (eds), *Money, Financial Instability and Stabilization Policy* (Aldershot: Edward Elgar).

Matthew, B. (2006) 'Greenspan, With a Calculated "Mumble," Left Markets Guessing', *Bloomberg*, January 26, http://www.bloomberg.com/apps/news?pid=10000103&refer=us&sid=armWJQf5Pn94.

McCallum, B.T. (1995) 'Two Fallacies Concerning Central Bank Independence', *American Economic Review*, 85(2): 207–11.

Meyer, L. (2000) *The Politics of Monetary Policy: Balancing Independence and Accountability*, Remarks by Governor L. Meyer at the University of Wisconsin, October 24, http://www.federalreserve.gov/boarddocs/speeches/2000/20001024.htm.

Meyer, L. (2003) 'Practical Problems and Obstacles to Inflation Targeting', Conference on 'Inflation Targeting: Prospects and Problems', *Federal Reserve Bank of Saint Louis Review*, 86(4): 151–60, http://research.stlouisfed.org/publications/review/04/07/Meyer.pdf.

Mishkin, F. (2004) *Can Central Bank Transparency Go Too Far?*, Reserve Bank of Australia's Conference on 'The Future of Inflation Targeting', Sydney, August, http://www.rba.gov.au/PublicationsAndResearch/Conferences/2004/index.html.

Persson, T. and Tabellini, G. (1993) 'Designing Institutions for Monetary Stability', *Carnegie Rochester Conference Series on Public Policy*, 39: 53–84.

Rogoff, K. (1985) 'The Optimal Degree of Commitment to an Intermediate Monetary Target', *The Quarterly Journal of Economics*, 100(4): 1169–90.

Scheller, H. (2004) The European Central Bank. History, Role and Functions (Frankfurt am Main: ECB), http://www.ecb.int/pub/pdf/other/ecbhistoryrolefunctions2004en.pdf.

Svensson, L.E.O. (1997) 'Optimal Inflation Targets, Conservative Central Banks and Linear Inflation Contracts', *American Economic Review*, 87(1): 98–114.

Thornton, D. (2002) *Monetary Policy Transparency: Transparent About What?*, Fed of St Louis, November, Working Paper 2002-028B, http://research.stlouisfed.org/wp/2002/2002-028.pdf.

Trichet, J. C. (2004) *Issues in Monetary Policy: Views from the ECB*, Speech at the Economic Club of New York, April 26, http://www.bis.org/review/r040430e.pdf.

Walsh, C. (1995) 'Optimal Contracts for Central Bankers', *American Economic Review*, 85(1): 150–67.

Werner R.A. (2006) 'What Accession Countries Need to Know about ECB: A Comparative Analysis of the Independence of ECB, Bundesbank and Reichsbank', in J.A. Batten and C. Kearney (eds), *Emerging European Financial Markets: Independence and Integration Post-Enlargement, International Finance Review*, 6: 99–116.

# 10
# AS–AD Disequilibrium Dynamics and the Taylor Interest Rate Policy Rule: Euro Area-Based Estimation and Simulation

*Peter Flaschel and Christian R. Proaño*

## Introduction

The future and the success of the European Monetary Union are still unclear in many respects. While some researchers think that monetary unification, with the subsequent higher economic integration and labour mobility between the EMU member countries, will lead to a synchronization of the business cycles of the participating economies, and therefore to a more harmonic macroeconomic environment within the EMU, other observers see great dangers for its stability and even its further existence, due to the present scenario of (competing) heterogeneous fiscal policies and the (non-cooperative) inflation developments in certain economies. In any case, even if such destabilizing factors decrease in the years ahead, the stability of the EMU depends to a large extent on the proper conduct of monetary policy by the ECB and the resulting changes in economic activity and in nominal wage and price adjustment in the EMU in particular.

This chapter presents and estimates a Keynesian AS–AD disequilibrium model for the Euro area which builds (as recent New Keynesian macrodynamic models, yet in a distinctively different way) on gradual wage and price adjustments. Our model employs two Phillips curves that relate the wage and price inflation dynamics to corresponding factor utilization rates and their link via a simple form of Okun's Law. Moreover, it uses a dynamic IS curve and a Taylor interest rate rule for policy analysis. It resembles the New Keynesian macromodels of staggered wage and price setting in that it also includes elements of forward-looking behaviour (by making use of a specific mix of perfect foresight on current wage and price inflation rates and a medium-run inflationary climate expression that is subject to adaptive learning).

It permits for non-clearing goods and labour markets, underutilized labour and capital stocks and also sluggish quantity adjustments. Although our model builds on the earlier traditional AS–AD model, the resulting nonlinear 5D model of non-clearing labour and goods market dynamics completely avoids the anomalies of the conventional AS–AD approach to the business cycle, as they are discussed in detail in Asada *et al.* (2006).

The chapter is organized as follows. The next section briefly discusses the theoretical framework underlying our analysis of the implications of monetary policy in the Euro area (and Germany). Then we provide our empirical estimates for the Eurozone – and Germany – and discuss the implied results, obtained by system GMM estimations of the semi-structural form of the theoretical model. Following this, numerical simulation results (based on the estimated parameters), in particular concerning the role of monetary policy in the Euro area for the stability and volatility of the system, will be presented. The fifth section concludes.

## Keynesian disequilibrium dynamics: a semi-structural baseline model

In this section we reformulate a theoretical disequilibrium model of AS–AD growth, introduced in Asada *et al.* (2006), towards a somewhat simplified form that is more suitable for empirical estimation than the original model and also handier for the study of the role of contemporary interest rate policy rules. We start from the observation that a Keynesian model of aggregate demand fluctuations should (independently of whether justification can be found for this in Keynes' General Theory) allow for under- (or over-) utilized labour as well as capital, in order to be general enough from the descriptive point of view. As Barro (1994), for example, observes, IS–LM is (or should be) based on imperfectly flexible wages and prices and thus on the consideration of wage as well as price Phillips curves. This is precisely what we will do in the following, augmented by the observation that medium-run aspects also count both in wage and price adjustments, here formulated in simple terms by the introduction of the concept of an inflation climate that is subject to adaptive learning. We have moreover short-term model-consistent expectations with respect to wage and price inflation. Our reformulation of the traditional AS–AD model thus treats expectations in a hybrid way, with crossover myopic perfect foresight on the currently evolving rates of wage and price inflation on the one hand and an adaptive updating of an inflation climate expression with exponential or any other weighting schemes on the other hand.

We consequently assume two Phillips curves in the place of only one. This means that we can discuss wage and price dynamics separately from each other, in their structural forms, both based on their own measure of demand pressure, $V^l - \overline{V}^l$, $V^c - \overline{V}^c$, in the market for labour and for goods, respectively. We denote by $V^l$ the rate of employment on the labour market and by $\overline{V}^l$ the NAIRU level of this rate, and similarly by $V^c$ the rate of capacity utilization of the capital stock and $\overline{V}^c$ the normal rate of capacity utilization of firms. These demand pressure influences on wage and price dynamics, or on the formation of wage and price inflation rates, $\hat{w}$, $\hat{p}$, are both augmented by Blanchard and Katz (1999) error correction terms (giving income distribution also a role to play in the modelled wage and price dynamics), by a weighted average of corresponding cost-pressure terms, based on forward looking myopic perfect foresight $\hat{p}$, $\hat{w}$, respectively, and a backward-looking measure of the prevailing inflationary climate, symbolized by $\pi^m$. We stress that we can include forward-looking behaviour here without need for an application of the jump variable technique of the rational expectations school as will be shown in the next section.[1]

The structural form of the wage-price dynamics:

$$\hat{w} = \beta_{w1}(V^l - \overline{V}^l) - \beta_{w2}\,(\ln \omega - \ln \omega_0) + \kappa_w \hat{p} + (1 - \kappa_w)\,\pi^m \qquad (10.1)$$

$$\hat{p} = \beta_{p2}(V^c - \overline{V}^c) - \beta_{p2}\,(\ln \omega - \ln \omega_0) + \kappa_p \hat{p} + (1 - \kappa_p)\,\pi^m \qquad (10.2)$$

Somewhat simplified versions of these two Phillips curves have been estimated for the US economy in various ways in Flaschel and Krolzig (2006), Flaschel, Kauermann and Semmler (2006) and Chen and Flaschel (2006), and have been found to represent a significant improvement over the conventional single reduced-form Phillips curve. A particular finding was that wage flexibility was greater than price flexibility with respect to their demand pressure measure in the market for labour and for goods,[2] respectively, and workers were more shortsighted than firms with respect to their cost-pressure terms. Note that such a finding is not possible in the conventional framework of a single reduced-form Phillips curve (PC).

Inflationary expectations over the medium run, $\pi^m$, i.e., the inflationary climate in which current inflation is operating, may be adaptively following the actual rate of inflation (by use of some linear or exponential weighting scheme), may be based on a rolling sample (with hump-shaped weighting schemes), or on other possibilities for updating expectations. For simplicity of the exposition we shall make use of the conventional adaptive expectations mechanism in the theoretical part of this chapter, namely:

$$\dot{\pi}^m = \beta_{\pi^m} (\hat{p} - \pi^m) \tag{10.3}$$

Note that for our current version of the wage–price spiral the inflationary climate variable does not matter for the evolution of the real wage $\omega = w/p$, the law of motion of which is given by (with $\kappa = 1/(1 - \kappa_w \kappa_p)$):

$$\hat{\omega} = k \begin{bmatrix} (1 - \kappa_p)(\beta_{w1}(V^l - \overline{V}^l) - \beta_{w2} (\ln \omega - \ln \omega_0)) \\ - (1 - \kappa_w)(\beta_{p1}(V^c - \overline{V}^c) - \beta_{p2} (\ln \omega - \ln \omega_0)) \end{bmatrix}$$

This follows easily from the following obviously equivalent representation of the above two PCs:

$$\hat{w} = \pi^m = \beta_{w1}(V^l - \overline{V}^l) - \beta_{w2} (\ln \omega - \ln \omega_0) + \kappa_w (\hat{p} - \pi^m)$$

$$\hat{p} = \pi^m = \beta_{p2}(V^c - \overline{V}^c) + \beta_{p2} (\ln \omega - \ln \omega_0) + \kappa_p (\hat{p} - \pi^m)$$

by solving for the variables $\hat{w} - \pi^m$ and $\hat{p} - \pi^m$. It also implies the following two across-markets or reduced form PCs:

$$\hat{w} = \kappa \begin{bmatrix} \beta_{w1}(V^l - \overline{V}^l) - \beta_{w2} (\ln \omega - \ln \omega_0) \\ + \kappa_w (\beta_{p1}(V^c - \overline{V}^c) - \beta_{p2} (\ln \omega - \ln \omega_0)) \end{bmatrix} + \pi^m$$

$$\hat{p} = \kappa \begin{bmatrix} \beta_{p1}(V^c - \overline{V}^c) + \beta_{p2} (\ln \omega - \ln \omega_0) \\ + \kappa_p (\beta_{w1}(V^l - \overline{V}^l) - \beta_{w2} (\ln \omega - \ln \omega_0)) \end{bmatrix} + \pi^m$$

which represent a considerable generalization of the conventional view of a single-market price PC with only one measure of demand pressure, the one in the labour market.

The remaining laws of motion of the private sector of the model are as follows:

$$V^c = -\alpha_{11}(V^c - \overline{V}^c) - \alpha_{12}((r - \hat{p}) - (r_0 - \overline{\pi})) \pm a_{13} (\alpha - \omega_0) \tag{10.4}$$

$$\hat{V}^l = -\alpha_{21}(V^c - \overline{V}^c) + \alpha_{22}\hat{V}^c \tag{10.5}$$

The first law of motion is of the type of a dynamic IS-equation, see also Rudebusch and Svensson (1999) in this regard, here represented by the growth rate of the capacity utilization rate of firms. It has three important characteristics; (i) it reflects the dependence of output changes on aggregate income and thus on the rate of capacity utilization by assuming a negative, i.e., stable dynamic multiplier relationship in this respect; (ii) it shows the joint dependence of consumption and investment on the real wage (which in the aggregate may in principle allow for positive or negative signs before the parameter $\alpha_w$, depending on whether consumption or investment is more responsive to real wage changes); and (iii) it shows finally the negative influence of the real rate of interest on the evolution of economic activity.

In the second law of motion, for the rate of employment, we assume that the employment policy of firms follows – in the form of a generalized Okun Law – the rate of capacity utilization (and the thereby implied rate of over- or underemployment of the employed workforce) partly with a lag (measured by $1/\alpha_{21}$), and partly without a lag (through a positive parameter $\alpha_{22}$). Employment is thus assumed to adjust to the level of current activity in somewhat delayed form which is a reasonable assumption from the empirical point of view. The second term, $\alpha_{22}\hat{V}^c$, is added to take account of the possibility that Okun's Law may hold in level form rather than in the form of a law of motion, since this latter dependence can be shown to be equivalent to the use of a term $(V^c/\overline{V}^c)^{\alpha_{22}}$ when integrated, i.e., the form of Okun's Law in which this law was originally specified by Okun (1970) himself.

The above two laws of motion therefore reformulate in a dynamic form the static IS-curve (and the employment this curve implies) that was used in Asada *et al.* (2006). They only reflect implicitly the assumed dependence of the rate of capacity utilization on the real wage, due to smooth factor substitution in production (and the measurement of the potential output this implies in Asada *et al.* 2006), which constitutes another positive influence of the real wage on the rate of capacity utilization and its rate of change. This simplification helps to avoid the estimation of separate equations for consumption and investment $C$, $I$ and for potential output $Y^p$.

Finally, we no longer employ a law of motion for real balances as was still the case in Asada *et al.* (2006). Money supply is now accommodating to the interest rate policy pursued by the central bank and thus does not feedback into the core laws of motion of the model. As interest rate policy we assume the following classical type of Taylor Rule:

$$r^* = (r_0 - \pi) + \hat{p} + \alpha_p\,(\hat{p} - \pi\text{–}) + \alpha_{V^c}\,(V^c - \overline{V}^c) \tag{10.6}$$

$$\dot{r} = \alpha_r(r^* - r) \tag{10.7}$$

The target rate of the central bank $r^*$ is here made dependent on the steady-state real rate of interest augmented by actual inflation back to a nominal rate, and is as usually dependent on the inflation gap and the capacity utilization gap (as measure of the output gap). With respect to this target there is then interest rate smoothing with strength $\alpha_r$. Inserting $r^*$ and rearranging terms we get from this expression the following from of a Taylor Rule

$$\dot{r} = -\gamma_1 (r - r_0) + \gamma_2 (\hat{p} - \bar{\pi}) + \gamma_3 (V^c - \bar{V}^c), \ \gamma_1 = \alpha_r \tag{10.8}$$

where we have $\gamma_2 = \alpha_r (1 + \alpha_p)$, i.e., $\alpha_p = \gamma_2/\alpha_r - 1$ and $\gamma_3 = \alpha_r \alpha_{V^c}$.

We thus allow for interest rate smoothing in this rule. Furthermore, the actual (perfectly foreseen) rate of inflation $\hat{p}$ is used to measure the inflation gap with respect to the inflation target $\bar{\pi}$ of the central bank. Note finally that we could have included (but have not done this here yet) a new kind of gap into the above Taylor Rule, the real wage gap, since we have in our model a dependence of aggregate demand on income distribution and the real wage. The state of income distribution matters for the dynamics of our model and thus should also play a role in the decisions of the central bank. All of the employed gaps are measured relative to the steady state of the model, in order to allow for an interest rate policy that is consistent with it.

We note that the steady state of the dynamics, due to its specific formulation, can be supplied exogenously. For reasons of notational simplicity we choose:

$$V_0^c = \bar{V}^c = 1, \ V_0^l = \bar{V}^l = 1, \ \omega_0 = 1, \ \pi_0^m = \bar{\pi} = 0.03, \ r_0 = 0.08$$

in the later simulation of the model by means of annualized quarterly Euro area data. As the model is formulated now it exhibits five gaps, to be closed in the steady state, and has five laws of motion, which, when set equal to zero, exactly imply this result, since the determinant of the Jacobian of the dynamics can be shown to be always non-zero.

The steady state of the dynamics is locally asymptotically stable under certain sluggishness conditions that are reasonable from a Keynesian perspective, loses its asymptotic stability cyclically (by way of so-called Hopf-bifurcations) if the system becomes too flexible, and becomes sooner or later globally unstable if (generally speaking) adjustment speeds become too high.[3] If the model is subject to explosive forces, it requires extrinsic nonlinearities in economic behaviour – like downward money wage rigidity – to manifest themselves at least far off the steady state in order to bound the dynamics to an economically meaningful domain in the considered 5D state space. Chen *et al.* (2006) provide a variety of numerical studies for such an approach with extrinsically motivated nonlinearities and thus undertake its detailed numerical investigation. In sum, therefore, our dynamic AS–AD growth model here and there will exhibit a variety of features that are much more in line with a Keynesian understanding of the characteristics of the business cycle than is the case for the conventional modelling of AS–AD growth dynamics or its radical reformulation by the New Keynesians (where – if non-determinacy can be avoided by the choice of an appropriate Taylor Rule – only the steady-state position is a meaningful solution in their baseline case with both staggered wages and prices).

Taken together, the model of this section consists of the following five laws of motion (with the derived reduced-form expressions as far as the wage–price spiral is concerned and with reduced form expressions by assumption concerning the goods and the labour market dynamics):[4]

Dyn. IS:

$$\hat{V}^c = -\alpha_{11}(V^c - \overline{V}^c) - \alpha_{12}\,((r - \hat{p}) - (r_0 - \bar{\pi})) \pm \alpha_{13}(\omega - \omega_0) \qquad (10.9)$$

Okun's Law:

$$\hat{V}^l = -\alpha_{21}(V^c - \overline{V}^c) + \alpha_{22}\hat{V}^c \qquad (10.10)$$

Taylor Rule:

$$\dot{r} = -\gamma_1(r - r_0) + \gamma_2(\hat{p} - \bar{\pi}) + \gamma_3(V^c - \overline{V}^c) \qquad (10.11)$$

Real wage Phillips curve (RWPC):

$$\begin{aligned}\hat{\omega} = \kappa[&(1 - \kappa_p)(\beta_{w1}(V^l - \overline{V}^l) - \beta_{w2}\,(\text{In}\ \omega - \ln \omega_0)) \\ &- (1 - k_w)(\beta_{p1}\,(V^c - \overline{V}^c) - \beta_{p2}\,(\text{In}\ w - \ln w_0))]\end{aligned} \qquad (10.12)$$

Inflationary climate:

$$\dot{\pi}^m = \beta_{\pi^m}\,(\hat{p} - \pi^m) \qquad (10.13)$$

The above equations represent, in comparison to the baseline model of New Keynesian macroeconomics (Galí 2000), the IS goods market dynamics, here augmented by Okun's Law as link between the goods and the labour market, and of course the Taylor Rule, and a law of motion for the real wage $\hat{\omega} = \hat{w} - \hat{p}$, and finally the law of motion

(10.13) that describes the updating of the inflationary climate expression. We have to make use here in addition of the following reduced-form expression for the price inflation rate or the price PC, our law of motion for the price level $p$ in the place of the traditional reduced-form expression for price inflation:

$$\hat{p} = \kappa \begin{bmatrix} \beta_{p1}(\bar{V}^c - (\bar{V}^c) - \beta_{p2}(\ln\omega - \ln\omega_0) \\ + \kappa_p(\beta_{w1}(V^l - \bar{V}^l) - \beta_{w2}(\ln\omega - \ln\omega_0)) \end{bmatrix} + \mu^m \qquad (10.14)$$

This law of motion for price inflation has to be inserted into the above laws of motion in various places in order to get an autonomous nonlinear system of differential equations in the state variables: capacity utilization $V^c$, the rate of employment $V^l$, the nominal rate of interest $r$, the real wage rate $\omega$ and the inflationary climate expression $\pi^m$. We stress that one can consider the equation (10.14) as a sixth law of motion of the considered dynamics which, however – when added – leads a system determinant which is zero and which therefore allows for zero-root hysteresis for certain variables of the model (in fact in the price level if the target rate of inflation of the Central Bank is zero and if interest rate smoothing is present in the Taylor Rule).

With respect to the empirically motivated restructuring of the original theoretical framework, the model is as pragmatic as the approach employed by Rudebusch and Svensson (1999). By and large we believe that it represents a working alternative to the New Keynesian approach, in particular when the current critique of the latter approach is taken into account. It overcomes the weaknesses and the logical inconsistencies of the old Neoclassical synthesis (see Asada *et al.* 2006), and it does so in a minimal way from a mature, but still traditionally oriented Keynesian perspective (and is thus not really 'New'). It preserves the problematic stability features of the real rate of interest channel, where the stabilizing Keynes effect or the interest rate policy of the central bank are interacting with the destabilizing, expectations-driven Mundell effect. It also preserves the real wage effect of the old Neoclassical synthesis, where – due to an unambiguously negative dependence of aggregate demand on the real wage – we had that price flexibility was destabilizing, while wage flexibility was not. This real wage channel is not really discussed in the New Keynesian approach, due to the specific form of wage-price dynamics there considered, see Woodford (2003), and it is summarized in the Figure 10.1 for the situation where investment dominates consumption with respect to real wage changes. In the opposite case, the situations considered in this figure will be reversed with respect to their stability implications.

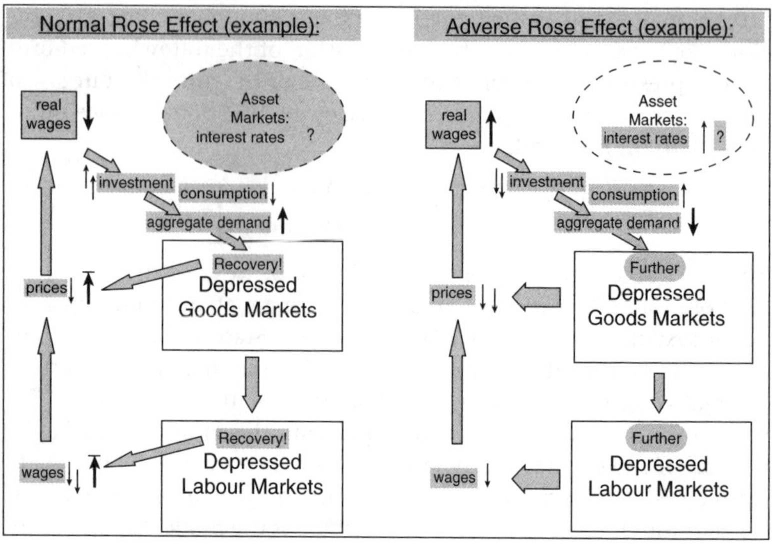


*Figure 10.1* The Rose effects: the real wage channel of Keynesian macrodynamics

The next section will provide estimates of the semi-structural form of the model for the Euro area (and for Germany), the implications of which for the stability of the economy and the working of monetary policy in such a framework will be considered in the fourth section.

## Estimating the model for the Euro area

In this section we provide empirical estimates for the parameter values underlying the laws of motion (10.9)–(10.13) of our disequilibrium AS–AD model. We do this by means of a system estimation of the originally semi-structural presentation of the model, i.e., of its wage and price Phillips curve, its dynamic multiplier equation, Okun's Law and an interest rate policy rule for the Euro area (and for Germany).

In the implied reduced form (10.9)–(10.13), these dynamics exhibit the following sign structure in their Jacobian, calculated at their interior steady state solution:

$$J = \begin{pmatrix} \pm & + & - & \pm & + \\ \pm & + & - & \pm & + \\ + & + & - & \pm & + \\ - & + & 0 & - & 0 \\ + & + & 0 & \pm & 0 \end{pmatrix}.$$

There are thus several signs in this Jacobian matrix which cannot be determined on purely theoretical grounds, due to the existence of ambiguous feedback effects: There is first of all, see equation (10.9), the ambiguous influence of real wages on (the dynamics of) the rate of capacity utilization, which should be a negative one if investment is more responsive than consumption to real wage changes and a positive one in the opposite case. There is secondly, with an immediate impact effect if the rates of capacity utilization for capital and labour are perfectly synchronized, the fact that real wages rise with economic activity through money wage changes on the labour market, while they fall with it through price-level changes on the goods market, see equation (10.12). Finally, we have in the reduced form equation for price inflation a further ambiguous effect of real wage increases, which lower $\hat{p}$ through their effect on wage inflation, while speeding up $\hat{p}$ through their effect on price inflation, effects which work into opposite directions in the reduced-form price PC, equation (10.14). Wage- vs profit-led situations, Rose-type real wage dynamics and Blanchard-Katz error-correction feedback channels therefore make the dynamics indeterminate on the theoretical level.

In all of the cases empirical analysis will now, however, provide us with definite answers as to which of these opposing forces will be the dominant ones. However, we will not attempt to estimate the parameter $\beta_{\pi^m}$ that describes the evolution of the inflationary climate characterizing our economy. Instead, we will use moving averages with linearly declining weights for its representation, which allows us to bypass the estimation of the law of motion (10.13). We consider this as the simplest approach to the treatment of our climate expression (comparable with recent New Keynesian treatments of hybrid expectation formation), which should later on be replaced by more sophisticated ones, for example one that makes use of the Livingston index for inflationary expectations as in Laxton *et al.* (2000) which in our view mirrors some adaptive mechanism in the adjustment of inflationary expectations.

We conduct our estimates in conjunction with time-invariant estimates of all the parameters of our model. This in particular implies that Keynes' (1936) explanation of the trade cycle, which employed systematic changes in the propensity to consume, the marginal efficiency of investment and liquidity preference over the course of the cycle, find no application here and that – due the use of detrended measures for income distribution changes and unit-wage costs – the role of technical change is also downplayed to a significant degree, in line with its neglect in the theoretical equations of the model presented in the second section of this chapter. As a result, we expect to obtain from our estimates long-phased economic fluctuations, but not yet long-waves, since important fluctuations in aggregate demand (based on time-varying parameters) are still ignored and since the dynamics are then driven primarily by slowly changing income distribution, indeed a slow process in the overall evolution of the Euro area (and Germany). Particularly with respect to the estimated structural parameters concerning the Euro area, we wish to point out that the parameter estimates presented below represent the numerical characteristics of an artificial, at that time not existing economy (as an economic area with a single currency), and therefore should not be considered as reliable proxies for the future macroeconomic development of the Euro area.

The relevant variables for the following econometric analysis are the wage (compensation per hour) inflation rate (backwardly dated), the price inflation rate (measured by the GDP deflator), the rates of utilization of labour and of capital, the nominal short-term interest rate, the log of the average unit wage costs and the labour productivity, to be denoted in the following by: $\hat{w}_t$, $\hat{p}_t$, $V^l_t$, $V^c_t$, $r_t$, $\ln(w_t)$, and $z_t$. The inflationary climate $\pi^m$ of the theoretical part of this chapter is approximated here in a very simple way by a linearly declining moving average of price inflation rates with linearly decreasing weights over the past 12 quarters. The empirical data have been extracted from OECD and DIW databases. The data are quarterly, seasonally adjusted (by the Census X12 ARIMA procedure) and concern the period from 1980:1 to 2004:4 for both economies.

In our econometric specification for Germany, we incorporate into the German Taylor Rule the Euro area wide inflation rate rather than the German inflation rate. By inserting the Euro area inflation rate in the German Taylor Rule we 'simulate' the consequences of a single, Euro area monetary policy for Germany. Additionally, given the predominant role of Germany in the EMU (and the high relative weight of the German inflation rate in the Euro area inflation), the assumption of the Bundesbank targeting the Euro area instead of only the German inflation rate (and so acting as a 'big brother' even before the factual adoption of the euro) is not completely unreasonable. Additionally, as Peersman and Smets (1999: 85) state, the 'Bundesbank arguably is a model central bank for the ECB' concerning the conduction of monetary policy, which indeed has been performed by the ECB in a very similar manner as the Bundesbank did before the currency unification.

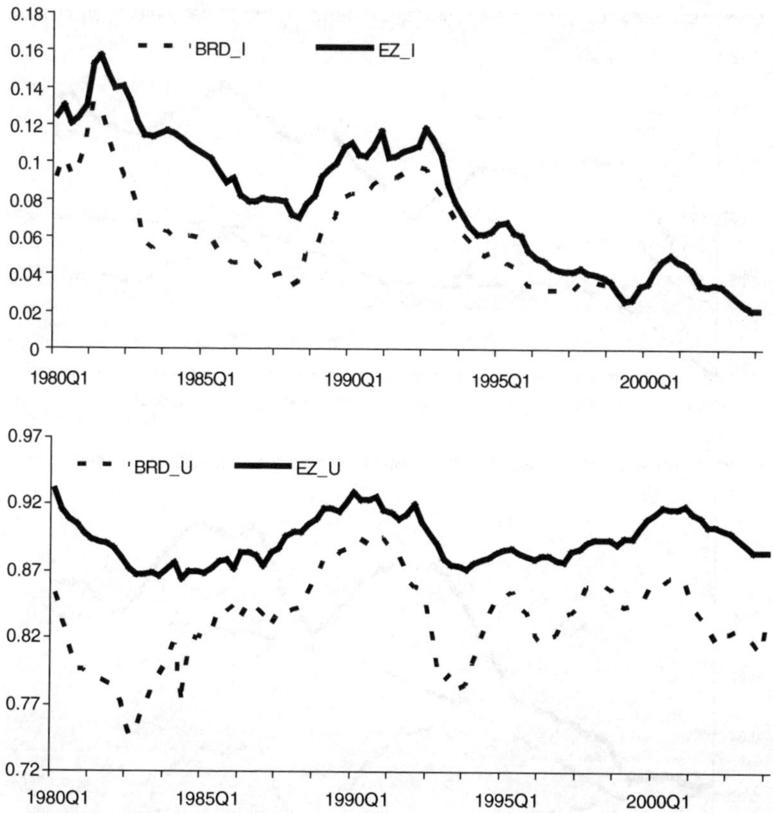


*Figure 10.2* Euro area (EZ) and German (BRD) nominal interest and capacity utilization rates

Concerning the dynamics of employment, a pronounced upward trend of unemployment rates over the last twenty years could be observed, as depicted in Figure 10.3. As discussed in Layard, Nickell, and Jackman (1991) and Ljungqvist and Sargent (1998), in Europe the main determinant for this development has been the overproportional increase in the number of long-term unemployed (i.e. workers with an unemployment duration over 12 months) as compared to short-term unemployed (workers with an unemployment duration of less than 12 months) and the phenomenon of hysteresis especially in the first group. Now, when the long-term unemployment is high, the aggregate unemployment rate of an economy 'becomes a poor indicator of effective labour supply, and the macroeconomic adjustment mechanisms –

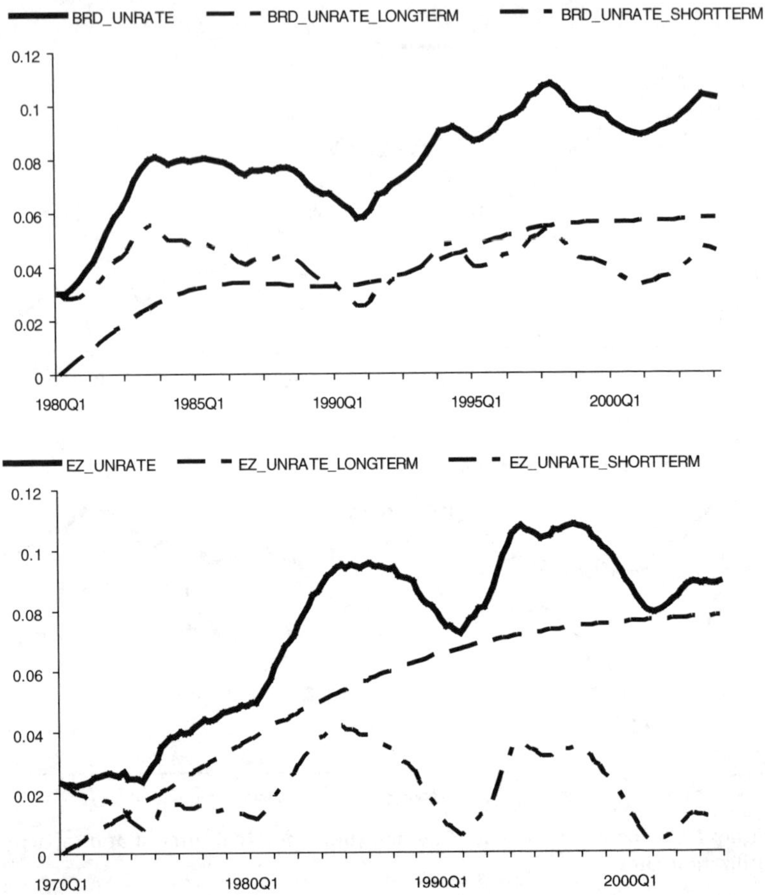


*Figure 10.3* Modified Euro area (EZ) and German (BRD) long- and short-term unemployment rates

such as downward pressure on wages and inflation when unemployment is high – will then not operate effectively' (OECD 2002: 189). Since time series data for long-term unemployment in the Euro area are not available, we try to approximate it in a rather simple way: We first perform the HP-filter on the Euro area unemployment rate with a high smoothing factor ($\lambda$ = 640000). We normalize the resulting smoothed series so that the 1970:1 value equals zero, implicitly assuming that in 1970:1 the number of long-term unemployed was negligibly small. Since before the oil price shocks in the 1970s unemployment – and also long-term unemployment – was extremely low in the

European continent, this assumption hence appears to be reasonable. We interpret this smoothed series as a proxy for the actual development of long-term unemployment. The difference between the aggregate unemployment rate and this series can be interpreted and handled as a proxy for short-term unemployment, and as providing the relevant demand pressure variable for the evolution of the wage inflation rate. The corresponding employment rate is calculated as $V^l = 1 - U^{st}$.

We carry out Phillips–Perron unit root tests for each series in order to account, besides residual autocorrelation as done by the standard ADF Tests, also for possible residual heteroskedasticity. The Phillips–Perron test results are shown in Table 10.1.

The applied unit root tests confirm our presumptions with the exception of the nominal interest rate $r$ and the capacity utilization $V^c$. Although the test cannot reject the null of a unit root, there is no reason to expect both series to be unit root processes. Indeed, we reasonably expect these rates to be constrained to certain limited ranges in both economies. Due to the generally known low power of unit root tests, we interpret these results as providing only a hint that both time series exhibit a strong autocorrelation.

As discussed above, the law of motion for the real wage rate, given by equation (10.12), represents a reduced-form expression of the two structural equations for $\hat{w}_t$ and $\hat{p}_t$. Noting again that the inflation climate variable is defined in the estimated model as a linearly declin-

*Table 10.1* Phillips–Perron unit root test results

| *Country* | *Variable* | *Sample* | *Lag length* | *Determ.* | *Test stat.* | *Prob.** |
|---|---|---|---|---|---|---|
| | $\mathrm{dln}(p)$ | 1975:1–2004:4 | 1 | — | −2.3464 | 0.0189 |
| Euro area | $\mathrm{dln}(w)$ | 1977:3–2004:4 | 1 | const. | −3.4567 | 0.0110 |
| | $\mathrm{dln}(V^l)$ | 1975:2–2004:4 | 1 | — | −3.6923 | 0.0003 |
| | $V^c$ | 1979:1–2004:4 | 1 | — | −0.8862 | 0.3298 |
| | $R$ | 1977:2–2004:4 | 1 | — | −1.0099 | 0.2792 |
| | $\mathrm{dln}(p)$ | 1980:1–2003:4 | 1 | const. | −7.1214 | 0.0000 |
| Germany | $\mathrm{dln}(w)$ | 1980:1–2003:4 | 1 | const. | −7.5909 | 0.0000 |
| | $\mathrm{dln}(V^l)$ | 1980:1–2003:4 | — | — | −4.1897 | 0.0001 |
| | $V^c$ | 1980:1–2003:4 | — | — | −0.2751 | 0.5844 |
| | $R$ | 1960:1–2003:4 | 1 | const. | −1.7458 | 0.0767 |

*Note*: *MacKinnon (1996) one-sided p-values.

ing function of the past twelve price inflation rates, the dynamics of the system given earlier can be reformulated as:

$$\hat{w}_t = \beta_{w1} V^l_{t-1} - \beta_{w2} \ln(y_{t-1}) + \kappa_{wp}\hat{p} + \kappa_{w\pi}\pi^m_t + \kappa_{wz}\hat{z}_t + \kappa_{wc} + \varepsilon_{1t}$$

$$\hat{p}_t = \beta_{p1} V^l_{t-1} - \beta_{p2} \ln(v_{t-1}) + \kappa_{pw}\hat{p} + \kappa_{p\pi}\pi^m_t + \kappa_{pz}\hat{z}_t + \kappa_{pc} + \varepsilon_{1t}$$

$$\hat{V}^c_t = \gamma_{Vc} \hat{V}^c_{t-1} - \alpha_{12}(r_{t-1} - \hat{p}_t) \pm \alpha_{13} v_{t-1} + \alpha_{14} + \varepsilon_{3t}$$

$$\hat{V}^l_t = \alpha_{21} \hat{V}^c_{t-1} - \alpha_{22} \hat{V}^c_{t-2} + \alpha_{23} \hat{V}^c_{t-3} + \alpha_{24} \hat{V}^c_{t-4} + \varepsilon_{4t}$$

$$r_t = \gamma_1 r_{t-1} + \gamma_2 \hat{p}_t + \gamma_3 V^c_{t-1} + \gamma_4 + \varepsilon_{5t}$$

with $\gamma_1 = 1 - \alpha_r$, $\gamma_{Vc} = 1 - \alpha_{11}$, and where the intercept terms in the equations are assumed to contain the steady-state values, and where $v$, the wage share, is replaced by its cyclical component calculated by the Hodrick-Prescott filter with the smoothing factor $\lambda = 640{,}000$ and where levels and not the growth rates (or first differences) of the capacity utilization and nominal interest rates are estimated.[5]

The structural model is estimated by means of the General Method of Moments (GMM) methodology. An estimation by means of GMM possesses several advantages with respect to more traditional estimation methods as OLS and 2SLS, especially in time series models, where heteroskedasticity in the residuals is a common feature: 'The optimal GMM estimator is asymptotically no less efficient than two-stage least squares under homoskedasticity, and GMM is generally better under heteroskedasticity' (Wooldridge 2001: 92). This and the additional robustness property of GMM estimates of not relying on a specific assumption with respect to the distribution of the residuals make the GMM methodology preferable and advantageous for our estimation.[6]

As instrumental variables in all five equations we use, besides the strictly exogenous variables, the last four lagged values of the employment rate, the labour share (detrended by the Hodrick–Prescott Filter) and the growth rate of labour productivity. We present the structural parameter estimates for the Euro area and German economies (*t*-statistics in brackets) in Table 10.2.

At a general level, the GMM parameter estimates shown above deliver empirical support for the specification of our theoretical disequilibrium model and confirm, especially for the Euro area, some of the empirical findings of Flaschel and Krolzig (2006) and Flaschel, Kauermann and Semmler (2006) for the US economy. In the first place we find that wage flexibility is greater than price flexibility in both

*Table 10.2* GMM parameter estimates of the structural model

Euro area: 1979:4–2004:4, Estimation Sample: Germany: 1981:4–2003:4
Kernel: Bartlett, Bandwidth: Euro area: 4, Germany: 3

| $dln(w_t)$ | $b_{w1}$ | $b_{w2}$ | $k_{wp}$ | $k_{wp}$ | $k_{wz}$ | $k_{wc}$ | $\bar{R}^2$ | $DW$ |
|---|---|---|---|---|---|---|---|---|
| Euro area | 0.547 | –0.464 | 0.662 | 0.502 | 0.213 | –0.774 | 0.706 | 1.584 |
| | [14.763] | [–13.650] | [18.808] | [12.839] | [19.450] | [–20.718] | | |
| Germany | 0.974 | –0.771 | 1.070 | — | 0.236 | –1.545 | 0.336 | 1.919 |
| | [6.721] | [–9.792] | [18.843] | | [5.240] | [–10.806] | | |
| $dln(p_t)$ | $b_{p1}$ | $b_{p2}$ | $k_{pw}$ | $k_{pp}$ | $k_{pz}$ | $k_{pc}$ | $\bar{R}^2$ | $DW$ |
| Euro area | 0.109 | 0.195 | 0.441 | 0.467 | — | — | 0.843 | 1.696 |
| | [8.567] | [8.643] | [26.554] | [22.593] | | | | |
| Germany | 0.061 | 0.073 | 0.438 | 0.796 | — | — | 0.150 | 1.822 |
| | [2.248] | [2.542] | [11.713] | [10.296] | | | | |
| $V_t^c$ | $g_u$ | — | — | $a_{12}$ | $a_{13}$ | $a_{14}$ | $\bar{R}^2$ | $DW$ |
| Euro area | 0.891 | — | — | –0.049 | –0.225 | 0.233 | 0.925 | 1.981 |
| | [98.548] | | | [–7.124] | [–17.263] | [17.350] | | |
| Germany | 0.892 | — | — | –0.091 | –0.624 | 0.374 | 0.899 | 1.842 |
| | [52.175] | | | [–4.336] | [–9.888] | [11.999] | | |
| $dln(V_t^l)$ | $a_{21}$ | $a_{22}$ | $a_{23}$ | $a_{24}$ | — | — | $\bar{R}^2$ | $DW$ |
| Euro area | 0.137 | 0.123 | 0.070 | 0.090 | — | — | 0.692 | 1.248 |
| | [25.884] | [28.586] | [10.086] | [19.203] | | | | |
| Germany | 0.042 | 0.034 | — | 0.041 | — | — | 0.301 | 1.135 |
| | [9.888] | [8.890] | | [5.982] | | | | |
| $r_t$ | $g_1$ | $g_2$ | $g^3$ | $g_4$ | — | — | $\bar{R}^2$ | $DW$ |
| Euro area | 0.927 | 0.114 | 0.130 | –0.116 | | | 0.981 | 1.431 |
| | [80.735] | [7.183] | [13.519] | [–13.900] | — | — | | |
| Germany | 0.810 | 0.174 | 0.205 | –0.180 | | | 0.956 | 1.093 |
| | [43.477] | [6.849] | [11.801] | [–11.690] | — | — | | |

| | |
|---|---|
| Determinant Residual Covariance | Euro area: 7.88E–23, Germany: 4.77E–21 |
| J-Statistic | Euro area: 0.215, Germany: 0.257 |

economies with respect to demand pressure in the labour and goods markets, respectively (though there is a larger amplitude in the capacity utilization series than in the one for the employment rate). Secondly, concerning the (log of the) wage share, the Blanchard–Katz error correction term, we find also a significant influence on the price inflation dynamics in both economies. In contrast, while the growth rate of labour productivity appears to influence positively, in a significant way and a similar extent wage inflation in the two economies (the parameter estimates equal 0.213 for the Euro area and 0.236 for the Germany), the same variable appears to be insignificant for the price inflation in both economies.

Additionally we find that the estimated parameter $\beta_{w1}$, which measures the flexibility of wages with respect to labour market developments, is higher in the Euro area than in Germany, if we make use of our proxy variable for the Euro area short term unemployed (on the relevant group in the wage bargaining process) instead of using the aggregate unemployment rate. Concerning the inflationary pressure terms, while in the estimated wage and price Phillips curves for the Euro area and in the price Phillips curve for Germany the influences of the perfectly foreseen price inflation and of the inflationary climate are quite similar (what supports our formulation of our joint effect as a weighted average), in the wage Phillips curve for Germany the latter variable turns out to be insignificant. The explanatory significance of the inflationary climate – which proxies the medium-run inflationary expectations of the economic agents – for aggregate price inflation delivers also empirical evidence for the presence of the Mundell effect – which influences aggregate production through the real interest rate channel – and this in both economies.

Concerning the influence of the real wage on capacity utilization rates, we find in the first place evidence for a principally profit-led goods markets dynamics in both countries, a result which supports the orthodox point of view (where from a non-Keynesian microeconomic point of view lower real wages, due to the profit maximizing behaviour of the firms, lead to a higher production level). In a Keynesian framework, however, it instead simply means that investment is more responsive to changes in the real wage than consumption. In addition, due to the openness of both economies to international trade (Germany being of course relatively more open than the Euro area), the negative influence of the real wages on the growth rate of capacity utilization of the economy might reflect in part the loss of competitiveness which higher wages cause, and thus not at all variants of the orthodox point of view of a profit-led economy.

The result that goods demand is profit led is associated in both economies with the result that real wage dynamics (ignoring Blanchard and Katz error correction) are labour market led – that is, wage flexibility dominates price flexibility (in combination with the result that wage earners are more myopic than firms as far as the $\kappa$ expressions are concerned. Combining these results thus leads (also in the case of the German economy) with respect to Figure 10.1 to the situation shown on its left-hand side which means that real wage adjustment is normal or stabilizing in the feedback chain leading from real wage changes to aggregate demand changes and from there back to real wage changes.

With respect to monetary policy and the estimated Taylor Rules for the Euro area and Germany, we find an empirical confirmation for an active interest rate policy in the Euro area as also found, for example, in Peersman and Smets (1999) and Gerlach and Schnabel (2000), when we derive the total impact of the price inflation on the interest rate. In the German Taylor Rule, where the Euro area-wide inflation rate was inserted, on the contrary, the Taylor principle, which requires a total effect of price inflation on the nominal interest rate above 1 is not fulfilled: in order to have 'controlled' Euro area and not only German price inflation, the Bundesbank should have acted in a more active manner than was historically the case.

In the next section we now simulate numerically, based on the estimated parameter values for the Euro area, some scenarios concerning private sector (in-) stability and the role of monetary policy in such a context.

## Private sector stability and the role of monetary policy

Using the parameter estimates for the Euro area we consider first, in Figure 10.4, impulse–response patterns for the various state variables of the model.[7] We apply a downward 5 per cent real wage shock in the figures top-right and top-left and an upward shock of 10 per cent to this state variable bottom-right and bottom-left. Since the economy has been estimated as being profit-led, the decrease in real wages (at time t=1) stimulates economic activity as measured by the rate of capacity utilization $V^c$. The rate of employment follows this increased activity to a certain degree due to the measured form of Okun's Law. The recovery of real wages and the return of economic activity to normal activity takes approximately 15 of the 40 years shown on the horizontal axis. This long transient behaviour may appear as too long, but is in fact not really so, since here we consider a Keynesian framework where no parameter is varying in time and where, therefore, important causes that shape the business cycle are absent (time-varying propensities to consume and to invest, for example).[8] In fact, the figure top-right also shows that the evolution of nominal variables back to normal takes even longer, indicating that the cost-pressure spiral of our wage-price module can obtain some independence from the real variables (can display extra inertia), enforcing the point that high nominal interest rates are needed for a longer time span (than appears as necessary from the real evolution of the economy) in order also to bring the wage–price spiral mechanism back to normal levels, in combination with slightly depressed economic activity.

In Figure 10.4 bottom-left and bottom-right we consider, by contrast, contractionary real wage shocks in this profit-led economy. In addition, we now assume a floor in the money wage PC. Bottom-left we consider situations where the floor is given by 0.02, 0.01, 0.00, –0.01, –0.02 respectively, and get for an inflation target $\bar{\pi} = 0$ the five shown impulse–response reactions for the rate of capacity utilization, with the recessions being deeper the higher the floor to the money wage PC. Due to this horizontal kink in the WPC we now also have path-dependence in the responses of capacity utilization. We remark that, for example, the worst situation (a floor of 2 per cent wage inflation, as it has been measured in Hoogenveen and Kuipers (2000) for several European countries, can be improved towards the one shown for a zero floor (in the middle), if the target rate $\bar{\pi}$ of the CB is increased from zero to 2 per cent. Monetary policy should therefore for its proper working be interested in finding out where the floors to money wage inflation or deflation in fact lie (a possibly ambiguous objective for the whole Euro area).

In Figure 10.4, bottom-right, we show the evolution of the inflationary climate expression of our economy for the assumed upward real wage shock. We consider first again a target inflation rate $\bar{\pi} = 0$ of the CB. The responses shown are (from the top to the bottom) ordered by money wage floors, here given by the sequence 0.02, 0.01, 0.00, –0.01, –0.02, $-\infty$ i.e., the deepest deflation (in terms of $\pi^m$) occurs if there is no floor to money wages. The working of the horizontal kink of the WPC is furthermore clearly visible for –0.02, –0.01.[9] We observe that this kink makes the considered deflation period the longer the earlier (from below) it occurs. From the nominal side the situation $\bar{\pi} = 0$ seems to be best, since there is then rapid return to the target of the CB. The highest level response that is shown, finally, considers the case $\bar{\pi} = 0.02$ and a WPC floor of which then provides a situation not very different from the zero target of the CB.

In Figure 10.5 we present the maximum real part of the eigenvalues of the Jacobian of the considered dynamics – evaluated at the steady state – as a function of crucial parameters of the Keynesian disequilib-

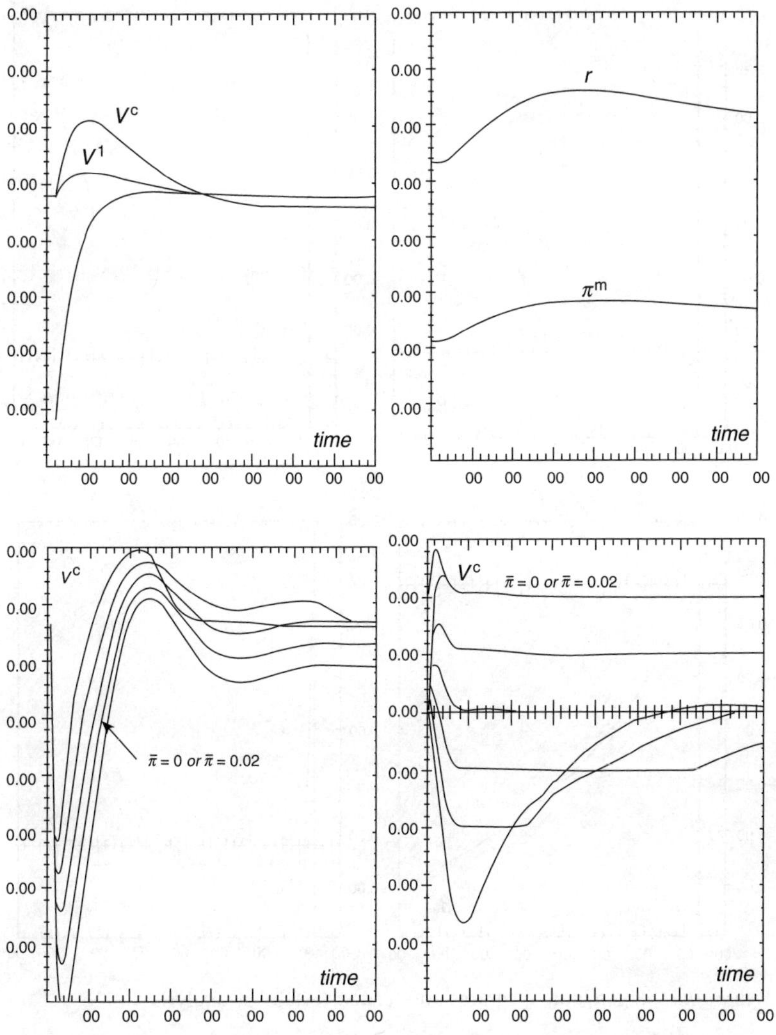


*Figure 10.4* Impulse response test and monetary policy reaction parameters

rium dynamics. If this maximum passes from below through zero there occurs a Hopf-bifurcation where the system switches from local stability to local instability in a cyclical way, i.e., by way of business fluctuations and thus not by monotonic convergence changing into monotonic explosiveness. We can see from these eigenvalue diagrams

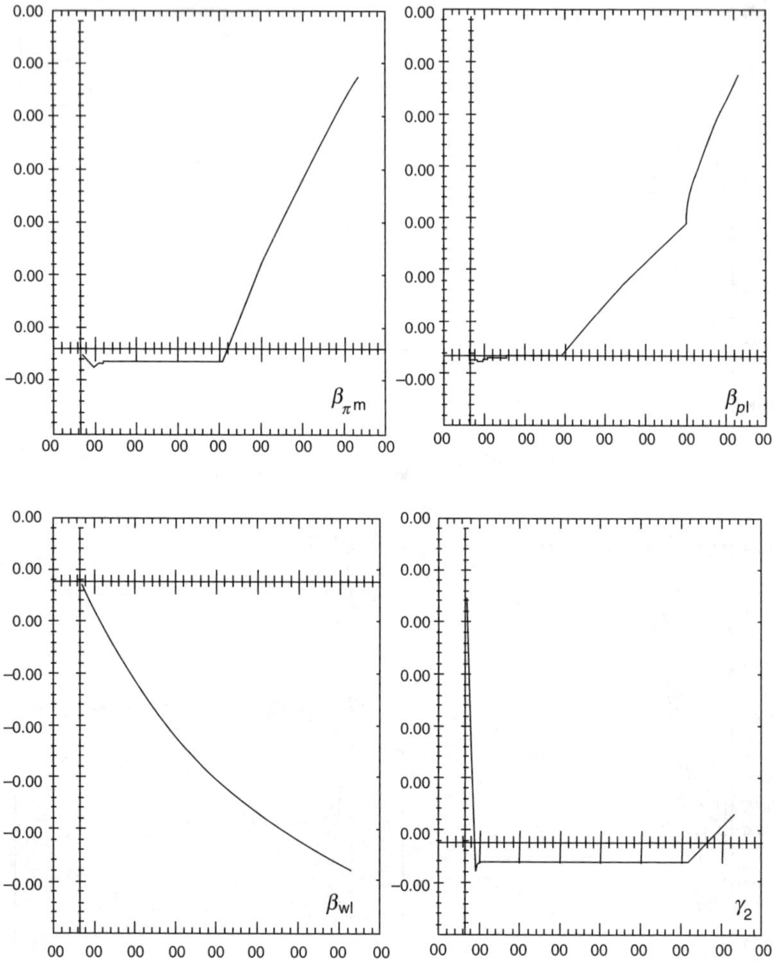


*Figure 10.5* Eigenvalue diagrams and feedback stability analysis

that wage flexibility with respect to demand pressure (on the labour market) is stabilizing if it increases, while price flexibility is not (here with respect to demand pressure on the market for goods). This is due to a working of the Rose real-wage effect, as shown on the left-hand side in Figure 10.1. Faster adjustment of the inflationary climate expression is also destabilizing, since it simply means that the conven-

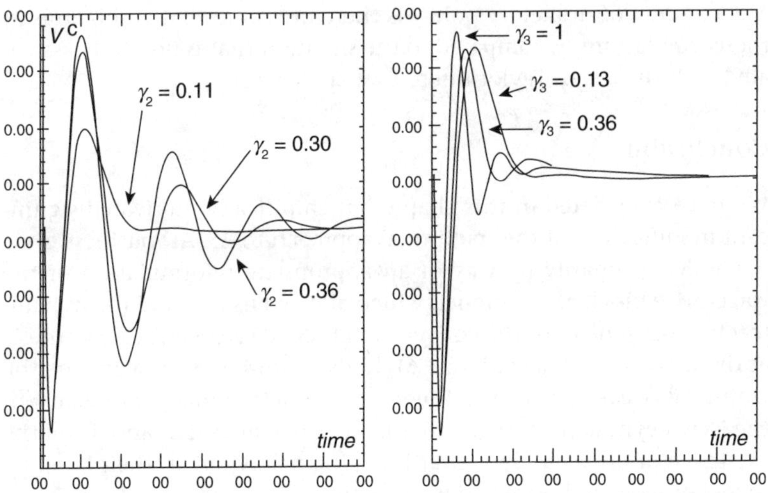


*Figure 10.6* Bifurcation diagrams for monetary policy reaction parameters

tional Mundell effect (working through the real interest rate channel in goods market dynamics) is becoming more pronounced. Finally, we see in Figure 10.5 bottom-right that an increased reaction strength of the CB with respect to the inflation gap is at first stabilizing (closely above zero), but later on can become destabilizing again, i.e., this speed of adjustment must be chosen in a certain corridor in order to work as suggested.

Figure 10.6 finally shows bottom-left and bottom-right, for the rate of capacity utilization, the influence of CB reactions to the inflation and the utilization gap, respectively. We see on the left-hand side that increasing the parameter $\gamma_2$ makes the dynamics more volatile, while the same does not happen equally strong bottom-left, where the parameter $\gamma_3$ is increased. These impulse response diagrams therefore suggest that a stronger reaction to the utilization gap may be preferable to a stronger reaction to the inflation gap, possibly, due to the fact that the first policy is more direct towards the fight against inflation than is the second one. The Figures 10.5 top-right and top-left finally show the same situation from the perspective of bifurcation diagrams. We there plot the local maxima and minima shown in its bottom for all parameter values $\gamma_2$, $\gamma_3$ in the interval [0.0.36] While the first local minimum stays constant as a consequence of the uniform initial shock to real wages in all these situations, we see again that there is an increase in volatility in the situation top-left, while the opposite occurs top-right.

The conduct of monetary policy is therefore somewhat ambiguous in these simulations as compared to the situation that is normally associated with the use of Taylor interest rate policy rules.

## Conclusion

We have considered in this chapter an empirically motivated significant modification of the traditional approach to AS–AD business cycle dynamics, primarily by way of an appropriate reformulation of the wage-price block of the model, which allowed us to avoid the dynamical inconsistencies of the conventional AS–AD Neoclassical Synthesis as discussed in Asada *et al.* (2006). It also allowed us to overcome the empirical weaknesses and theoretical indeterminacy problems of the New Keynesian approach to inflation dynamics that arise from the existence of only purely forward looking behaviour in their baseline model of staggered price and wage setting.

By contrast, our alternative approach – which allows for gradual wage as well as price adjustment, driven by labour and goods market imbalances, respectively, and also for certain economic climate variables, representing the medium-run evolution of inflation – completely bypasses the purely formal imposition of New Keynesian boundedness assumptions. Instead, it allows us to obtain, guided by the intuition behind important Keynesian macro-feedback channels, local asymptotic stability under certain plausible assumptions on the model's parameters[10] (indeed very plausible from the perspective of Keynesian feedback mechanism), cyclical loss of stability when these assumptions are violated (if speeds of adjustment become sufficiently high), and even explosive fluctuations in the case of further increases of the crucial speeds of adjustment of the model. In the latter case further behavioural nonlinearities have to be introduced in order to tame the explosive dynamics, as in Chiarella and Flaschel (2000: chs 6, 7), where a kinked Phillips curve (downward wage rigidity) was employed in order to achieve global boundedness.

In the present chapter we have studied such disequilibrium AS–AD dynamics primarily from the empirical and the numerical point of view. In particular, our parameter estimates for the Euro area confirmed the sign restrictions that are imposed by theory on the parameters of the model. In addition, such estimates suggested (for the theoretically indetermined parameter signs) that aggregate demand is profit-led and that real wage dynamics are labour-market-led; which in sum implies that the real wage feedback channel works in a stabilizing way. Numerical simulations finally showed strong, though – due to the neglect of the possibility of time varying parameter values – slowly convergent behaviour for the estimated model. On this basis we, in particular, found that increasing parameter sizes work as claimed by partial Keynesian feedback reasoning and that policy must be exercised with care in order to not increase the volatility of the dynamics of the private sector.

## Notes

1. For a detailed comparison with the New Keynesian alternative to our model type see Chiarella, Flaschel and Franke (2005). Note also that the shown restriction that cost-pressure weights sum up to '1' will be relaxed in the empirical section and that the growth rate of labor productivity will play a role then in addition.
2. For lack of better terms we associate the degree of wage and price flexibility with the size of the parameters $\beta_{w1}$, $\beta_{p1}$, though of course the extent of these flexibilities will also depend on the size of the fluctuations of the excess demands in the market for labour and for goods, respectively.
3. See Asada *et al.* (2006), Chen *et al.* (2006) for details.
4. As the model is formulated we have no real anchor for the steady-state rate of interest (via investment behavior and the rate of profit it implies in the steady state) and thus have to assume here that it is the monetary authority that enforces a certain steady-state value for the nominal rate of interest.
5. Multi-equation GMM estimations carried out alternatively with the first differences – instead of the levels – of the nominal interest and capacity utilization rates deliver quite similar results.
6. In a wage equation estimation Wooldridge (2001: 94) shows that 'the GMM estimates and standard errors are very similar to those for two-stage least squares. [...] using GMM does not hurt anything, and perhaps [*it might offer*] greater precision.'
7. For Okun's Law we use in all of the following the form: $\hat{V}^l = 0.3\hat{V}^c + 0.05V^c$ in order to enforce convergence back to the steady state (since det $J \neq 0$ is then ensured).
8. See also Keynes (1936: ch. 22) on this matter.
9. And also for where the climate and actual inflation stays above the target set by the CB.
10. See Asada *et al.* (2006) for details.

## References

Asada, T., Chen, P., Chiarella, C. and Flaschel, P. (2006) 'Keynesian Dynamics and The Wage-Price Spiral: A Baseline Disequilibrium Approach', *Journal of Macroeconomics,* 28: 90–130.

Barro, R. (1994) 'The Aggregate Supply/Aggregate Demand Model', *Eastern Economic Journal,* 20: 1–6.

Blanchard, O.J. and Katz, L. (1999) 'Wage Dynamics: Reconciling Theory and Evidence', *The American Economic Review,* 89: 69–74.

Chen, P., Chiarella, C., Flaschel, P. and Hung, H. (2005) 'Keynesian Disequilibrium Dynamics. Estimated Convergence, Roads to Instability and the Emergence of Complex Business Fluctuations', in H. Galler and C. Dreger (eds), *Advances in Macroeconometric Modeling*. Papers and Proceedings of the 5th IWH Workshop in Macroeconometrics (Baden-Baden: Nomos), forthcoming.

Chen, P. and Flaschel, P. (2006) 'Measuring the Interaction of Wage and Price Phillips Curves for the US Economy', *Studies in Nonlinear Dynamics and Econometrics*, 10(3), forthcoming.

Chiarella, C. and Flaschel, P. (2000) *The Dynamics of Keynesian Monetary Growth: Macro Foundations* (Cambridge: Cambridge University Press).

Chiarella, C., Flaschel, P. and Franke, R. (2005) *Foundations for a Disequilibrium Theory of the Business Cycle: Qualitative Analysis and Quantitative Assessment* (Cambridge: Cambridge University Press).

Flaschel, P., Kauermann, G. and Semmler, W. (2006) 'Testing Wage and Price Phillips Curves for the United States', *Metroeconomica*, forthcoming.

Flaschel, P. and Krolzig, H.M. (2006) 'Wage and Price Phillips Curves and Macroeconomic Stability: Basic Structural Form, Estimation and Analysis', in C. Chiarella, P. Flaschel, R. Franke and W. Semmler (eds), *Quantitative and Empirical Analysis of Nonlinear Dynamic Macromodels: Contributions to Economic Analysis* (Amsterdam: Elsevier).

Galí, J. (2000) 'The Return of the Phillips Curve and Other Recent Developments in Business Cycle Theory', *Spanish Economic Review*, 2: 1–10.

Gerlach, S. and Schnabel, G. (2000) 'The Taylor Rule and Interest Rates in the EMU Area', *Economics Letters*, 67(2): 165–71.

Hoogenveen, V. and Kuipers, S. (2000) 'The Long-Run Effects of Low Inflation Rates', *Banca Nazionale del Lavoro Quarterly Review*, 53: 267–86.

Keynes, J.M. (1936) *The General Theory of Employment, Interest and Money* (New York: Macmillan).

Laxton, D., Rose, D., and D. Tambakis (2000) 'The US Phillips-Curve: The Case for Asymmetry', *Journal of Economic Dynamics and Control*, 23: 1459–85.

Layard, R., Nickell, S. and Jackman, R. (1991) *Unemployment: Macroeconomic Performance and the Labour Market* (Oxford: Oxford University Press).

Ljungqvist, L. and Sargent, T.J. (1998) 'The European Unemployment Dilemma', *Journal of Political Economy*, 106(3): 514–50.

MacKinnon, J.G. (1996) 'Numerical Distribution Functions for Unit Root and Cointegration Tests', *Journal of Applied Econometrics*, 11: 167–76.

OECD (2002) 'The Ins and Outs of Long-Term Unemployment', *OECD Employment Outlook* (Paris: OECD), pp. 189–239.

Okun, A.M. (1970) *The Political Economy of Prosperity* (Washington DC: The Brookings Institution).

Peersman, G. and Smets, F. (1999) 'The Taylor Rule: A Useful Monetary Policy Benchmark for the Euro Area?', *International Finance*, 1: 85–116.

Rudebusch, G.D. and Svensson, L.E. (1999) 'Policy Rules for Inflation Targeting', in J.B. Taylor (ed.), *Monetary Policy Rules* (Chicago: The University of Chicago Press).

Woodford, M. (2003) *Interest and Prices: Foundations of a Theory of Monetary Policy* (Princeton: Princeton University Press).

Wooldridge, J. (2001) 'Applications of Generalized Method of Moments Estimation', Journal of Economic Perspectives, 15(4): 87–100.

# 11
# How the Maastricht Regime Fosters Divergence as Well as Instability*

*Jörg Bibow*

## Introduction

This chapter investigates the phenomenon of persistent macroeconomic divergence that has occurred across the Euro area in the fragile macroeconomic environment of recent years. Optimal currency area theory would point toward asymmetric shocks and structural factors as the foremost candidate causes. The alternative hypothesis pursued here focuses on the working of the Maastricht regime itself, highlighting that the regime features powerful built-in de-stabilizers that foster divergence as well as instability. Supposed adjustment mechanisms have turned out to actually undermine the operation of the currency union by making it ever less 'optimal', that is, less subjectable to a 'one-size-fits-all' monetary policy and common nominal exchange rate in view of the resulting business cycle de-synchronization and related build-up of financial imbalances.

The issue of divergence across the Eurozone has gained some prominence in recent years. Often attention is primarily focused on inflation differentials, which are, however, not necessarily judged undesirable. For instance, in its May Bulletin of 2005, the European Central Bank (ECB) observed that:

> Inflation differentials can be an integral part of the adjustment mechanism resulting from dispersion of economic developments

*The author gratefully acknowledges comments from the participants at the 9th Workshop of the Research Network 'Alternative Macroeconomic Policies' (theme: 'Macroeconomics and Macroeconomic Policies – Alternatives to the Orthodoxy') in Berlin, 28–9 October 2005, where a preliminary draft of this essay was presented.

> across the participating countries, a mechanism which in turn reflects the impact of various economic shocks as well as the fact that the economic structures in place vary from country to country. Inflation differentials are, then, the product of an equilibrating adjustment process within a monetary union and, as such, are not only unavoidable, but also desirable. At the same time, lasting inflation differentials in the Euro area are, to some extent, also a product of misaligned fiscal policies, diverging wage developments and deep-seated structural inefficiencies such as nominal and real rigidities in product and factor markets. (ECB 2005: 61)

Note that inflation differentials are seen here as part of an *equilibrating adjustment mechanism* featuring wage and price flexibility. A related issue is that structural reforms enhancing flexibility are then seen as bolstering the working of these supposedly equilibrating forces. By contrast, the analysis here will pinpoint that powerful forces of divergence triggered in the process are ignored in the official flexibility doctrine and that substituting structural reform and flexibility for proper demand management is doomed to failure.

The analysis starts in the second section with the ill-conceived 'convergence process' of the 1990s. Developments since the euro's launch are the subject of the third section. The fourth section then turns to optimum currency area theory for advice on the issue of divergence within currency areas. A thorough analysis of the 'competitiveness channel', the various forces of divergence kicked off thereby, and their joint effect on internal economic stability of individual member states is provided in fifth section. The accompanying build-up of intra-Eurozone imbalances is the subject of the sixth section, which also identifies the key flaws in the reasoning behind the official flexibility doctrine. The seventh section concludes the analysis and offers recommendations for regime reform targeting the divergence issue.

## Divergence during the 'convergence process' of the 1990s

Before setting out to investigate the phenomenon of persistent divergence in inflation and economic activity across Euroland since 1999 two issues require prior clarification. One concerns the catching-up process of lower-income EU members with their higher-income partners. Another is that persistent inflation differentials and cyclical divergence are not new phenomena in Europe.

As to the first, growth theory would lead one to expect that, for instance, the latecomers in Europe's south, Greece, Portugal and Spain, just like the new EU members in Europe's east, will grow faster than the 'old EU core' for as long as their catching up and convergence to a supposedly common (long-run) growth trend is taking place. Essentially, this can be thought of as an equilibrium phenomenon during which both higher- and lower-income countries can grow at their respective potential trend rates. And long-run catching up is not the issue in what follows. Instead, at issue are pronounced *out-of-sync* deviations from steady-state growth and persistent inflation differentials not attributable to the Balassa–Samuelson effect. In principle, cyclical divergence can become either amplified or effectively counterbalanced, and by either market mechanisms and/or stabilizing policies.

In practice, pronounced cyclical divergence has characterized the situation since 2001. In particular, while domestic demand and economic activity in Germany has remained severely depressed, France fared significantly better until recently, and Spain experienced boom conditions throughout the period. In other words, while Germany has suffered from protracted cyclical slack, Spain enjoyed sustained above-trend growth, with France and Italy falling somewhere in between. Similarly, persistent inflation differentials remain in place, with Germany well below and Italy and Spain well above the Eurozone average. Among smaller countries Portugal and the Netherlands have been persistent laggards and Ireland and Greece persistent star performers. The point is that for members of a common currency area such a lack of synchronization of business cycles can represent a serious problem since the common monetary policy stance and external exchange rate tend to become increasingly less 'optimal' the further member countries are drifting apart.

And this leads me to the second issue, the fact that cyclical divergence and persistent inflation differentials are not new phenomena in Europe at all, but have characterized the whole postwar era up to EMU. In the past, such diverging trends led to external imbalances and periodic exchange rate adjustments or crises. These were, however, always considered a threat to the common market and further economic integration, which is exactly why Europe undertook a fresh attempt at creating a 'zone of monetary stability' in the late 1970s (the EMS), and then embarked on the common currency project in the late 1980s (EMU). EMU was supposed to end the possibility of competitive devaluations that could disturb or even undermine the common market and European integration more generally.

However, by the time this was agreed upon in the early 1990s Europe suffered from very severe divergences indeed, in both inflation and economic activity. It was to prepare the launching of the common currency into a more stable environment that a period of convergence was prescribed to precede the euro's introduction. The Maastricht Treaty features certain criteria that countries had to fulfil in order to be allowed into the club. These criteria set limits for inflation, nominal interest rates, nominal exchange rate changes, and public finances; apart from requiring the release into independence of national central banks before merging them into the Eurosystem.

As it turns out, actual occurrences over the 1990s foretold many of the problems that countries were also to experience under EMU conditions more recently. While inflation and nominal interest rates generally fell to low levels and budget deficits declined to just below 3 per cent of GDP by 1997–98, too, developments in the real economy during the 1990s were anything but harmonious (Arestis and Sawyer 2001).

The decade started out in 1990 with what represented a sizeable asymmetric shock hitting the anchor currency. In Germany's case, unification extended the belated boom that had reached the country only by 1988, after subdued growth, ever since the early 1980s recession. Among other things, Germany's miraculous four-year span of high growth at stable and low inflation paid put to the popular contemporary view that Germany was suffering from all-pervasive structural problems that prevented it from growing. By contrast, and despite export spill-overs from Germany's so-called unification boom, much of the rest of Europe was facing stagnation if not outright recessionary conditions, by that time.

This marked de-synchronization of business cycle conditions, together with the Bundesbank's extraordinarily tight money course embarked upon in 1991, led to the ERM crises of 1992/93. The sizeable devaluations 'suffered' by many satellite currencies *vis-à-vis* the deutschmark in these events corrected for Germany's creeping competitiveness gains that had accumulated during the 'hard EMS' period. While it would be wrong, therefore, to conclude that Germany had to restore its competitiveness lost through these events, their impact no doubt represented the first source of subsequent divergence, with competitiveness gains boosting exports in countries like Italy and Spain, but having the opposite impact on Germany. The loss of Germany's previous (undervaluation) advantage was one of two main factors that reversed the direction of diverging trends over the course of the 1990s:

Germany had started out as the strongest economy in Europe when the common currency was agreed upon, but turned out to be its weakest when the euro was actually launched.

The turning point occurred around the middle of the decade. By that time, however, all of 'Euroland to be' found itself in the doldrums. It is worthwhile to recall here that even in mid-1997 it appeared that only a very small group of countries would qualify for an early euro adoption. The fiscal contractions inflicted upon Europe at the time – although at varying degrees and timings – proved rather less expansionary than its propagators had promised. Accompanied by the Bundesbank's conspicuous reluctance to ease policy, referring to a stability-oriented need for a 'steady hand' policy, an argument never heard of when the bank envisions reasons to hike rates, the predictable consequence was subdued growth.

Luckily, the US's 'new economy' boom and associated US dollar strength provided a last-minute lifeline for the struggling EU economies; just in time for the 'convergence test' of spring 1998 leading to a broad EMU after all.

Luck proved short-lived, however, as the Asian and Russian crises soon afterwards delivered a sizeable external demand shock. Germany was especially hard hit because by that point the country had already become overly reliant on export-driven growth. In Germany, domestic demand failed to ever recover from the Bundesbank's tight money crusade that accompanied the severe and procyclical fiscal contraction between 1992 and 1997 – an exceptionally (and counterproductively!) tight macro policy stance that diverged from the situation in much of the rest of Europe.

For one thing, other countries, like France, Spain, and Austria for instance, wisely delayed the bulk of their fiscal consolidation efforts until the worst was over, thereby avoiding the strongly pro-cyclical impact that characterized Germany's situation. For another, the years 1996–98 saw non-deutschmark interest rates across Europe converge (i.e. decline) to German levels, traditionally the European interest rate floor (except for the Swiss franc) related to Germany's EMS lead role. To this decline in interest rates corresponds a rise in asset prices, with strong credit growth boosting domestic demand during the adjustment process.

In summary, cyclical divergence during the 1990s occurred primarily between Germany on the one hand and former EMS-satellite countries on the other. These developments were inevitable only in the sense and to the extent that the deutschmark had been undervalued prior to the ERM crises and Germany bound to lose its former (key currency) interest-rate bonus with the launch of the common currency. At that time Germany was free to compensate for these factors, however. In particular, there was nothing to stop the relevant German authorities from conducting less inappropriate macroeconomic policies. For one thing, the Bundesbank was still in charge of German monetary policy and charged with a German mandate. For another, it was quite unnecessary to inflict a fiscal contraction upon Germany that lacked any historical parallel in the developed world. Behind all this was a deliberate abstention to address the problem of protracted domestic demand stagnation on the part of Germany's key authorities. Since the 1980s a peculiar 'structuralist' (or, 'supply-side-only') view is running high in German policy-making circles.

In the event, having lost both of its former competitive advantages during the run-up to EMU, the DM undervaluation that had been accumulated during the hard EMS era as well as its traditional (key currency) interest-rate bonus, Germany was in a poor shape to cope with the Asian and Russian crises that struck its economy at the very time when Germany finally surrendered its monetary policy sovereignty, too. It so happened that Germany became quickly dubbed the 'sick man of the euro' when the new currency started on its steep decline in 1999 in view of a perceived growth disadvantage compared to the roaring US economy. In retrospect, one is truly taken aback by the degree of ineptness that characterized the German authorities' macro policy response to the unification challenge by means of which the Western German economy has been lastingly derailed – until today (Bibow 2005).

## After briefly abating early on, divergence has quickly re-emerged with protracted stagnation since the 2001 downturn

Between two long spans of subdued growth or near stagnation Germany actually experienced a brief burst of growth, beginning in mid-1999 and lasting for a little over a year. After the export slump of 1998–99, exports recovered strongly, amplified by the fall of the euro. Moreover, as fiscal consolidation briefly paused domestic demand growth accelerated to an annual rate of 2.5 per cent in 1999–2000, so that GDP growth reached a remarkable 3.5 per cent in 2000.

Unfortunately, however, the euro's plunge also magnified the rise in oil prices and lifted import prices more generally, which pushed headline HICP inflation above the ECB's declared 2-per cent ceiling by mid-2000. Importantly, while the strength of these price effects differed significantly across Europe, core inflation remained very low and showed relatively little dispersion at this time.

Things have changed again with the return of subdued growth since 2001, as, for instance, a report prepared in 2003 by the Monetary Policy Committee of the Eurosystem observed that:

> With the exception of Luxembourg, Belgium and Finland, all countries have experienced inflation persistently above or below the Euro area average since 1999... A related issue is that differences in the evolution of inflation among the three largest euro area countries appear to have increasingly diverged since 2002. Despite the common slowdown in economic activity experienced by France, Italy and Germany, and notwithstanding the relatively similar cyclical positions of the latter two countries, inflation in core HICP components in Germany declined throughout 2002, whereas it was more or less flat in France and increased in Italy. (ECB 2004: 7)

*Figure 11.1* HICP inflation since 1999: level up, but dispersion stable

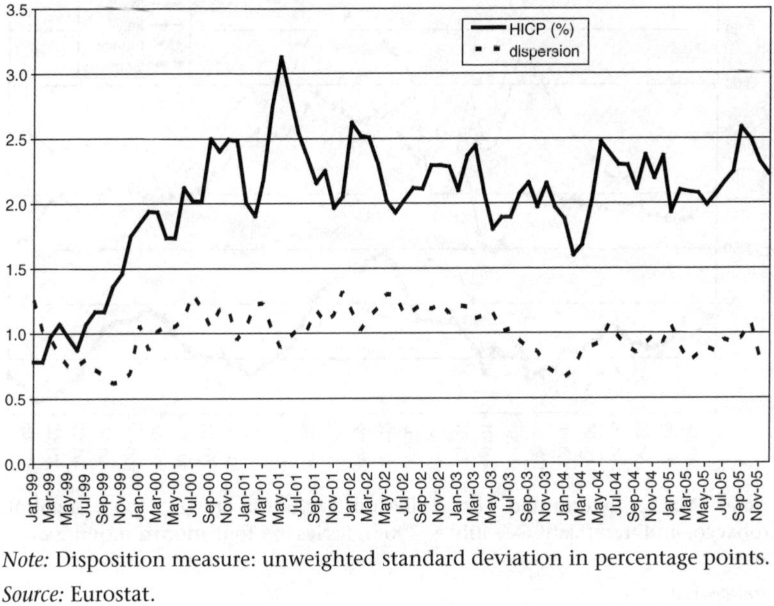


*Note:* Disposition measure: unweighted standard deviation in percentage points.
*Source:* Eurostat.

It is of great interest that this report refers to a 'common slowdown in economic activity' and to core rather than headline inflation. For the issue is barely discernible from the evolution of the dispersion in headline inflation across all Euro area countries shown in Figure 11.1. Measured by the (unweighted) standard deviation of the ECB's chosen inflation index, dispersion has stayed fairly stable throughout.

Yet, as the above report suggests and Figure 11.2 confirms, persistent inflation differentials have characterized developments in core prices in the largest Eurozone economies. Spain was added to the analysis here despite not being fully comparable with 'the big three', given its remaining scope for catching up with the core countries in terms of income levels. Spain may be even less comparable with the smaller Eurozone economies, however, for which the argument developed here applies less fully.

The key feature emerging from Figure 11.2 is the decline in German (market-determined)[1] core inflation to close to zero, while price trends in the other countries have been running at significantly higher levels until today.

*Figure 11.2* Persistent differentials in market-determined core inflation (big four)

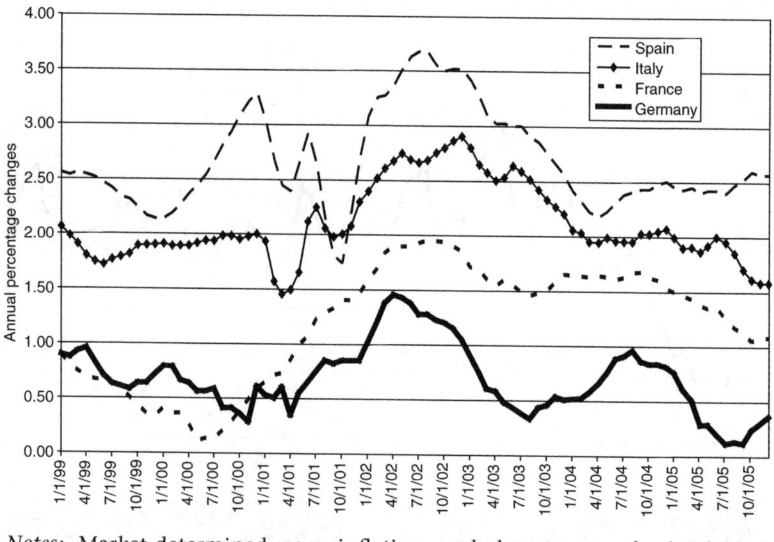


*Notes:* Market-determined core inflation excludes: energy, food, alcohol, tobacco, and 'tax push' (see Bibow 2006). Series are four-month moving averages.

*Source*: Eurostat.

*Figure 11.3* Diverging wage inflation trends, with Germany as the outlier

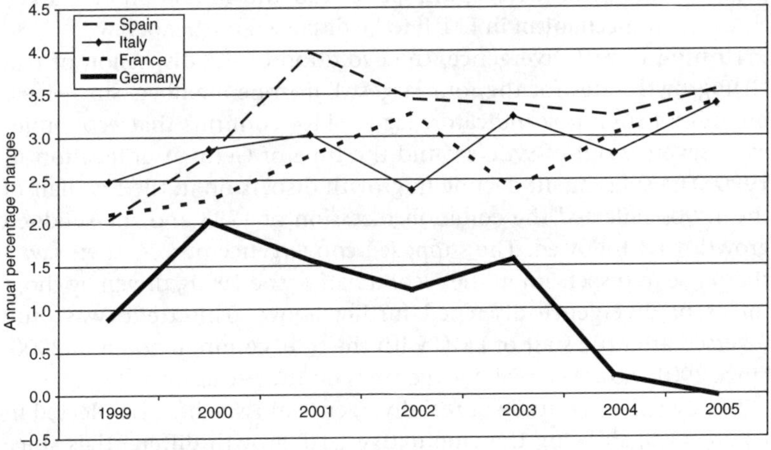


*Note:* Compensation per employee in the business sector.
*Source: OECD Economic Outlook* No. 78 (December 2005).

The underlying reason for this divergence in core inflation can be seen in Figure 11.3, which shows that German wage inflation declined to zero by 2005, with annual rates between 2.5–3.5 per cent for the

*Figure 11.4* Dispersion in big four's GDP growth rate since 1988

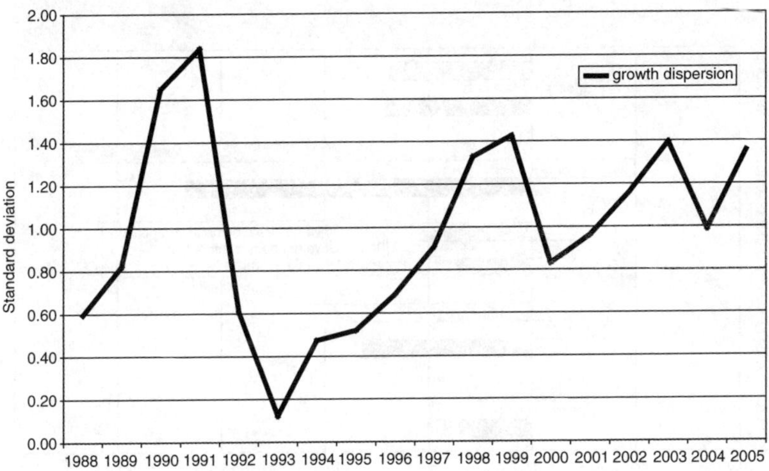


*Note:* 'Big four' are: Germany, France, Italy, and Spain.
*Source: OECD Economic Outlook* 78 (December 2005).

other three countries. This is a rather crucial fact in view of the proposition that flexible wages and prices can and should provide a key adjustment mechanism in EMU; to be discussed further below.

Turning to real divergence, the evolution of the dispersion of real GDP growth rates for the four largest Eurozone members since 1988 provides a summary indicator. Figure 11.4 confirms that economies were severely out-of-sync around the time of German unification in 1990. The subsequent decline in growth dispersion in the first half of the 1990s reflected the common recession of 1993 and the subdued growth that followed. The supposed convergence process then saw a sharp rise in dispersion in the second half of the 1990s, driven by those forces of divergence discussed further above. This trend was only reversed after the start of EMU with the brief common boom in 2000. Since 2001, however, real divergence is on the rise again.

The overall magnitude of real divergence at issue here is reflected in Figure 11.5, showing the cumulative GDP growth differentials since 2001 and also the respective cumulative net trade contributions to GDP growth over this period. While Spain's superior performance may partly reflect catch up, this case can hardly be made for France growing so much faster than Germany and Italy. As to the composition of GDP growth, note that Germany's growth over this period was driven more than exclusively by foreign trade! This is another crucial fact in view of the proposition that flexible wages and prices should provide the key adjustment mechanism in EMU.

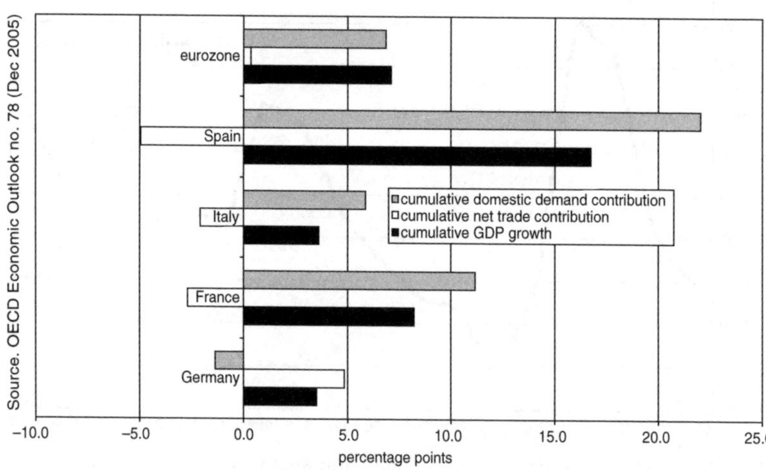


*Figure 11.5* Cumulative GDP growth and its composition (2001–2005)

## Revisiting optimum currency area (OCA) theory

The issue of persistent divergence is important to EMU since member states have surrendered their ability to use national monetary and exchange rate policies to deal with it individually, while the common 'one-size-fits-all' policy stance decided for them as a group actually becomes ever less fitting the more they drift apart. Worst, if such drift became self-reinforcing. Best, if automatic market mechanisms alone re-equilibrated the system. For the sustainability of EMU it is a vital matter whether market forces alone can be relied upon as drivers of supposedly equilibrating adjustment processes, or what role deliberate policies might have to play in all this.

Traditionally, this issue has been at the very heart of 'optimum currency area' theory (OCA). Starting in the context of the fixed-versus-flexible-exchange-rates debate of the 1960s, OCA has identified certain properties that members of a currency union should possess to make the union function in a sustainable fashion. The central idea is that the more these properties were shared by all members, the more this would tend to reduce the need and usefulness of nominal exchange rate adjustments in achieving internal and external balance; namely, by reducing the likelihood and impact of certain types of shocks and/or in facilitating adjustment thereafter. On the basis of OCA, what was to be expected for Euroland?

Mundell's (1961) starting point was that real world economies might lack the degree of price and wage flexibility which neoclassical theory postulates would assure a quick convergence back toward equilibrium, following shocks. The kind of shocks Mundell focused on where asymmetric demand shocks, with demand shifting away from the products of one country towards those of another. Notice here that overall aggregate demand in the two countries together is not the issue. Rather, whereas one country suffers from a slump, the other experiences overheating. With wages and prices falling in the former while rising in the latter, or at least the relative pace of wage and price changes diverging appropriately, competitiveness of the two countries would adjust in ways that tend to restore both full employment as well as external equilibrium in both countries, and in a mutually beneficial way too.

As alternative adjustment mechanisms and criteria for evaluating the fitness for currency union membership, Mundell and later contributors to OCA emphasized the following aspects: factor mobility, fiscal policy, diversified industry structures, openness and trade relations, and financial integration. All along, the key question was how useful and effective national exchange rate and monetary policies might be in the event of asymmetric shocks, given the particular properties of the economies involved. More recently, the idea has gained ground that the rather static OCA perspective on the matter may be misleading if the very establishment of a monetary union itself tends to align countries more closely together in relevant respects, so that 'optimality' of currency areas features important elements of endogeneity. As a summary measure of OCA wisdom (or, 'meta-criterion'), business cycle synchronicity comes top.[2]

At least until recently, in applying OCA to EMU in Europe, there was never any question that wage and price flexibility might ever be sufficient to assure short-run stabilization. And, arguably, no real world economy really fulfils what seems to be required along these lines anyway; leaving aside for the moment Keynes's (1936) fundamental reservations against this supposed route of macroeconomic adjustment. Instead, labour mobility featured most prominently as a potential alternative, although empirical studies always found Europe lagging the US in this respect.

Be that as it may, given that the EU features 'cohesion' and 'solidarity' among its long-term goals, and uses regional policies to prevent regions from falling further behind, it would seem that large-scale permanent migration is not desired in the EU anyway. Moreover, as to the more relevant short-run too, labour mobility can hardly play more than a fairly limited role, given the immense costs involved in temporarily resettling families across the continent.

Mobility of capital in the form of real capital investment, on the other hand, has never really been seen as a major adjustment mechanism. For packing up factory plants and shuffling them across the continent is an unlikely event, especially for cyclical reasons. Similarly, running down existing real capital in one place, while starting afresh elsewhere, does not look like a viable strategy for short-run adjustment either. This is especially so as depressed regions are rarely seen as the location to be by greenfield investors. Also, in a monetary union, financing cost may not be lower there than elsewhere in the union, while overcapacities and depressed sales and profit expectations would, if anything, seem to work against the depressed region's attractiveness, too.

Things may be different as far as cross-border mergers and acquisitions are concerned, since at sales prices troubled local firms in depressed regions might become attractive targets for foreign predators.

That national authorities may be tempted to resist such penetration is one thing. More importantly, the key question is whether this can be expected to be conducive to short-run stabilization – given the manifold frictions and large-scale labour shedding often involved in such scenarios.

This leaves mobility of financial capital. And in this area a fairly advanced state of financial integration may be attested across Europe with respect to both financial intermediaries and markets. Whether the current degree of financial integration may be sufficient to deliver much in the form of risk diversification and insurance across the union, and whether this can be reasonably expected to be more than a minor factor anyway, is one thing. But certainly the financing of soaring intra-union (current account) imbalances has not yet met any resistance in the financial system. The real question is to what extent the financial system plays any equilibrating role, or merely facilitates growing divergences, or might even accentuate them.

Prior to the start of EMU some observers stressed the potential disciplining role that could be played by financial markets as far as public finances are concerned; with market discipline thus seen as a force that may be conducive to securing convergence and long-run equilibrium. In practice, with the disappearance of currency risk, sovereign credit spreads have also shrunk to very low levels over recent years and today very few people seem to really expect markets to play any disciplining role at all. In my view, this whole issue pertains to private financial relations within the union every bit as much, if not more so, than it does to any exposure to public debt.

Yet given a common monetary policy stance, to what extent can the financial system be expected to play any stabilizing role – tightening financial conditions in booming countries, while simultaneously easing them in depressed ones? To my mind, it is not clear that finance necessarily plays any equilibrating role at all. It even seems possible that the financial system might actually amplify divergence apart from facilitating imbalances. Today, external imbalances within the Eurozone feature both depressed countries (Portugal) as well as booming ones (Spain) with large current account deficit positions. And the same holds on the surplus side, with Germany and Ireland as prominent examples.

That leaves us with fiscal policy, stressed by OCA as the key policy instrument. The point is, however, that there is no proper fiscal policy possible at the union level as the current degree of fiscal integration is minuscule. Reflecting the hybrid state of political integration, budgets and hence fiscal policy remain under national sovereignty. In fact, Goodhart (1998) argues that standard OCA analysis fails to appreciate the fundamental 'link between political sovereignty and fiscal authority on the one hand and money creation... on the other', emphasizing that EMU in Europe represents an 'unprecedented divorce between the main monetary and fiscal authorities' (Goodhart 1998: 3) – with possible side-effects yet to be acknowledged.

In principle, fiscal policy is the only traditional stabilization policy tool left to members of EMU. Remarkably, the Maastricht regime's designers foresaw neither any need to coordinate national fiscal policies, so as to assure an appropriate aggregate fiscal stance, nor to establish coordination with other policy areas so as to assure an appropriate mix of policies at any time. German policy wisdom suggested that policy responsibilities be kept clearly separate and monetary policy independent from any political control and accountability at all costs.[3]

While predictably detrimental for aggregate stability in the union, one might at first even see some virtue in this non-coordination as far as the flexibility of national fiscal policies in coping with the key OCA concern of asymmetric shocks and business cycle asynchronicity across the union is concerned. In practice, however, EMU in Europe was designed primarily with a view of disciplining national fiscal policies, which gave rise to the institutionalized fiscal straitjacket erroneously labelled 'Stability and Growth Pact'. While the idea was to establish a more or less automatic, rule-based fiscal regime that relies on the free working of built-in fiscal stabilizers only, this pact is unlikely to deliver on either stability or growth.

Some of the most serious flaws in this dysfunctional fiscal regime stem from the unwarranted presumptions that the supposed budgetary equilibrium (i.e. a budget that is in balance or surplus) has already been achieved at the outset and that adverse conditions would never be severe enough to actually trigger the procyclical discretionary measures that breaching the 3 per cent deficit limit legally calls for.

In the event, EMU started with an aggregate budget position that fell well short of its supposed equilibrium position. And, contrary to popularly held beliefs, this was not due to insufficient ambition in the run-up to EMU, but subdued GDP growth; which itself was partly the result of the counterproductive approach to fiscal consolidation followed during the 1990s. The slowdown of 2001 and protracted stagnation that followed then provided the very kind of adverse conditions which the pact was not designed to cope with. After quickly exhausting the rather limited fiscal leeway available according to the rules, pro-cyclical discretionary consolidation attempts characterized the true working of the 'Instability and Stagnation Pact' (Bibow 2001), further destabilizing the respective countries and the Eurozone.

Arguably, this situation arose because the only stabilization policy instrument fully available in the Eurozone, monetary policy, failed to stem the plight. Although he was merely spelling out textbook wisdom, it is worthwhile to recall here Horst Koehler's reminder issued to the ECB (in his capacity as IMF Chairman) in 2002 that 'monetary policy [was] the first line of defence'. Remarkably, ECB president Duisenberg responded that 'he had never heard of that' (WSJE 2002).

In summary, it was quite clear from the start what is and what is not to be expected in the Eurozone in terms of OCA adjustment mechanisms. And in view of actual developments since 1999 there have not been any real surprises at this front either. What is surprising, then, is that the thoroughly disillusioning experiences with the working of the ill-designed Maastricht regime have given rise to a remarkably hypocritical defence against the regime's urgently needed reform. Today, and quite in conflict with the previous OCA focus, official doctrine is to put all the emphasis on the supposedly self-equilibrating role of wage and price flexibility; to be augmented not by demand-side (stabilization) policies, but supply-side (structural) reforms of market institutions that enhance allegedly lacking market 'flexibility'. The supposed flexibility ideal Euroland is aiming for may not exist anywhere on this planet. But hypocrisy and denial still prevent a sober assessment of the fact that the US and UK, for instance, use demand management policies to stabilize their respective economies.

The next section analyses whether the peculiarly one-sided policy approach favoured in Euroland due to German power can be expected to deliver stability and growth, or might actually foster divergence – apart from instability.

## All bets on the 'competitiveness channel': explaining divergence as caused by the working of the Maastricht regime

The proposition that wage and price flexibility, accompanied by structural reforms that further enhance the flexible working of product and labour markets, play a key role in fostering convergence and the smooth functioning of EMU was most clearly expressed by the ECB in the quotation in the introductory section above. The ECB refers there to inflation differentials as a 'desirable' product of an 'equilibrating adjustment process' within a monetary union (ECB 2005: 61). And, as an institution supposedly charged with the allegedly purely technical task of monetary policy that appears to justify its political independence, the ECB never tires of calling for reforms eliminating structural inefficiencies that allegedly give rise to undesirable inflation differentials.

A vital implication is that adjustment to shocks is supposed to work primarily through changes in competitiveness, featuring net exports as a key pull or drag factor on GDP growth. Indeed, the ECB is very optimistic about the effectiveness of this supposed equilibrating adjustment mechanism, asserting that the 'competitiveness ('real exchange rate') channel, although slow to build up, eventually becomes the dominating adjustment factor' (ECB 2005: 77). Similarly, the OECD (2004; emphasis added) observed that 'in the absence of monetary policy instruments, and with the leeway for fiscal policy also limited, adjustment *will have to* rely on changes in external competitiveness *operating through wages and prices'*.

The 'there-is-no-alternative' claim is always easily made. But developments since 2001 have provided an interesting experiment along these lines. It is thus appropriate to scrutinize the outcomes. Certainly, wage and price developments between Germany and Spain have moved in accordance with the above proposition. Wage and (core) price inflation have fallen to historically low levels in stagnant Germany, but stayed at well above Eurozone average levels in booming Spain, with France falling somewhere in between as regards both inflation and growth performance and Italy as something of an outlier (featuring *relatively* high wage and price inflation despite even worse performance than Germany since 2004).

The idea is that these developments would tend to drive diverging Eurozone countries back to their converging steady-state growth paths. Alas, it is overlooked that important forces of divergence are also at work that amplify rather than counterbalance growth and inflation divergence. These are summarized in Figure 11.6, contrasting stagnant Germany and booming Spain.

Given the budgetary consequences of protracted stagnation versus protracted boom conditions, the SGP's inherent asymmetry provides a first important amplifier. For in booming Spain the SGP does not provide any effective discipline at all. In fact, Spain can even employ its favourable budgetary position to further stimulate domestic demand.[4] In depressed Germany, by contrast, the deflationary bias in the SGP springs to life as stagnation leads to a breach of the 3 per cent deficit

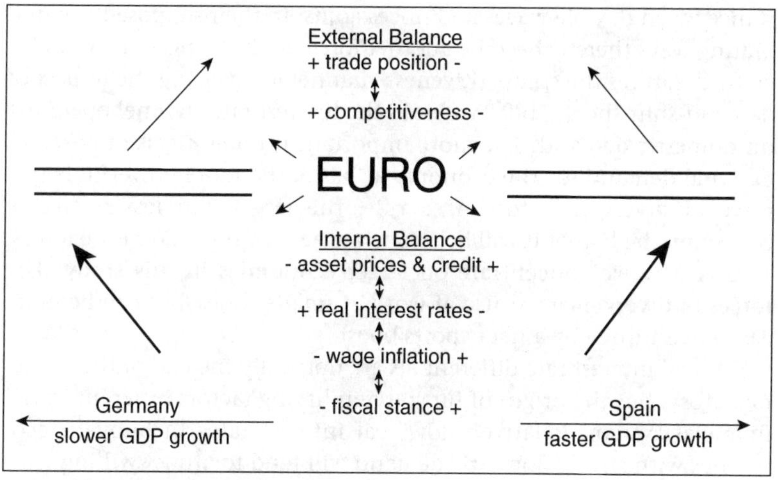


*Figure 11.6* Partners drifting apart until...

limit (or threatens to do so), triggering procyclical *discretionary* consolidation attempts.

Further forces of divergence feature wages and prices. Although diverging in their supposed way, the supposedly equilibrating adjustment role of flexible wages and prices itself amplifies cyclical divergence at the domestic front, both directly and indirectly. To begin with, wage growth (apart from labour market strength and job security) directly bolsters private consumption in booming countries. By contrast, wage moderation (apart from labour market weakness and widespread job fears) further undermines private consumption by depressing disposable incomes of wage earners in depressed countries. In this context, proponents of structural reform will be quick to assert that positive confidence effects would easily do the trick and boost growth overall (just as positive confidence effects are routinely asserted for fiscal contractions and the ECB's notorious refusal to ease policy). Reality may not comply, however. As to labour market reforms, too, German experience since 2001 points clearly in the opposite direction.

At the same time, wage trends are a most powerful force behind inflation trends, with further indirect effects. An important factor is that diverging inflation trends in a monetary union with common nominal interest rates imply that real interest rates can be highest precisely in those countries with already weak economies. The real interest rate differentials resulting from a 'one-size-fits-all' monetary policy stance when flexible wages and prices adjust in their supposedly equilibrating ways thereby become another force of divergence. The OCA literature features the competitiveness channel in reversing the impact of demand-shift shocks, but overlooks the interest rate channel operating on domestic demand. The more important is domestic as opposed to external demand for the economy at hand, the more powerful is this force of divergence, too. As a rule, the larger and less open the economy, the harder it will be to operate against these domestic forces. This is why we concentrate on larger economies in this study. The forces of divergence are also at work in smaller ones, but can be more easily overturned by a net exports boost.

Yet, real interest rate differentials are not really the end of the monetary story, but the origin of further amplifying factors inherent in the financial system. Relatively low real interest rates in buoyant economies with strong domestic demand will tend to attract willing (corporate and household) borrowers as well as willing lenders, nourishing credit growth and rising asset prices in self-reinforcing ways. By contrast, relatively high real interest rates in stagnant economies can arouse the exact opposite kind of financial propagation mechanisms in stagnant economies – providing yet another important source of divergence.

Perhaps the most crucial insight is that these various forces of divergence do not operate independently, but reinforce each other. For in each country they all operate in one and the same direction. As a result, partners continue drifting apart and may get ever further away from reattaining a balanced position, both individually and as a union. Focusing on the internal balance issue up to this point, the analysis will now turn to the external part of the supposedly equilibrating adjustment process since external imbalances are bound to arise in the process too.

## Intra-euro area imbalances soar as misdiagnosis and flawed advice hold sway

It is clear that, diverging wage and price developments are key driving forces behind changes in competitiveness and, over time, impact on trade positions accordingly. The ECB (2005) asserts that the competitiveness channel 'eventually becomes the dominant factor'. The problem is that reliance on the competitiveness channel may not only be ineffective (or worse) in fostering internal balance in the short run, i.e. over the cycle, but may also cause diverging trends and the build-up of external imbalances over the longer run. Especially in large economies reliance on the competitiveness channel comes at the price of depressing domestic demand through the various operative channels analysed above. A liberalized and integrated financial system can facilitate and accommodate growing (intra-union) 'external imbalances' for a long time without prompting any self-equilibrating forces. Worse, procyclical propagation mechanisms inherent in the financial system can even be a continuing force of divergence – up to a point.

In the fourth section above I have emphasized that Germany's GDP growth since 2001 derived (more than) exclusively from net trade.[5] In Spain, by contrast, net trade has been a persistent sizeable drag on GDP growth, while France and Italy have seen their net trade shift from contributor to drag on growth since 1999. With Germany's current account surplus forecast to climb towards 5 per cent of GDP in 2005, the absolute swing in its current account balance since 2000 amounts to some $140bn, the largest swing in any surplus country in the world. This is not only highly relevant in the context of global imbalances. A good part of the swing in Germany's trade balance occurred within the Eurozone – to the detriment of Germany's European partners.

In other words, while Germany's reliance on the competitiveness channel may have backfired internally by depressing its domestic

*Figure 11.7* Germany's growing trade surpluses with its partners

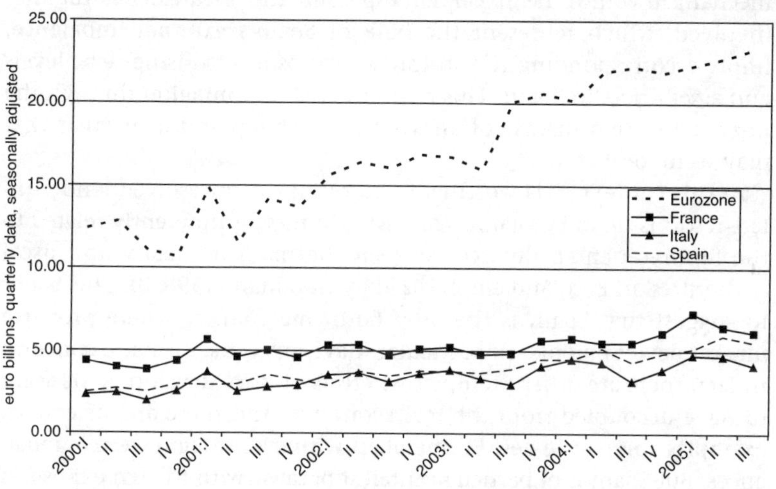


*Source:* Reuters.

economy, to this point it has clearly worked externally, namely by passing the buck to those partners that have been less negligent with respect to their domestic economies – such as, for instance, like France and Italy. And in this way, Germany's 'beggar-thy-neighbour' strategy can work towards eventual convergence. But convergence towards a depressed level of activity it will be, especially if Germany's weakening partners respond to the increasing external drag by deflating their economies too; convergence through spreading the German disease. Clearly, this strategy is self-defeating for the union as a whole and it is thus quite astonishing that the euro's supposed guardians should find so much praise for Germany's pursuits. Essentially, Germany follows the very kind of 'beggar-thy-neighbour' competitive devaluation which the euro was meant to ban forever.[6]

Interestingly, the external drag has so far failed to derail Spain's decade-long boom. Spain's current account deficit is forecast to reach double-digit territory by 2006. A good part of this deficit is with Spain's partners in the Euro area, where current account imbalances allegedly do not matter any more. Yet, do not overlook that with Spain's public budget roughly in balance an important implication is that Spain's fast-deteriorating international investment position is driven by private sector financial deficits of corresponding magnitude.

True, some part of this imbalance may have its counterpart in Germans acquiring vacation domiciles in Spain. And another part is in the form of equity flows which supposedly serve as an equilibrating mechanism within the union. But especially the private debt structures involved, which represent the bulk of Spain's external imbalance, imply a corresponding rise in foreign exposures to rising debt levels and asset prices in Spain. This raises the risk of contagion through the financial system in case of an asset price slump and debt crisis that may seem local at first.

In this context, it is worthwhile to recall the unresolved lender-of-last-resort issue in Euroland. This issue, in turn, is inherently related to the 'unprecedented divorce between the main monetary and fiscal authorities' in Euroland emphasized by Goodhart (1998: 3). This is not to suggest that Spain is the only Eurozone country where property market developments, in particular, have given rise to some concern. In fact, there are other examples where asset price developments seem to have decoupled from the real economy. And there are, of course, examples among the new EU members with even larger external imbalances. But Spain is of particular interest because with foreign exposures to private credit risks in Spain soaring the competitiveness channel is predicted to 'eventually become the dominating adjustment factor' (ECB 2005) while the nominal exchange rate can play no part in it.

In summary, sole reliance on the competitiveness channel, that is, on wage and price flexibility as well as structural reforms intended to enhance their flexibility, ignores important forces of divergence that not only tend to depress domestic demand in the deflating country. In addition, to the extent that its competitiveness actually improves, the deflating country's export success will come through spreading its problems to its trading partners, getting dragged down through their deteriorating export performance and/or experiencing the built-up of external imbalances; which will unravel at some point.[7]

The two key flaws in Europe's official flexibility doctrine featuring wage-price flexibility and the competitiveness channel may thus be pinpointed. One is to ignore Keynes's chapter 19 insight that wage flexibility essentially means monetary policy conducted by the trade unions. The other is to ignore that Mundell focused on the competitiveness channel specifically in the context of asymmetric shocks.

As to the first flaw, recall Keynes's conclusion in chapter 19 that money wage flexibility may be both less effective as well as riskier than stable wage inflation combined with deliberate stabilizing monetary policies by a competent central bank. The point is that downward wage flexibility effectively works through forcing expansionary monetary policy upon the central bank; apart from whatever net exports pull this strategy might elicit through the competitiveness channel. The trouble is that this may not work for a large economy with a slow central bank, either because the economy slips into deflation before the central bank dares to act or because factors other than wages keep up inflation and thereby forestall monetary easing.

The latter case describes developments in the Eurozone as a whole where the budgetary consequences of stagnation led to a sizeable upward distortion in headline inflation as finance ministers raised indirect taxes and administered prices in view of their ongoing struggle with the SGP. Bibow (2006) identified the resulting 'tax-push' inflation as a symptom of ill-guided macroeconomic policies that have caused macroeconomic instability in the Eurozone as a whole. The value added of the analysis in this chapter was to investigate the forces of divergence at work when a large member country like Germany follows the flexibility prescription. The point is that the competitiveness channel is not the only channel at work and that in large economies the overall effect may be to destabilize the deflating economy, in addition to spreading domestic problems to partners and causing divergence within the union.

As to the second flaw, it should not be forgotten that Mundell's OCA was about asymmetric shocks that resulted in demand imbalances while overall effective demand was sufficient. For there is no denying that the '2001 global slowdown' was in the nature of a common shock – a shock which required a common response boosting depressed overall demand. In such a situation reliance on the competitiveness channel does not foster a mutually beneficial rebalancing of overall demand, but represents a 'beggar-thy-neighbour' policy plain and simple.[8] Only that the policy's intricate workings may not be so plain and simple, owing to the complex forces of divergence involved in the process. *It was only through the working of these forces of divergence within the framework of the Maastricht regime that the originally symmetric shock attained its asymmetric characteristics as well.*

## Concluding observations and proposals for reform

The analysis in this chapter has identified important forces of divergence that are inherent in the working of the Maastricht regime of EMU. Featuring the supposedly equilibrating role of wage and price flexibility, it is shown that detrimental effects are to be expected both for larger countries relying on their working and the union as a whole. The official flexibility doctrine therefore offers misguided advice in stressing the role of the competitiveness channel in rebalancing divergence in economic activity and persistent inflation differentials as experienced across the Eurozone since 2001. This advice ignores fundamental insights of Keynes and Mundell.

For the Eurozone as a whole Keynes taught us that downward wage flexibility can only work through inducing timely and well-measured monetary easing; which is anathema to the 'stability-oriented' mindset and approach ruling at the ECB. Otherwise this strategy is a risky one as it can lead to either stagflation (as occurred since 2001) or even outright deflation. For a large economy like Germany's, for instance, downward wage and price flexibility triggers powerful adverse domestic channels that can for long over-compensate the competitiveness channel, fostering fragility as well as divergence and the built-up of imbalances along the way instead.

No less important is the fact that Mundell stressed the competitiveness channel as rebalancing two countries that were hit by an *asymmetric* shock. By contrast, when the '2001 global slowdown' hit the

Eurozone, this was originally a symmetric or common shock that required a common policy response – which was not forthcoming. This policy failure occurred due to crucial flaws in the Maastricht regime – a failure that can not be rectified by then relying on the competitiveness channel instead. For in case of symmetric shocks the working of the competitiveness channel will not be of a mutually beneficial kind at all, but represent 'beggar-thy-neighbour' instead. This is a recipe not for rebalancing, but for undermining the euro. It is invoking what EMU was supposed to ban forever – competitive devaluations.

It thus reflects flawed thinking to assume that structural reforms are the answer to the current situation and to assert that a more flexible Eurozone economy might cope better with the same kind of shocks next time they occur. Union-wide downward wage flexibility raises the risk of deflation, a sure recipe for disaster in conjunction with a slow-to-ease central bank. If downward wage flexibility in Germany alone were enhanced, the forces analysed above might work faster – although with unclear ramifications! – but the 'beggar-thy-neighbour' character of the strategy would not change. At best, enhanced two-way [sic!] wage-price flexibility might speed up the rebalancing of countries through the competitiveness channel in a mutually beneficial way in response to properly *asymmetric* shocks of the demand-shift type, although the forces of divergence operative within the Maastricht regime that were identified above remain relevant even then.

The bottom line is that micro flexibility is no substitute for proper aggregate demand management and that structural reform of markets are no substitute for reforming the flawed Maastricht regime of EMU. The Maastricht regime fosters divergence as well as instability. The latter problem arises because no one is keeping the domestic demand store – unless the ECB chooses to do so. And the former problem is bound to even worsen with and reinforce aggregate instability, especially in case of ill-guided reliance on the competitiveness channel as a substitute for appropriately designed policies addressing, as the case may be, common shocks and/or asymmetric shocks and divergence.

Apart from the macro regime reforms I suggested elsewhere (Bibow 2003), I recommend that wage inflation in the larger countries needs to be aligned, both for their own good as well as in view of the sustainability of EMU. By coordinated effort a stable long-run (4–5 per cent) trend of wage inflation should be established, with persistent divergence in productivity trends and external imbalances justifying deviations from the established wage norm. For smaller countries the situation is somewhat different because in their case (due to a greater degree of openness) the competitiveness channel might dominate the domestic channel (with its inherent forces of divergence) even in the short run.[9] Yet, while wage-price flexibility can play a stabilizing role in their case, there should be safeguards in place against using this route in a free-riding way – that is, at the expense of partners. Again, external positions might provide guidance on tolerable deviations from the wage norm.

Finally, throughout the analysis the important fact was ignored that the Eurozone is part of an increasingly integrated global economy. So let me add here that it is clearly not advisable for the second largest economic area on this globe to rely on the competitiveness channel, especially in view of mounting global imbalances (Kregel 1999). Until today, a favourable global environment has helped to offset the Maastricht regime's deflationary bias. The real test will come when the Eurozone can no longer 'freeload' on external stimuli. A serious risk is that a US slowdown will prompt US dollar depreciation. A rising euro together with falling oil prices can have a strongly deflationary impact. Whether this will boost domestic demand sufficiently enough to offset any external demand weakness, as some seem to hope, remains to be seen.

## Notes

1. Apart from energy, food, alcohol and tobacco, this measure of core inflation also excludes the (approximated) price effects of 'tax-push', i.e. hikes in indirect taxes and administered prices. See Bibow (2006).
2. See De Grauwe and Mongelli (2005) for an overview of OCA.
3. On the design of the Maastricht regime and critiques thereof see: Allsopp and Vines (1998), Bibow (2001), Dyson and Featherstone (1999), and Tietmeyer (1991).
4. In fact, Spain's finance minister Pedro Solbes plans tax cuts for 2007 in the order of magnitude of 0.5 per cent of GDP – the 'magic number' the same man asked 'SGP sinners' like stagnant Germany to at least impose on their economies in his previous life as EU Commissioner. See *Financial Times Deutschland*, 25 January 2006.
5. And to the extent that business investment have picked up since 2004 this was concentrated in the export-oriented sectors, too (Loose and Ludwig 2005).
6. A popular – but thoroughly confused – view holds that Italy, in particular, still has to go through the wage deflation Germany has already accomplished. Of course internal imbalances can also be dealt with by raising the German wage level accordingly (instead of deutschmark revaluations as in the old days). Neither course will do anything to address the aggregate demand deficiency in the Eurozone.

7. Nonetheless many observers today appear to be even surprised that the 'eurozone fails to match Germany's revival' (FT.com, 1 February 2006).
8. Whereas Mundell (1961) focused on asymmetric (demand-shift) shocks, Friedman's (1953) case for flexible exchange rates was inspired by the idea that this would free macro policy to focus on internal balance; following Keynes (1923) of course.
9. The 'Dutch miracle' of the 1980s and 90s is a case in point here; although a miracle ending in boom and bust as the bigger neighbor retaliated by wage deflation. See also Fritsche *et al.* (1999) and Hein and Truger (2005).

## References


Allsopp, C. and Vines, D. (1998) 'The Assessment: Macroeconomic Policy after EMU', *Oxford Review of Economic Policy*, 14(3): 1–23.

Arestis, P. and Sawyer, M. (2001) *The Euro: Evolution and Prospects* (Aldershot: Edward Elgar).

Bibow, J. (2001) 'Making EMU Work: Some Lessons from the 1990s', *International Review of Applied Economics*, 15(3): 233–59.

Bibow, J. (2003) *Is Europe Doomed to Stagnation?* Working Paper No. 379, Levy Economics Institute.

Bibow, J. (2005) 'Germany in Crisis: The Unification Challenge, Macroeconomic Policy Shocks and Traditions, and EMU', *International Review of Applied Economics*, 19(1): 29–50.

Bibow, J. (2006) *Inflation Persistence and Tax-push Inflation in Germany and the Euro Area: A Symptom of Macroeconomic Mismanagement?*, IMK Studies 1/2006.

De Grauwe, P. and Mongelli, F.P. (2005) *Endogeneities of Optimum Currency Areas: What Brings Countries Sharing a Single Currency Closer Together?*, ECB Working Paper Series No. 468, April.

Dyson, K. and Featherstone, K. (1999) *The Road to Maastricht: Negotiating EMU* (New York: Oxford University Press).

ECB (2004) *Inflation Differentials in the Euro Area: Potential Causes and Policy Implications*, Working Paper No. 388, September. http://www.ecb.int/pub/pdf/scpwps/ecbwp388.pdf.

ECB (2005) 'Monetary Policy and Inflation Differentials in a Heterogeneous Currency Area', *Monthly Bulletin*, May: 61–77.

Financial Times Deutschland (2006) Kritik an Madrids Steuergeschenk, written by K. Finkenzeller and S. Dullien, 25 January, p. 16.

Friedman, M. (1953) 'The Case for Flexible Exchange Rates', in M. Friedman (ed.), *Essays in Positive Economics* (Chicago: Chicago University Press).

Fritsche, U. *et al.* (1999) 'Is There a Need for a Co-ordinated European Wage and Labour Market Policy?', in G. Huemer, M. Mesch, M. and F. Traxler (eds), *The Role of Employer Associations and Labour Unions in the EMU* (Aldershot: Ashgate).

FT.com 2006. 'Eurozone Fails to Match Germany's Industrial Revival' (R. Atkins), February 1.

Goodhart, C.A.E. (1998) 'The Two Concepts of Money: Implications for the Analysis of Optimal Currency Areas', *European Journal of Political Economy*, 14: 407–32.

Hein, E. and Truger, A. (2005) 'European Monetary Union: Nominal Convergence, Real Divergence and Slow Growth?', *Structural Change and Economic Dynamics,* 16: 7–33.

Keynes, J.M. (1923) *A Tract on Monetary Reform* (London: Macmillan).

Keynes, J.M. (1936) *The General Theory of Employment, Interest and Money* (London: Macmillan).

Kregel, J. (1999) 'Can EMU Combine Price Stability with Employment and Income Growth?', *Eastern Economic Journal,* 25(1): 35–47.

Loose, B. and Ludwig, U. (2005) 'Deutschland nach dem Boomjahr 2000: Gespaltene Konjunktur – Gespaltenes Investitionsverhalten', *Wirtschaft im Wandel,* 12: 367, Wirtschaftsforschungsinstitut Halle.

Mongelli, F. (2002) *'New' Views on the Optimum Currency Area Theory: What is EMU Telling Us?,* ECB Working Paper Series, No. 138, April.

Mundell, R.A. (1961) 'A Theory of Optimum Currency Areas', *American Economic Review,* 51: 657–75.

OECD (2004) *Euro Area Survey* (Paris: OECD).

Tietmeyer, H. (1991) 'The Role of an Independent Central Bank in Europe', in P. Downes and R. Vaez-Zadeh (eds), *The Evolving Role of Central Banks* (Washington, DC: IMF).

WSJE (2002) 'Duisenberg Defends Holding Rates Steady', 9 October (T. Sims and B.A. Grow).

# 12
# Germany's Post-2000 Stagnation in the European Context – a Lesson in Macroeconomic Mismanagement

*Eckhard Hein and Achim Truger*

## Introduction

Since the mid-1990s Germany's economic performance with respect to GDP growth, the development of unemployment and also the budget deficit has been considerably worse than the Euro area average (Hein and Truger 2005a, 2005b). However, this relative economic weakness might have gone almost unnoticed if it had not been for the slowdown of the world economy after 2000. By the end of 2002 it had become obvious that Germany had been hit much harder by this slowdown and did not manage to recover. For the first time unemployment rose above the Euro area average and the budget deficit exceeded the 3 per cent limit of the European Stability and Growth Pact (SGP).

Now, more than five years after the beginning of the slowdown – and perhaps on the verge of an uncertain recovery – the whole extent of the German crisis can be evaluated: Real GDP growth more or less stagnated from late 2001 to 2003. 2004 then saw a mild recovery with a growth rate of 1.6 per cent, but in 2005 growth faltered again and fell to below 1 per cent. Unemployment rose to its post-war maximum. The budget deficit, though still not excessively high by international standards, has been increasing despite strong consolidation efforts since 2001. In 2005 it has exceeded the 3 per cent (of GDP) deficit limit of the Maastricht Treaty and the Stability and Growth Pact (SGP) for the fourth time in four consecutive years.

The economic crisis had serious consequences both for the economic policy debate and also for economic policy itself. The debate that had been biased by a Monetarist/new classical or simple supply-side view became even more radical. For most of the German – and to some extent also the international – mainstream economists, journalists and business lobbyists Germany seemed stuck in a deep 'structural' crisis caused by tightly regulated labour markets and an overly generous welfare state. In their view the long duration of the stagnation excluded demand-side factors as an explanation. Therefore, they recommended radical 'structural' reforms, i.e. a large-scale deregulation of the labour market, a dismantling of the welfare state, together with an accelerated policy of fiscal consolidation by means of public expenditure cuts.

The proponents of radical reforms have been politically successful: Six months after the beginning of the red-green government's second term, Chancellor Schroeder's 'AGENDA 2010' presented in March 2003 was the turning point towards the implementation of far reaching structural reforms to overcome the (perceived) institutional sclerosis (Schroeder 2003). Above all the duration and the level of unemployment benefits have been drastically reduced by 2005 ('Hartz IV' laws). And in November 2005 the newly elected grand coalition government, formed by the conservative party (CDU) and the social democrats (SPD) under Chancellor Angela Merkel, has made it very clear that it is determined to continue the way of 'structural' reforms and to tighten fiscal policy even further (Coalition Contract 2005).

In this chapter we question the mainstream diagnosis as well as the prescribed remedies. We show that the underlying 'institutional sclerosis' view of Germany's stagnation is unfounded and that, therefore, the political measures proposed and actually taken are misguided. Instead, we claim that macroeconomic mismanagement explains Germany's absolute and relative stagnation compared with the Euro area as a whole and with the USA. If the problem of macroeconomic mismanagement is not addressed and solved, irrespective occasional cyclical upswings, we predict a continuing stagnation tendency for the German economy. And we argue that this is not only a German problem, but a matter of European concern: The macroeconomic policies which have caused the German constellation might have major negative feedback effects on the other Euro area countries in the near future.

The chapter is organized as follows. The second section presents the facts to be explained, namely the different economic performances of Germany, the Euro area as a whole and the USA after the economic slowdown in 2000/2001. The third section sketches 'institutional sclerosis' and a lack of 'structural reforms' as the dominant mainstream explanation and shows that it cannot be reconciled with the standard empirical indicators for institutional sclerosis. The fourth section presents our macroeconomic policy explanation and demonstrates that macroeconomic mismanagement of the post-2000 slowdown is the key to understand the prolonged German stagnation. The final section concludes and gives some economic policy conclusions and a rather pessimistic outlook.

## Germany's stagnation since 2000/2001

During the recent years the Euro area as a whole has been facing serious economic problems and has been faring considerably worse than the USA.[1] But in comparison to the Euro area as a whole Germany's performance has been even worse since the mid-1990s, and Germany was hit much harder by the economic slowdown in 2000/2001 (Table 12.1). During the period 2001–2005 average annual GDP growth in Germany has amounted to only 0.7 per cent which was only half of the Euro area growth of 1.4 per cent.

In contrast to the entire Euro area, Germany's weak growth is completely driven by export surpluses. The contribution of domestic demand to GDP growth has been negative on average over this period. Whereas

*Table 12.1* Real GDP growth, growth contributions of demand aggregates, unemployment rate and inflation rate, in Germany, the Euro area and the USA, average values for 2001–2005*

| | *Germany* | *Euro area* | *USA* |
|---|---|---|---|
| Real GDP, annual growth rate (per cent) | 0.7 | 1.4 | 2.6 |
| Growth contribution of domestic demand including stocks (percentage points) | –0.3 | 1.3 | 3.0 |
| Growth contribution of private consumption (percentage points) | 0.2 | 0.8 | 2.2 |
| Growth contribution of public consumption (percentage points) | 0.0 | 0.3 | 0.5 |
| Growth contribution of gross fixed capital formation (percentage points) | –0.4 | 0.1 | 0.4 |
| Growth contribution of balance of goods and services (percentage points) | 1.0 | 0.1 | –0.5 |
| Employment, annual growth (per cent) | –0.1 | 0.8 | 0.7 |
| Unemployment rate (per cent) | 8.7 | 8.5 | 5.4 |
| Inflation rate (Germany, Euro area: HICP, USA: national ICP) (per cent) | 1.6 | 2.2 | 2.5 |

*Notes*: *Forecast values for 2005.

*Source*: European Commission (2005), OECD (2005a), authors' calculations.

private and public consumption in real terms have almost stagnated during the period 2001–2005, private and public investment have decreased and have contributed negatively to GDP growth. Without the huge growth contribution of export surpluses, which amounted to one percentage point per year on average, Germany would not only have faced a period of stagnation but would have suffered from a deep recession. Taken together, Germany's economy has performed very well on international markets and has gained considerable export surpluses in the period 2001–2005, but has suffered from weak domestic demand.

Between 2001 and 2005, GDP growth in the Euro area has been higher than in Germany but more than one percentage point per year below US growth. The growth contribution of external demand is positive but low. The USA has done well after the recession of 2000/1 and seems to have returned to the growth path of the second half of the 1990s. It is relying completely on domestic demand with external demand contributing negatively to real GDP growth. As in the 1990s, US investors and, in particular, US consumers, supported by public expenditures on investment and consumption, are again the world demand locomotive.[2]

Because of weak growth, German employment has even shrunken during the period 2001–2005, whereas employment in the Euro area and in the USA has increased by 0.8 and 0.7 per cent per year. Therefore, German unemployment, which had always been below the Euro area average until 2002, now exceeds this average. The unemployment rate in the Euro area is still more than 3 percentage points higher than in the USA. Inflation in Germany is well below the Euro area average, as it has been since the mid 1990s. And Euro area inflation is slightly below US inflation.

Taken together, the development following the 2000/1 growth slowdown has made clear that Germany, the former key currency country of the European Monetary System (EMS) has indeed become 'Europe's sick man'. This is not associated with a loss of international competitiveness but rather with stagnating domestic demand.

## The mainstream interpretation: lack of structural reforms

For most of the German – and to a somewhat lesser extent also the international – economics profession, the analysis of the German growth and employment problem is clear and simple: Institutional sclerosis, i.e. rigid and over-regulated labour markets and too generous welfare state institutions have driven Germany into crisis.[3] We have argued elsewhere (Hein and Truger 2005a, 2005b) that the institutional sclerosis view in general suffers from serious deficiencies with respect to both its theoretical as well as its empirical foundations. What is even more important in the particular German case is that the empirical conditions for deriving an institutional sclerosis explanation of its absolute and relative economic weakness are hardly ever verified.

In order to convincingly apply the institutional sclerosis explanation to Germany's current economic crisis it would have to be shown that German labour market and welfare state institutions have taken an unfavourable path, both over time and in international comparison. The supposed 'lack of reforms' should be observable somewhere in the data. As we have demonstrated in greater detail elsewhere (Hein and Truger 2005a, 2005b), using the set of six institutional indicators usually applied in this kind of analysis (index of employment protection, benefit replacement rate, benefit duration, union density, bargaining coordination and tax wedge) from Baker *et al.* (2004), this is not the case. Table 12.2 presents the most important results for our present purpose in a nutshell. It shows the total indicator of institutional sclerosis for Germany, the OECD, the European Union, the Euro area and the United States which we calculated from the set of six single indicators for the first half of the 1980s and the second half of the 1990s. Higher values indicate higher levels of institutional sclerosis. Focusing first on Germany alone, it can easily be seen that within the covered 20 year period, it has succeeded in reducing its institutional sclerosis by about 5 percentage points. Obviously, in contrast to popular wisdom, there has been considerable reform activity. This becomes even more striking in international comparison, where Germany seems to have outperformed the OECD, EU, Euro area and the US with respect to reform activity: The average total indicator for the OECD, the EU and the US has been reduced by only 2 percentage points, the Euro area average has even risen by 1 percentage point. Starting from above average values, by the end of the 1990s Germany has managed to bring down its level of institutional sclerosis to the average EU level and even below the Euro area average. Of course it still cannot 'compete' with the free-market USA.

Although there is no complete data set comparable to that of Baker *et al.* (2004) for the more recent past, there are strong indications that there has been no reversal of the reform trend in Germany. The analysis by Mabbett and Schelkle (2005) on the basis of the Fondazione Rodolfo Debenedetti Social Reforms Data Base (Fondazione 2005) shows that, at least in the case of employment protection legislation

*Table 12.2* Total indicator of institutional sclerosis,* 1980–1984 and 1995–1999

| | *1980–84* | *1995–99* |
|---|---|---|
| Germany | 57 | 52 |
| OECD[1] | 49 | 47 |
| European Union[2] | 53 | 52 |
| Euro area[2] | 52 | 53 |
| USA | 20 | 18 |

*Notes*: *Arithmetic mean of six single indicators for employment protection legislation, benefit replacement rate, benefit duration, union density, bargaining coordination and the tax wedge previously scaled to the interval [0; 100]. An exact definition and a documentation of the origin of the data is given by Nickell *et al.* (2002) and Baker *et al.* (2004). A more detailed presentation of the German data in international comparison is given in Hein and Truger (2005a).

[1] Australia, Austria, Belgium, Canada, Denmark, Finland, France, Germany, Ireland, Italy, Japan, Netherlands, New Zealand, Norway, Portugal, Spain, Sweden, Switzerland, United Kingdom, USA.

[2] Excluding Greece and Luxembourg.

*Source*: Baker *et al.* (2004), authors' calculations.

and the system of unemployment benefits, the earlier reform trend has continued until 2002. Table 12.3 displays indicators summarizing the intensity of welfare state reform with respect to employment protection and unemployment benefits for 14 EU countries in the period 1986–2002 divided into two sub-periods. Positive (negative) values indicate a decrease (increase) in institutional sclerosis. As can easily be seen, Germany had a rather 'bad start' during the first sub-period 1986–1994, when welfare state institutions slightly 'worsened', whereas most of the other countries 'improved' them by small amounts. However, in the second period (1995–2002) Germany 'improved' its welfare state institutions by 17 points – more than any other country except for the Netherlands.

We can conclude: In comparison with the Euro area average the indicators prove that Germany is less sclerotic and has shown above-average efforts to improve its structural conditions in the recent past.

## Another view: macroeconomic mismanagement

In order to provide a macroeconomic policy explanation for Germany's recent stagnation, it has to be shown that since 2001 monetary, fiscal and wage policies for Germany have indeed been less favourable than for the Euro area average or for the USA (Table 12.4).[4]

*Table 12.3* Intensity of welfare state reform[1] in 14 EU countries

| | *1987–1994* | *1995–2002* | *1987–2002* |
|---|---|---|---|
| Austria | –1 | 13 | 12 |
| Belgium | 5 | 7 | 12 |
| Denmark | 4 | 10 | 14 |
| Finland | 4 | 16 | 20 |
| France | –3 | –12 | –15 |
| Germany | –2 | 17 | 15 |
| Greece | 0 | 9 | 9 |
| Ireland | 5 | 3 | 8 |
| Italy | 1 | 13 | 14 |
| Netherlands | 2 | 24 | 26 |
| Portugal | 0 | –3 | –3 |
| Spain | 5 | 0 | 5 |
| Sweden | 4 | 15 | 19 |
| United Kingdom | 5 | 5 | 10 |

*Notes*: [1] Sum of the two single reform intensity values assigned by Mabbett and Schelkle (2005), i.e. the sum of reform intensity values of reform measures in employment protection and non-employment benefits for each country in the relevant period, on the basis of the Fondazione Rodolfo Debenedetti Social Reforms database (Fondazione 2005). A plus indicates 'increasing flexibility' (making systems less protective or generous). A minus indicates 'decreasing flexibility' (making systems more protective or generous). Mabbett and Schelkle (2005) measure the intensity of any reform package by assigning a value of ±1 to reform measures the database classifies as 'marginal' and ±2 to those classified as 'structural'. Reform packages containing a series of measures get an intensity value of 2 if they contain two or more marginal measures and an additional 2 for including a structural measure (so ±4 is the maximum for the intensity of any one reform package, ±2 if it contains only marginal measures).

*Sources*: Fondazione (2005), Mabbett and Schelkle (2005), authors' calculations.

## Monetary policy

Monetary policy will be assessed by the development of the short-term real interest rate. It is now widely accepted that modern central banks use the short-term nominal interest rate as an economic policy instrument. But if central banks target inflation they have to set nominal interest rates with an eye to the ensuing real rate, as proposed, for example, in the famous Taylor rule (Taylor 1993). In order to take into account the underlying economic situation, we consult the differences between both short- and long-term real interest rates and real GDP growth. We expect a negative influence of real interest rates on economic growth working through different transmission channels (money, credit, asset prices, exchange rates) (Bernanke and Gertler 1995; Cecchetti 1995).

*Table 12.4* Indicators for monetary, wage and fiscal policies in Germany, the Euro area, and the USA, 2001–2005*

| | *Germany* | *Euro area* | *USA* |
|---|---|---|---|
| *Monetary policy* | | | |
| Short-term real interest rate (per cent) | 1.2 | 0.6 | –0.2 |
| Long-term real interest rate (per cent) | 2.6 | 2.1 | 1.9 |
| Short-term real interest rate minus real GDP growth (percentage points) | 0.5 | –0.8 | –2.7 |
| Long-term real interest rate minus real GDP growth (percentage points) | 1.9 | 0.7 | –0.7 |
| *Fiscal policy* | | | |
| Budget balance (per cent of GDP) | –3.6 | –2.6 | –3.5 |
| Cyclically adjusted budget balance (per cent of cyclical adjusted GDP), annual change, percentage points | –0.1 | –0.1 | –0.9 |
| Output gap (per cent of cyclical adjusted GDP), annual change (percentage points) | –0.8 | –0.6 | –0.3 |
| Number of years with pro-cyclical fiscal policy during an economic slowdown | 3 (2003–5) | 3 (2003–5) | 0 |
| Negative fiscal stimulus in economic slowdown, cumulated (per cent of potential GDP) | 1.1 | 0.5 | — |
| *Wage policy* | | | |
| Nominal compensation per employee, annual growth (per cent) | 1.7 | 2.5 | 4.0 |
| Nominal unit labour costs, annual growth (per cent) | 0.3 | 1.7 | 1.7 |
| Labour income share (per cent)[1] | 58.1 | 58.0 | 62.6 |
| Change in labour income share to previous year (percentage points) | –0.5 | –0.2 | –0.4 |

*Notes*: *Forecast values for 2005, [1] compensation per employee divided by GDP at current market prices per person employed.

*Sources*: European Commission (2005), OECD (2005a), authors' calculations.

With respect to monetary policies, Germany has lost its former status as the key currency country within the European Monetary System (EMS) at the start of the European Monetary Union (EMU) in 1999. Since then it has no longer been in a position to reap the advantages of lower interest rates it used to have compared to the other EMS countries. During the process of convergence these countries gained from a considerable decrease of short- and long-term nominal interest rates towards the lower German level. The decrease in nominal interest rates was associated with a stronger decrease in real interest rates for the other Euro area countries than for Germany over the 1990s. This has been conducive to relative growth in these countries and has established a more favourable real interest rate–real GDP growth relationship compared to Germany since the mid-1990s (Figure 12.1). In the USA monetary policies have even been more conducive to growth with a negative short-term interest rate–real GDP growth difference almost throughout since the early 1990s.

As the German inflation rate has been lower than the Euro area average and the nominal interest rates have almost completely converged since 1999, Germany's real interest rates have even been higher than the Euro area average since then. On average over the period 2001–2005 the ECB policies generated a short-term real interest rate of 1.2 per cent in Germany which was now twice as high as in the Euro area as a whole with 0.6 per cent (Table 12.4). Whereas the Euro area short-term real interest rate was positive on average over the period after the 2000/1 growth slowdown, the Federal Reserve managed to

*Figure 12.1* Short-term real interest rate minus real GDP growth in Germany, the Euro area and the USA, 1992–2005 (percentage points)

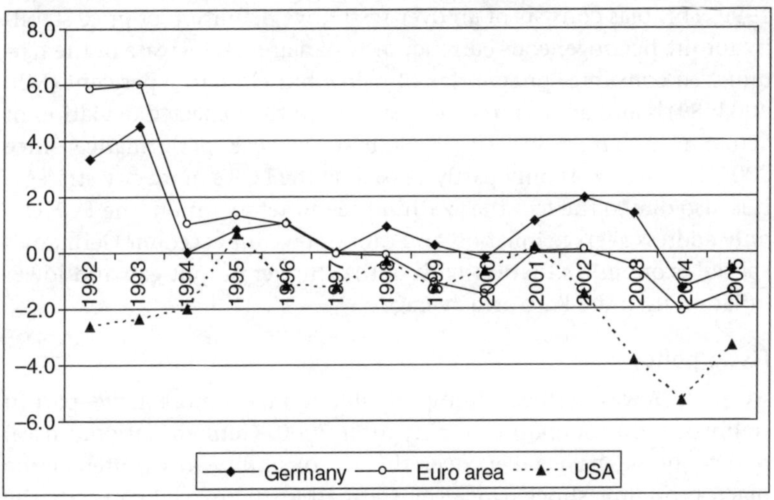


*Source:* European Commission (2005), OECD (2005a), authors' calculations.

establish a negative short-term real interest rate of –0.2 per cent in the USA. These expansionary monetary policies contributed to the quick recovery of the US economy. Already in 2002 the USA saw again – as in the years before 2001 – a negative short-term real interest rate–real GDP growth rate-difference, whereas in the Euro area this difference became negative only in 2003 and in Germany only in 2004 (Figure 12.1). On average over the recent years, the Fed established a favourable short-term real interest rate–real GDP growth difference (–2.7 percentage points), and also a growth-friendly long-term real interest rate–real GDP growth constellation (–0.7 percentage points). The ECB has been much more reluctant to stimulate the economy by means of cutting interest rates in the face of the 2000/1 slowdown and has thereby contributed to weak growth in the Euro area, and particularly in Germany since then. Whereas on average over the period 2001–2005 in the Euro area as a whole the short-term real interest rate–real GDP growth-difference has been at least slightly negative (–0.8 percentage points), in Germany this difference has even been positive (0.5 percentage points). And the long-term real interest rate-real GDP growth-difference has been positive in the Euro area as whole (0.7 percentage points) with the German value (1.9 percentage points) exceeding the Euro area average by a considerable amount.

Therefore, Germany has not only suffered from European monetary integration losing the interest rate advantage it had enjoyed before, but it has also particularly suffered from the ECB's 'anti-growth bias' since 1999. This bias consists of an over-restrictive definition of price stability for the heterogeneous currency area – an annual increase of the harmonized consumer price index of below but close to 2 per cent (ECB 2003: 89) – and an asymmetric response to the expected deviation of actual from target inflation.[5] Germany's weak performance since 2000/1, however, is only partly caused by the ECB's monetary strategy. It is also due to the fact that within the monetary union, the ECB can only address average inflation and cannot take into account Germany's special economic situation with both a higher output gap and lower inflation than the Euro area average.

## Fiscal policy

As the ECB was neither willing nor able to take a more active part in stabilizing the German economy after 2000, German national fiscal policy should have taken over the responsibility to counteract the macroeconomic shock. However, German fiscal policy did exactly the opposite by switching to a policy of pro-cyclical budget consolidation, thereby further worsening the crisis. The German budget deficit over the period 2001–2005 has averaged 3.6 per cent of GDP (Table 12.4), leading many professional observers to believe that fiscal policy was useless, because permanently 'high' deficits seemingly have been unable to make the German economy recover. However, such reasoning is obviously simplistic. It ignores the fact that high or even growing deficits may well be the result of an economic slump rather than an indicator of active fiscal policy.

The extent to which fiscal policy exerts a stabilizing or destabilizing influence on the business cycle can be assessed by comparing changes in the output gap and the cyclically adjusted budget balance–potential GDP ratio (CBR).[6] The output gap serves as an indicator of the current state of economic activity. If it is positive, then capacity is outstripped, if it is negative, this means that capacity is not fully utilized. Consequently, a positive change in the output gap indicates a cyclical upturn, whereas a negative change points to a cyclical downturn. If there is a positive (negative) change in the CBR, then structural deficits fall (rise) or structural surpluses rise (fall), and fiscal policy provides a restrictive (expansive) stimulus to demand. If the CBR remains constant when there is a change in the output gap, then fiscal policy is neither expansive nor restrictive and the automatic stabilizers are simply left to take effect.

Measured in this way, German fiscal policy from 2001 to 2005 has been restrictive in three years in the face of a slowdown in economic activity, destabilizing the economy and pro-cyclically worsening the crisis. The cumulative negative fiscal stimulus from this pro-cyclical policy amounted to 1.1 per cent of potential GDP over the whole period, acting as a substantial brake for the recovery. For the Euro area as a whole fiscal policy was pro-cyclically restrictive, too. However, the negative fiscal stimulus amounted to only 0.5 per cent. So, despite the fact that the economic slowdown was considerably worse in Germany than in the Euro area as a whole (0.8 percentage points average annual fall in the output gap as compared to 0.6 percentage points in the Euro area), German fiscal policy was more restrictive. In striking contrast to the European practice, US fiscal policy has been a strong countercyclical stabilizer: During the observation period there was not a single year in which US fiscal policy reduced the CBR in the face of an economic slowdown. Quite the opposite, it boosted the US economy by reducing the CBR by 0.9 percentage points of potential GDP on average over the last five years. In both the Euro area and Germany the stimulus was only 0.1 percentage points on average.[7]

The restrictive and destabilizing impact of German fiscal policy becomes even more obvious if one considers the growth rates of some fiscal policy aggregates in more detail (Table 12.5). Public expenditure growth has been weak, all the relevant numbers being far below average real GDP growth of 0.7 per cent. Real total public expenditure actually declined by an annual average of –0.2 per cent. Real public final consumption stagnated and public investment declined dramatically by an annual 3.7 per cent leading to an historically low average share of public investment in GDP of only 1.5 per cent (1.3 per cent in 2005). The latter development is particularly distressing as public investment is not only an essential component of aggregate demand in the short run, but also a provider of public infrastructure making it a key condition for growth in the long run. Expenditure growth has not only been weak in absolute terms but also in comparison with the Euro area and the USA. The corresponding average expenditure growth rates for the Euro area are in the range between 1.4 and 1.8 per cent and therefore rather well in line with or even slightly above-average real GDP growth. The same is true for the USA where all the relevant expenditure growth rates are above 3 per cent. In both the USA and the Euro area with an average 2.7[8] and 2.5 per cent of GDP respectively the level of public investment is much higher than in Germany.

Another striking feature of German fiscal policy over the last five years has been the remarkable decrease of real total public revenue by 1.4 per cent per year, whereas both the Euro area and the US have had at least a slow positive revenue growth. In the absence of any tax policy

*Table 12.5* Annual growth rates of selected fiscal policy aggregates in Germany, the Euro area, and the USA, average values, 2001–2005* (percentages)

| | *Germany* | *Euro area* | *USA* |
|---|---|---|---|
| Real total government expenditure[1] | –0.2 | 1.4 | 3.6 |
| Real government final consumption expenditure | 0.0 | 1.8 | 3.1 |
| Real government gross fixed capital formation[2] | –3.7 | 1.5 | 3.1 |
| Real government total revenue[1] | –1.4 | 0.6 | 0.3 |
| Gross fixed government capital formation (percentage of GDP) | 1.5 | 2.5 | 2.7 |

*Notes*: *Forecast values for 2005; [1]deflated with the (harmonized) consumer price index; [2]deflated with the deflator of total fixed capital formation.

*Sources*: European Commission (2005), authors' calculations.

measures one would expect the revenue side to be growing somewhat faster than GDP due to a progressive tax system. It should be noted that there is a link between fiscal policy and wage policy through the revenue generation process of the tax system. In Germany the process of revenue generation and, therefore, also the process of fiscal consolidation has been harmed by the extremely moderate wage development owing to the progressive tax system and also to the fact that the German social security system is mainly financed by wage based contributions.

Apart from such effects, the weak development of revenue in Germany and also the USA reflects the effects of the substantial tax cuts by the former red-green government in Germany (Truger and Jacoby 2004) and by the Bush Administration in the USA. For Germany, however, this means that the small average expansionary effects of fiscal policy have almost exclusively come from the revenue side through tax cuts, while the expenditure side has been on a tight restrictive path. If one takes into account the fact that the usual empirical estimates for expenditure multipliers are about double the size of the tax multipliers (Arestis and Sawyer 2003), the German policy of fiscal consolidation additionally destabilized the economy by its particularly ill designed and counterproductive structure.

## Wage policy

Wage policies can be assessed by nominal wage growth (compensation per employee), unit labour cost growth and the labour income share. Nominal wage setting affects unit labour cost growth and inflation. If nominal wages increase at a faster pace than productivity plus the price level do, unit labour cost growth and inflation will speed up.[9] This will cause real interest rates to fall and may make the central bank increase nominal interest rates in order to reach its inflation target. If nominal wages increase at a rate below the sum of productivity growth and inflation, unit labour cost growth will slow down and cause disinflation. Finally, deflation may be the consequence. Deflation causes increasing real interest rates and rising real debts with potentially negative effects on investment and growth.[10] If deflationary processes have started, monetary policies lowering interest rates may be ineffective.

Wage policies, however, may not only affect prices, but may also change distribution if firms do not completely pass unit labour cost variations to prices or if prices of other inputs do not change in step with unit labour costs (Hein, Schulten and Truger 2006). Under these conditions, nominal wage moderation causes the labour income share to fall. Hypothetically, the effects of income shares on GDP growth are ambiguous (Bhaduri and Marglin 1990). With the propensity to save out of wages falling short of the saving propensity out of profits, a falling labour income share means a cutback in consumption demand and capacity utilization with directly contractive effects on investment and GDP growth. On the other hand, a fall in labour income shares that is associated with nominal wage restraint will improve international competitiveness and, therefore, stimulate demand for exports, investment and growth. With a slowdown in inflation, the central bank may also cut interest rates and stimulate investment and growth. Finally, a falling labour income share is associated with rising unit profits which may also improve investment and growth.

Since the stimulating effects of wage moderation and declining labour income shares for investment and growth are rather indirect and uncertain, in particular in large and rather closed economies, the direct and contractive effects will dominate presumably. And since nominal wage increases, which will shift distribution in favour of labour income, will also trigger inflation and concomitant restrictive central bank interventions, nominal wage growth according to the sum of long-run productivity growth and the central bank's inflation target, and hence roughly constant labour income shares, should be generally favourable conditions for growth and employment in large and rather closed economies.

Germany's overly moderate nominal wage increases are the major cause for the below-average inflation rate. Since 1995 unit labour cost growth in Germany has undercut the Euro area average (Hein, Schulten and Truger 2006). This is due to overly moderate wage development in Germany. On average over the period 2001–2005 nominal compensation per employee has only increased by 1.7 per cent per year (Table 12.4). Taking into account inflation (Table 12.1), this means that real compensation per employee has stagnated in Germany since 2001. In the Euro area as a whole nominal compensation per employee has increased at a faster pace (2.5 per cent per year) and real compensation has at least slightly increased (0.3 per cent per year). The USA has witnessed a much higher average rate of increase of nominal compensation per employee (4.0 per cent) and also of real compensation per employee (1.5 per cent). Because of overly moderate wage increases nominal unit labour cost growth in Germany has on average between 2001–2005 amounted to 0.3 per cent, whereas the Euro area as a whole, as well as the USA, have seen an average annual increase of 1.7 per cent.

Slower unit labour cost growth and lower inflation in Germany were also observed before European monetary integration when Germany's

*Table 12.6* Unit labour costs and inflation in Germany and the Euro area, 2001–2005

| | *2001* | *2002* | *2003* | *2004* | *2005* |
|---|---|---|---|---|---|
| *Germany* | | | | | |
| 1. Compensation per employee hour, annual increase (per cent) | 2.4 | 2.1 | 1.9 | 0.0 | 0.8 |
| 2. Productivity per hour, annual increase (per cent) | 1.8 | 1.5 | 1.2 | 0.9 | 1.5 |
| 3. Nominal unit labour cost growth (per cent) | 0.6 | 0.6 | 0.6 | –0.8 | –0.7 |
| 4. Market-determined core inflation[1] (per cent) | 0.7 | 1.3 | 0.5 | 0.8 | 0.3 |
| 5. Inflation rate (HICP) (per cent) | 1.9 | 1.3 | 1.1 | 1.7 | 2.0[2] |
| *Euro area* | | | | | |
| 1. Compensation per employee, annual increase (per cent) | 2.7 | 2.5 | 2.3 | 2.0 | 1.5[3] |
| 2. Productivity per employee, annual increase (per cent) | 0.5 | 0.2 | 0.5 | 1.1 | 0.5[3] |
| 3. Nominal unit labour cost growth (per cent) | 2.3 | 2.2 | 1.8 | 0.9 | 1.1[3] |
| 4. Market determined core inflation[1] (per cent) | 1.7 | 2.2 | 1.6 | 1.3 | 1.1 |
| 5. Inflation rate (HICP) (per cent) | 2.3 | 2.3 | 2.1 | 2.1 | 2.2[2] |

*Notes*: [1]without energy, food, alcohol, tobacco and administered prices according to Bibow (2006a), [2]European Commission (2005) forecast, [3]average of first 2 quarters.

*Sources*: Bibow (2006a), ECB (2005), European Commission (2005), Statistisches Bundesamt (2006), authors' calculations.

absolute and relative economic performance was much better (Hein and Truger 2005a, 2005b). But then unit labour cost growth and the resulting low inflation rates were the basis for the deutschmark's status as the regional key currency within the EMS, allowing the German Bundesbank to set substantially lower nominal and actually real interest rates than in the other EMS countries. Since the beginning of the interest rate convergence process in the mid 1990s and with the completion of Euro area in 1999, however, lower inflation rates for Germany do no longer pay off in terms of lower interest rates.

High unemployment, weak trade union bargaining power, the erosion of the German wage bargaining system, and the recent labour market reforms (AGENDA 2010, 'Hartz'-laws) have recently increased the risk of deflation for the German economy.[11] Unit labour cost growth has been negative in 2004 and 2005. This has not yet triggered actual deflation due to increasing import prices (crude oil and oil derivatives) and to increasing administered prices.[12] But it has certainly increased deflationary risks if we take a look at the development of the market determined core inflation (Table 12.6). This risk threatens to spread to the Euro area as a whole. Here nominal unit labour cost growth has come down to around 1 per cent in 2004 and 2005, and the market determined core inflation has also declined to close to 1 per cent in 2005. Of course, this development is dominated by Germany as the largest Euro area economy. But German wage restraint, increasing German competitiveness relative to the other Euro area countries and hence rising German export surpluses with the rest of the Euro area will increase the pressure on the other Euro area countries to reduce wage costs, too. And since the competitive price advantage which German producers have gained during the recent decade would be maintained even if unit labour costs in Germany and the rest of the Euro area would now start to move in

*Figure 12.2* Labour income share in Germany, the Euro area and the USA, 1992–2005

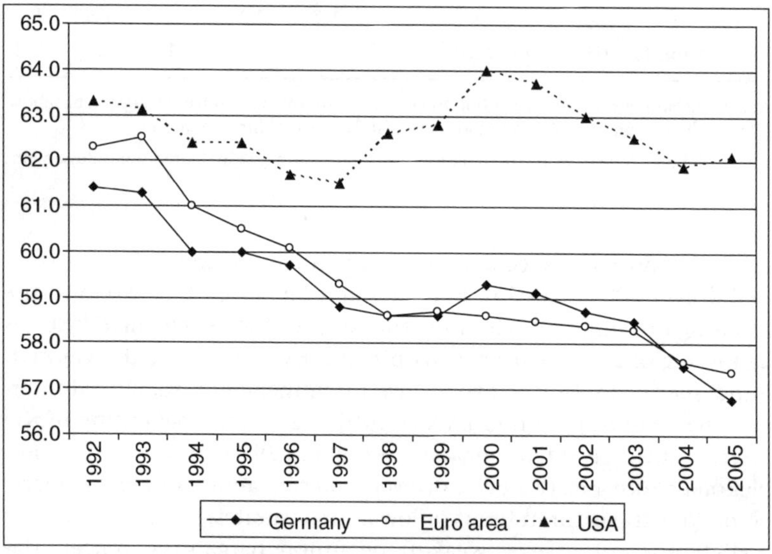


*Source*: European Commission (2005).

*Table 12.7* Current account balances as a percentage of GDP in Euro area countries and the USA, 2001–2005

| | *2001* | *2002* | *2003* | *2004* | *2005* |
|---|---|---|---|---|---|
| Germany | 0.2 | 2.3 | 2.2 | 3.8 | 4.1 |
| France | 1.6 | 0.9 | 0.4 | –0.4 | –1.6 |
| Italy | –0.1 | –0.8 | –1.3 | –0.9 | –1.5 |
| Spain | –3.9 | –3.3 | –3.6 | –5.3 | –7.7 |
| Austria | –1.9 | 0.3 | –0.5 | 0.3 | –0.4 |
| Belgium | 3.4 | 4.6 | 4.1 | 3.3 | 1.4 |
| Finland | 7.2 | 7.6 | 3.8 | 5.3 | 3.5 |
| Greece | –8.1 | –7.5 | –7.2 | –6.3 | –7.0 |
| Ireland | –0.6 | –1.0 | 0.0 | –0.8 | –1.5 |
| Netherlands | 2.4 | 2.9 | 2.8 | 3.3 | 5.8 |
| Portugal | –8.4 | –8.0 | –0.9 | –3.6 | –6.7 |
| Euro area | 0.1 | 0.7 | 0.3 | 0.5 | –0.2 |
| USA | –3.8 | –4.5 | –4.7 | –5.7 | –6.5 |

*Source*: OECD (2005a).

step, this pressure will continue and deflationary risks for the Euro area will inevitably have to increase.

The overly moderate wage setting in Germany did not only cause below average inflation rates. This wage policy also contributed to the acceleration of a tendency of declining labour income shares which had already started in the early 1980s and continued during the 1990s (Figure 12.2). This redistribution at the expense of labour has contributed to the weak development of domestic demand and hence to Germany's weak performance – in particular, since 2001 when the labour income share declined by 0.5 percentage points per annum. However, a declining labour income share trend can also be witnessed in the Euro area as a whole, but not in the USA since the early 1990s, so that on average over the period 2001–2005 the labour income share in the USA (62.6 per cent) exceeded the labour income share in the Euro area (58.0 per cent) and in Germany (58.1 per cent) by more than 4 percentage points. Redistribution at the expense of labour can hence only add to the explanation of Germany's *relative* performance compared with the USA but not compared with the rest of the Euro area.

On the other hand, moderate wage policies in Germany have improved the price competitiveness and profitability of German firms which made German export surpluses almost quadruple between 2001 and 2005. But this extraordinary export performance was insufficient to compensate for the associated deficiencies in domestic demand, as has been shown above (Table 12.1). And since more than 40 per cent of German exports go to the Euro area, increasing German export surpluses cause major problems for the other Euro area countries: Whereas Germany has continuously increased its current account surplus, amounting to 4.1 per cent of GDP in 2005, the other larger Euro area countries (France, Italy, Spain) are increasingly driven into current account deficits (Table 12.7). Some of the smaller countries either see their surpluses decline (Belgium, Finland) or are not allowed to improve their huge deficits (Greece, Portugal).

### A restrictive macroeconomic policy mix in Germany

In sum, macroeconomic policy variables have indeed been less favourable in Germany than in the Euro area as a whole and in the USA since 2001, as had already been the case since the mid-1990s (Hein and Truger 2005a, 2005b). Macroeconomic mismanagement, therefore, can be considered to be the main cause of Germany's stagnation. This is partly due to the integration of a former key currency country into a monetary union and the associated loss of the interest rate advantage, and is hence inevitable. But it is also caused by the restrictive macroeconomic policy mix implemented at the Euro area level, which is particularly affecting a slowly growing low-inflation country like Germany: the overly restrictive ECB monetary policy strategy and the SGP enforcing a restrictive stance on the member countries' fiscal policies. A major contribution to macroeconomic mismanagement has come from German wage developments, which seem to be completely inappropriate for the largest economy in a monetary union.

## Economic policy conclusions

Since the main cause for Germany's absolute and relative stagnation can be found in macroeconomic mismanagement, the economic policy recommendations seem to be quite straightforward: apply more expansive monetary and fiscal policies and stabilizing wage policies. However, such an approach faces serious institutional problems associated with the Maastricht economic policy regime dominating the Euro area: the ECB's monetary policy strategy and practice displaying a serious 'anti-growth' bias, the SGP imposing a restrictive fiscal stance on the Euro area, and the focus on labour market deregulation which systematically undermines the ability of bargaining parties to establish wage settlements with an eye to macroeconomic requirements.[13] Under these conditions, the combination of a pronounced trend towards stagnation and significant deflation risks caused by overly moderate wage developments in the largest Euro area country represents a major challenge:

First, reduction of deflation risks and nominal stabilization in Germany requires nominal wage growth to rise in order to achieve the sum of long-term productivity growth plus the ECB's target inflation rate. However, given the deterioration of the German wage bargaining system and the weak bargaining position of the trade unions, an increase in nominal wage and unit labour cost growth requires improved employment and higher GDP growth as a precondition. But more expansive macroeconomic policies at the national level generating more employment are difficult to achieve given the restrictions by the Euro area policy mix, i.e. the ECB policies and the SGP.

Secondly, even if German trade unions – assisted by more expansive fiscal and monetary policies – managed to increase nominal wage und unit labour cost growth, and if inflation in Germany rose, such a rise would lead to a Euro area inflation rate above the ECB's target as long as other Euro area countries have inflation rates considerably above that target rate. Restrictive monetary policies will then be unavoidable if the ECB is not prepared to increase its inflation target substantially in order to allow the slowly growing larger economies more room to achieve a recovery.

Thirdly, if the ECB is not prepared to raise its inflation target, it will be necessary to reduce inflation in the other Euro area countries in order to allow Germany to have more inflation. It is therefore important for the bargaining parties and in particular the trade unions to intensify their efforts towards European-level effective coordination of wage policies. The aim of this process should be for each country to increase wages on the basis of its long-term domestic productivity growth rates plus the ECB's target inflation rate.[14] There are, however, major obstacles for wage bargaining coordination across Europe arising from the different degrees of coordination within the national bargaining systems, from the overall weakness of trade unions in the larger Euro area countries, from the tendency towards decentralization of bargaining imposed by labour market policies, etc. In addition, reducing inflation in the rapidly growing high inflation Euro area countries would mean higher real interest rates and lower growth for these countries.

If it proves impossible either to convince the ECB to raise its inflation target or to coordinate wage policies across the Euro area in the way described above, even more expansive fiscal policies would have to be undermined by restrictive ECB policies. Under these conditions Germany's stagnation and deflation risks will continue to spread to the other Euro area countries. Excessive wage restraint in Germany will not only fuel national economic stagnation but will also increase the already existing pressure on wage policies in the other Euro area countries. If wage policies are widely used to protect or improve price competitiveness, then further redistribution at the expense of labour, rising effective demand problems and the threat of deflation will spread accordingly. If this happens, then even a more growth-friendly monetary policy by the ECB might be ineffective when in the next cyclical downturn the deflation risks become actual deflation – in Germany but perhaps also in the Euro area as a whole, with serious consequences for the economic and political future of the Euro area.

## Notes

1. See Hein and Niechoj (2007) and Hein and Truger (2005a, 2005b) for a detailed analysis of the long-run trends and the macroeconomic policy causes for the differences between the countries or currency areas referred to above.
2. The willingness of the USA to spend beyond their means has been a welcomed source of world demand and has contributed to a quick recovery of the world economy from the 2000/1 growth slowdown. But the associated world imbalances, in particular the enormous US current account deficit and the rising indebtedness of US private households, question the sustainability of this constellation. See for a discussion Godley *et al.* (2005) and Papadimitriou *et al.* (2005, 2006).
3. See, for instance, the annual reports of the German council of economic experts (SVR 2004, 2005), the majority view in the semi-annual joint reports of the leading economic research institutes in Germany (Institute 2004, 2005) and, in particular, an economic policy paper by the German central bank (Deutsche Bundesbank 2003). The OECD and IMF reports on the German and European economy also aim at structural reforms (IMF 2006, OECD 2004, 2005a). The same is true for the European Commission (2002).
4. See Hein and Truger (2005a) for the discussion of some theoretical foundations of macroeconomic policy coordination as a key to growth and employment from New Keynesian and, in particular, Post Keynesian perspectives. For the limitations and problems associated with the New Keynesian and the New Consensus models seen from a Kaleckian/Post Keynesian perspective see Hein (2006b).
5. The ECB has tended to tighten whenever inflation increased above the target without relaxing when inflation expectations came down. For a general critique of the ECB's 'anti-growth bias' see Bibow (2002, 2005a, 2005b) and Hein (2002).

6. Of course, such cyclically adjusted measures can be criticized for a number of theoretical and empirical reasons and should therefore be interpreted with great care. Theoretically, they are very close to the idea embedded in the standard NAIRU models that there is a long-run equilibrium determined by structural characteristics of the labour market which is independent of the short-run fluctuations generated by demand shocks or macroeconomic policy. We do not share this view (Hein 2002, 2006a). Empirically, these measures are very sensitive to the exact method used and to the choice of observation period. Despite these serious problems with the measures we consider them as useful. Even more: If it can be shown that certain empirical findings about the stabilising or destabilising effects of fiscal policy can be derived even within such a mainstream framework, then this strengthens the point from a heterodox perspective. Of course, the results for a given set of countries and a given time period should be more or less robust to the method used and to additional observations due to new data over time. In order to ensure the first, in this chapter we undertook some sensitivity analysis with regard to different methods. With respect to the latter most of the results have proven to be very robust to new data, because we conducted this kind of analysis with almost every new edition of the OECD Economic Outlook data since 2001 (Hein, Muelhaupt and Truger 2001; Hein and Truger 2005a, 2005b, 2005c, 2005d; Truger and Hein 2002).
7. Our results have been derived using the cyclically adjusted data and output gaps estimated by the OECD (2005a). As these estimates are considerably different from the two alternative estimates published by the European Commission (2005) based on a potential and a trend approach for Germany and the Euro area (there is no estimate for the USA), we checked whether our results still hold for these data. Qualitatively the results do hold, only the number of years with destabilising fiscal policy is reduced from three to two and the extent of the negative cumulative fiscal stimuli for both Germany and the Euro area are considerably lower.
8. In some of the earlier papers which we authored or one of us co-authored (Hein and Truger 2005d; Hein and Niechoj 2007) we displayed a substantially higher share of public investment for the USA well above 3 per cent. The difference is exclusively due to different data sources. The OECD Economic Outlook used in the earlier papers has data received from the BEA (OECD 2005b: 70). The European Commission data we used for this chapter subtracts the item 'gross investment national defence' from the primary US data, and adds it to government final consumption, hence the difference. This also has a visible effect on the growth rates of public consumption and investment calculated in Table 12.4. With the OECD data the growth rate of public investment would be higher by about 0.4 percentage points, those of public consumption would be lower by about 0.3 percentage points. We are grateful to Antonis Avdoulos and Noël Doyle from the European Commission for the statistical information.
9. See Arestis and Sawyer (2005) and Hein (2006a) for recent Post Keynesian models of distribution conflict and inflation.
10. See Hein (2006a, 2006b) for the integration of real debt effects into Kaleckian models of distribution and growth with conflict inflation.

11. See the IMF (2003) on deflation risks in Germany. For a more extensive discussion of deflation risks in Germany and the Euro area see Hein, Schulten and Truger (2006).
12. See Bibow (2006a, 2006b) on the relevance of tax-push inflation in Germany and other European countries.
13. On the Maastricht economic policy regime and European macroeconomic policies see the more extensive treatment in Hein and Truger (2005c, 2005d). On the interaction of the ECB's monetary policy with wage bargaining in Europe see Hein (2002).
14. For more detailed information on the various trade union coordination initiatives see Schulten (2003, 2004) and Traxler and Mehrmet (2003).

## References

Arestis, P. and Sawyer, M. (2003) 'Reinventing Fiscal Policy', *Journal of Post Keynesian Economics*, 26: 3–25.

Arestis, P. and Sawyer, M. (2005) 'Aggregate Demand, Conflict and Capacity in the Inflationary Process', *Cambridge Journal of Economics*, 29: 959–74.

Baker, D., Glyn, A., Howell, D. and Schmitt, J. (2004) 'Labour Market Institutions and Unemployment: A Critical Assessment of the Cross-Country Evidence', in D.R. Howell (ed.), *Fighting Unemployment: The Limits of the Free Market Orthodoxy* (Oxford: Oxford University Press).

Bernanke, B. and Gertler, M. (1995) 'Inside the Black Box: The Credit Channel of Monetary Policy Transmission', *Journal of Economic Perspectives*, 9: 27–48.

Bhaduri, A. and Marglin, S. (1990) 'Unemployment and the Real Wage: The Economic Basis for Contesting Political Ideologies', *Cambridge Journal of Economics*, 14: 375–93.

Bibow, J. (2002) 'The Monetary Policies of the European Central Bank and Euro's (Mal)performance: A Stability-oriented Assessment', *International Review of Applied Economics*, 16: 31–50.

Bibow, J. (2005a) *Europe's Quest for Monetary Stability: Central Banking Gone Astray*, The Levy Economics Institute of Bard College, Working Paper No. 428.

Bibow, J. (2005b) *Bad for Euroland, Worse for Germany – the ECB's Record*, The Levy Economics Institute of Bard College, Working Paper No. 429.

Bibow, J. (2006a) *Preistreiber Staat: Zur Inflationspersistenz im Euroraum*, IMK Report, 6/2006, Macroeconomic Policy Institute (IMK) in the Hans Boeckler Foundation, Duesseldorf.

Bibow, J. (2006b) *Inflation Persistence and Tax-push Inflation in Germany and in the Euro Area: A Symptom of Macroeconomic Mismanagement?*, IMK Studies, 1/2006, Macroeconomic Policy Institute (IMK) in the Hans Boeckler Foundation, Duesseldorf.

Cecchetti, S.G. (1995) 'Distinguishing Theories of the Monetary Transmission Mechanism', *Federal Reserve Bank of St. Louis Review*, 77(3): 83–97.

Coalition Contract (2005) *Gemeinsam für Deutschland – mit Mut und Menschlichkeit*, Koalitionsvertrag zwischen CDU, CSU und SPD vom 11.11.2005, Berlin.

Deutsche Bundesbank (2003) *Wege aus der Krise – Wirtschaftspolitische Denkanstöße für Deutschland* (Frankfurt: Deutsche Bundesbank).

ECB (2003) 'The Outcome of the ECB's Evaluation of its Monetary Policy Strategy', *Monthly Bulletin*, June: 79–92.

ECB (2006) *Monthly Bulletin*, January.

European Commission (2002) *Germany's Growth Performance in the 1990's*, Economic Paper No. 170, Mai 2002 (Brussels: European Commission, Directorate General for Economic and Financial Affairs).

European Commission (2005) *Annual Macro-economic Database* (AMECO), December 2005, http://europa.eu.int/comm/economy_finance/indicators/annual_macro_economic_database/ameco_en.htm.

Fondazione (2005) *The Fondazione Rodolfo Debenedetti Social Reforms Database*, http://www.frdb.org/documentazione/centro_doc.php.

Godley, W., Papadimitrou, D.B., Dos Santos, C.H. and Zezza, C. (2005) *The United States and Her Creditors, Can the Symbiosis Last?*, The Levy Economics Institute of Bard College, Strategic Analysis, September.

Hein, E. (2002) 'Monetary Policy and Wage Bargaining in the EMU: Restrictive ECB Policies, High Unemployment, Nominal Wage Restraint and Inflation above the Target', *Banca Nazionale del Lavoro Quarterly Review*, 55: 299–337.

Hein, E. (2006a) 'Wage Bargaining and Monetary Policy in a Kaleckian Monetary Distribution and Growth Model: Trying to Make Sense of the NAIRU', *Intervention. Journal of Economics*, 3: 305–29.

Hein, E. (2006b) 'On the (In-)stability and the Endogeneity of the "Normal" Rate of Capacity Utilisation in a Post-Keynesian/Kaleckian "Monetary" Distribution and Growth Model', *Indian Development Review*, 4: 129–50.

Hein, E., Muelhaupt, B. and Truger, A. (2001) 'WSI-Standortbericht 2001: Eine makroökonomische Perspektive', *WSI Mitteilungen*, 54: 351–8.

Hein, E. and Niechoj, T. (2007) 'Guidelines for Sustained Growth in the EU? The Concept and the Consequences of the Broad Economic Policy Guidelines', in J. McCombie and C. Rodriguez (eds), *Institutions, Public Policy and Governance* (Basingstoke: Palgrave Macmillan), forthcoming.

Hein, E., Schulten, T. and Truger, A. (2006) 'Deflation Risks in Germany and the EMU: The Role of Wages and Wage Bargaining', in E. Hein, A. Heise and A. Truger (eds), *The European Union: Current Problems and Prospects* (Basingstoke: Palgrave Macmillan).

Hein, E. and Truger, A. (2005a) 'What Ever Happened to Germany? Is the Decline of the Former European Key Currency Country Caused by Structural Sclerosis or by Macroeconomic Mismanagement?', *International Review of Applied Economics*, 19: 3–28.

Hein, E. and Truger, A. (2005b) 'A Different View of Germany's Stagnation', *Challenge. The Magazine of Economic Affairs*, 48 (6): 64–94.

Hein, E. and Truger, A. (2005c) 'European Monetary Union: Nominal Convergence, real Divergence and Slow Growth?', *Structural Change and Economic Dynamics*, 16: 7–33.

Hein, E. and Truger, A. (2005d) 'Macroeconomic Coordination as an Economic Policy Concept – Opportunities and Obstacles in the EMU', in E. Hein, T. Nichoj, T. Schulten and A. Truger (eds), *Macroeconomic Policy Coordination in Europe and the Role of the Trade Unions* (Brussels: ETUI).

IMF (2003) *Deflation: Determinants, Risks and Policy Options – Findings of an Interdepartmental Task Force* (Washington, DC: IMF).

IMF (2006) *Germany: Selected Issues,* Country Report No. 06/17, http://www.imf.org/external/pubs/ft/scr/2006/cr0617.pdf.

Institute (2004) Arbeitsgemeinschaft deutscher wirtschaftswissenschaftlicher Forschungsinstitute, 'Die Lage der Weltwirtschaft und der deutschen Wirtschaft im Herbst 2004', *DIW Wochenbericht,* 43: 629–82.

Institute (2005) Arbeitsgemeinschaft deutscher wirtschaftswissenschaftlicher Forschungsinstitute, 'Die Lage der Weltwirtschaft und der deutschen Wirtschaft im Herbst 2005', *DIW Wochenbericht,* 43: 605–55.

Mabbett, D. and Schelkle, W. (2005) *Bringing Macroeconomics Back into the Political Economy of Reform: the Lisbon Agenda and the 'Fiscal Philosophy' of EMU,* mimeo.

Nickell, S., Nunziata, L., Ochel, W. and Quintini, G. (2002) *The Beveridge Curve, Unemployment and Wages in the OECD from the 1960s to the 1990s,* Centre for Economic Performance, Discussion Paper 502 (Version May 2002) (London: London School of Economics and Political Science).

OECD (2004) *Economic Survey – Germany 2004* (Paris: OECD).

OECD (2005a) *Economic Outlook,* No. 78, December 2005, http://www.oecd.org/document/61/0,2340,en_2649_201185_2483901_1_1_1_1,00.html.

OECD (2005b) *The Economic Outlook Database Inventory,* http://www.oecd.org/dataoecd/47/9/2742733.pdf

Palley, T. (1998) 'Restoring Prosperity: Why the U.S. Model is not the Answer for the United States or Europe', *Journal of Post Keynesian Economics,* 20: 337–52.

Papadimitriou, D.P., Shaikh, A.M., Dos Santos, C.H. and Zezza, G. (2005) *How Fragile is the U.S. Economy*?, The Levy Economics Institute of Bard College, Strategic Analysis, March.

Papadimitriou, D.P., Chilcote, E. and Zezza, G. (2006) *Are housing prices, household debt, and growth sustainable?,* The Levy Economics Institute of Bard College, Strategic Analysis, January.

Schroeder, G. (2003) 'Niemand darf sich künftig zu Lasten der Gemeinschaft zurücklehnen', *Frankfurter Rundschau,* 15.3.2003: 7.

Schulten, T. (2003) 'Europeanization of Collective Bargaining: Trade Union Initiatives for the Transnational Coordination of Collective Bargaining', in H.-W. Platzer and B. Keller (eds), *Industrial Relations and European Integration: Trans- and Supranational Developments and Prospects* (Aldershot: Ashgate).

Schulten, T. (2004) *Solidarische Lohnpolitik in Europa. Zur Politischen Oekonomie der Gewerkschaften* (Hamburg: VSA).

Statistisches Bundesamt (2006) *Volkswirtschaftliche Gesamtrechnungen, Inlandsproduktsberechnung, Erste Jahresergebnisse 2005,* Fachserie 18, Reihe 1.1 (Wiesbaden: Statistisches Bundesamt).

SVR (2004) Sachverständigenrat zur Begutachtung der gesamtwirtschaftlichen Entwicklung, *Jahresgutachten 2004/2005, Erfolge im Ausland – Herausforderungen im Inland* (Berlin), http://www.sachverstaendigenrat-wirtschaft.de/gutacht/ga-content.php?gaid=40&node=f.

SVR (2005) Sachverständigenrat zur Begutachtung der gesamtwirtschaftlichen Entwicklung, *Jahresgutachten 2005/2006, Die Chance nutzen – Reformen mutig vorantreiben* (Berlin), http://www.sachverstaendigenrat-wirtschaft.de/gutacht/ga-content.php?gaid=45&node=f.
Taylor, J.B. (1993) 'Discretion versus Policy Rules in Practice', *Carnegie Rochester Conference Series on Public Policy*, 39: 195–214.
Traxler, F., Mehrmet, E. (2003) 'Coordination of Collective Bargaining: The Case of Europe', *Transfer. European Review of Labour and Research*, 9: 229–46.
Truger, A. and Hein, E. (2002) '"Schlusslicht Deutschland" – Makroökonomische Ursachen', *Wirtschaftsdienst*, 82: 402–10.
Truger, A. and Jacoby, W. (2004) 'Tax Reforms and "Modell Deutschland" – Lessons from Four Years of Red-Green Tax Policy', in J. Sperling (ed.), *Germany at 55: Berlin is not Bonn* (Manchester: Manchester University Press).

# 13

# Macroeconomic Policy in the UK under New Labour: The End of Boom and Bust?

*Philip Arestis and Malcolm Sawyer*

## Introduction

The Labour government elected in May 1997 came into office stressing that it was 'New Labour' and pursuing a 'third way'. In macroeconomic terms, the emphasis was on the avoidance of 'tax and spend' policies and restraints on public expenditure along with the adoption of the so-called 'golden rule' of public finances (as discussed below). There was something akin to a disavowal of a Keynesian approach to macroeconomic policies and specifically the use of fiscal policy to help steer the economy. There was an emphasis on labour market reforms and flexibility, which would, in effect, lower the 'non-accelerating rate of unemployment' and thereby lower unemployment. Whereas previous Labour governments had pursued a range of industrial and regional development policies to stimulate economic growth and lower unemployment, there was a major shift from those policies to those of labour (and to some degree product) market 'flexibility'.

This approach was reflected in New Labour's belief in a 'flexible labour market that serves employers and employees alike' (Labour Party 1997); also that

> The more our welfare to work reforms allow the long-term unemployed to re-enter the active labour market, the more it will be possible to reduce unemployment without increasing inflationary pressures. And the more our tax and benefit reforms remove unnecessary barriers to work, and the more our structural reforms promote the skills for work, the more it is possible to envisage long-term increases in employment, without the fuelling of inflationary pressures. (Brown 1999: 10)

Furthermore,

> The sustainable rate of unemployment, or NAIRU, is believed to have risen in the UK during the 1970s and 1980s, but there is broad agreement that this increase has been partly reversed since the late 1980s. Although the magnitude of any fall is very difficult to estimate, most estimates of the current level of the NAIRU lie in the range of 6 to 8 per cent on the LFS measure of unemployment. However, considerably lower levels should be achievable in the long run through re-integrating the long-term unemployed back into the labour market, upgrading skills, and reforming the tax and benefit systems to promote work incentives. (Treasury 1997: 82)

However, the idea of a fixed natural rate of unemployment consistent with stable inflation was discredited by the evidence of the 1980s, presumably on the grounds that unemployment and the estimates of the natural rate moved higher during the 1980s. In effect, 'the new government has taken a decisively different approach to employment policy over the past two years aimed at reducing the NAIRU' (Brown 1999: 10).

This chapter seeks a preliminary evaluation of the effects of the macroeconomic policies, which emerged from the 'third way', and whether they have delivered growth and stability. The chapter first considers (rather briefly) macroeconomic performance under the Labour government since 1997. It then considers the nature of fiscal and monetary policy since 1997, and the effects which those policies may have had on macroeconomic performance. The next section considers the performance in terms of unemployment and the final main section considers the question of whether Gordon Brown, Chancellor of the Exchequer throughout the period, has been a lucky chancellor in terms of whether the relatively good macroeconomic performance since 1997 can be ascribed to his policies or to the general national and global macroeconomic environment.

## Recent macroeconomic performance

Table 13.1 summarizes some of the aspects of recent macroeconomic performance. In growth terms, GDP has grown at an average annual rate of 2.8 per cent over the period 1997–2005, slightly above the presumed trend rate of growth. In the preceding seven years the average had been 2.05 per cent, but that included the recession years of 1990/91 (not included in Table 13.1); over the previous five years of

*Table 13.1* Summary macroeconomic data (percentage)

| | *Real GDP growth rate* | *Inflation rate* | *Unemployment rate (claimant count)* | *Unemployment rate (ILO)* |
|---|---|---|---|---|
| 1992 | 0.28 | 3.76 | 9.18 | |
| 1993 | 2.43 | 1.57 | 9.80 | 10.38 |
| 1994 | 4.41 | 2.49 | 8.88 | 9.50 |
| 1995 | 2.85 | 3.41 | 7.63 | 8.63 |
| 1996 | 2.73 | 2.41 | 6.95 | 8.05 |
| 1997 | 3.16 | 3.16 | 5.30 | 6.95 |
| 1998 | 3.24 | 3.42 | 4.50 | 6.25 |
| 1999 | 3.03 | 1.51 | 4.13 | 6.05 |
| 2000 | 4.03 | 2.97 | 3.58 | 5.45 |
| 2001 | 2.22 | 1.78 | 3.18 | 5.08 |
| 2002 | 2.00 | 1.69 | 3.08 | 5.18 |
| 2003 | 2.52 | 2.90 | 2.98 | 5.03 |
| 2004 | 3.12 | 2.98 | 2.75 | 4.75 |
| 2005 | 1.80 | 2.84 | 2.75 | 5.0 |

*Source*: Calculated from Economic Trends Annual Supplement and Economic Trends (June 2006).

1992 to 1997 the average growth rate was 2.9 per cent. Growth has been relatively stable, and in particular there has been no period of negative growth, whereas in the preceding quarter of a century there had been three recessions (1974/5, 1980/1, 1990/1). Inflation has remained low and consistently met the Chancellor's target of 2 per cent plus or minus 1 per cent.[1] Unemployment fell continuously from 1993 until 2005, but has been rising over the past 15 months to reach a four-year high in May 2006.

Figures such as those in Table 13.1 are used to support the view that macroeconomic performance in the past decade or so has been rather good – in the phrase used by the governor of the Bank of England, Meryvn King, the 'NICE' decade – 'Non-Inflationary Continuous Expansion'. The government and Chancellor, amongst others, have strongly promoted the idea that macroeconomic performance, in terms of the level (e.g. of inflation, growth) and variability ('stability'), has been particularly good. Recent endorsements have come from the OECD and IMF. For example, in their report on the UK, the OECD writes that:

> Macroeconomic performance over the last decade has been a paragon of stability: GDP growth has remained closer to potential than

> for almost any other OECD country; the unemployment rate has fallen to its lowest level and has been the least volatile since the 1970s; and inflation has remained stable and close to the official target. Perhaps most surprisingly, in the period since the current monetary and fiscal framework has been in place, not only has the effective exchange rate been more stable than at any time since the Bretton Woods period, but it is also among the most stable in the OECD and more stable than for the major euro area countries.

This performance is ascribed

> to the strength of the institutional arrangements for setting monetary and fiscal policy... as well as to the flexibility of labour and product markets. (OECD 2005b: 24)

It is, thus, argued that flexible labour and product markets have underpinned the recent impressive macroeconomic performance. Moreover, sectoral policies have not attempted to foster 'national champions'. The United Kingdom is among the leading countries in the OECD in terms of liberal product market regulation (OECD 2005b) and ranks highly in most aspects of labour market flexibility. Recent OECD work which constructed a composite policy indicator of flexibility ranked the United Kingdom the highest among all OECD countries. It also found cross-country evidence that this flexibility is important in facilitating growth in the service sector: 'One area where macroeconomic policy does, however, require attention is fiscal policy' (OECD 2005b: 34). We return to this below. The rest of the paper attempts to evaluate the contribution of macroeconomic policy to this performance, and specifically whether the policy regime introduced by the incoming Labour government in 1997 has made a major contribution.

## Fiscal policy

The Chancellor's Budget of March 2006 provides a recent summary of government's objectives and policy instruments.

> This Budget describes the next steps the Government is taking to enhance its long term goals of:
>
> - **maintaining macroeconomic stability**, ensuring the fiscal rules are met and that inflation remains low;

- **raising the sustainable rate of productivity growth**, through reforms that promote enterprise and competition, enhance flexibility and promote science, innovation and skills;
- **providing employment opportunity for all**, by promoting a flexible labour market which sustains a higher proportion of people in employment than ever before;
- **ensuring fairness**, by providing security for people when they need it, tackling child and pensioner poverty, providing opportunity for all children and young people and delivering security for all in retirement;
- **delivering world-class public services**, with extra investment alongside efficiency, reform and results; and
- **addressing environmental challenges**, such as climate change and the need for energy efficiency in response to rising oil prices. (Treasury 2006: 3, emphasis in original)

The six goals highlighted here provide a good summary of the objectives of the government as they see them, and in this chapter we pay particular attention to the first, third and fourth ones listed. The Treasury has argued that

> despite this [world] slowdown, the Government's macroeconomic framework has continued to deliver the UK's longest period of sustained and stable economic growth since records began fifty years ago. UK GDP has now expanded for 53 consecutive quarters. Moreover, the current economic expansion has now persisted for well over twice as long as the duration of the previous period of unbroken growth. (Treasury 2005: 3)

The operation of fiscal policy has been subject throughout the period to the operation of:

> – *the golden rule* – on average over the economic cycle, the Government will borrow only to invest and not to fund current spending; and, – *the sustainable investment rule* – the public sector net debt as a proportion of GDP will be held over the economic cycle at a stable and prudent level. (Treasury 1999: 19)

> The Government's primary objective for fiscal policy is to ensure sound public finances in the medium term. This means maintaining public sector net debt at a low and sustainable level. To meet the

> sustainable investment rule with confidence, net debt will be maintained below 40 per cent of GDP in each and every year of the current economic cycle. (Treasury 2005: 35)

This refers to public sector net debt: the figure calculated according to the Maastricht Treaty rules is around 6 to 7 per cent of GDP higher than 40 per cent.

In the 'golden rule' itself nothing is said on the extent of public investment, and hence of the extent of borrowing. But it is well known that an overall budget deficit to GDP ratio ($d$) would lead to debt to GDP ratio ($b$) stabilizing at: $b = d/g$, where $g$ is the nominal growth rate. Hence with a nominal growth rate of around 5 per cent (real growth of 2.5 per cent, inflation of 2.5 per cent say), a 40 per cent debt to GDP ratio would be consistent with a 2 per cent average budget deficit.

These fiscal rules are significantly less restrictive than those imposed on Euro area governments by the Stability and Growth Pact (SGP). An overall budget deficit of the order of 2 per cent of GDP as compared with the balanced budget or small surplus envisaged in the SGP. Further there is no upper limit placed on the size of budget deficit during a recession. As an aside it can be noted that the UK has been criticized by the European Commission (EC) for exceeding the 3 per cent figure:

> The European Commission will next week raise the chancellor's hackles by setting the Treasury a deadline of just 15 months to bring the government's budget deficit under control in a fresh row over Britain's deteriorating public finances... The strict deadline for bringing the deficit below the 3% limit set by the Maastricht treaty will be adopted by the commission on Wednesday. Brussels no longer believes the government's 'excessive' spending and borrowing is temporary. According to a draft recommendation circulating yesterday, 'the UK authorities should put an end to the present excessive deficit situation as soon as possible and by financial year 2006–2007 at the latest'. Britain, formerly hailed by the commission as a model of sustained growth and sound finances, is now being placed in the same camp as France and Germany, with the deficit expected to breach the 3% limit for four years in a row... The commission estimates that the deficit, which was 3.3% of GDP in 2003 and 3.2% in 2004, will have risen to 3.4% last year and will be 3.3% in 2006. It will decline to 3% in 2007, but still be above the Maastricht ceiling... The Treasury disputes the commission's

> estimates, arguing that the chancellor remains on course to meet his 'golden rule' over the economic cycle and that Britain has below-average levels of debt and deficit, with the bulk of increased borrowing designed for investment. (Gow 2006)

The OECD has commented that:

> Over the past few years, fiscal policy has moved from a significantly expansionary to a slightly contractionary stance. Nevertheless, the general government deficit, on a Maastricht basis, continues to exceed 3% of GDP and only a very gradual narrowing in the cyclically-adjusted deficit is expected by the OECD, so additional revenue or expenditure measures would be needed to reduce the deficit more quickly. In comparison, the official budget projections suggest that the deficit will narrow more rapidly, thanks to faster growth in corporate tax revenues than projected by the OECD. The government also estimates the cyclically-adjusted current budget deficit to be smaller than that of the OECD due to a larger output gap estimate. Whether or not the government meets the golden rule fiscal objective depends heavily on output gap estimates as well as on the dating of the business cycle, both of which are uncertain and vulnerable to data revisions. In the medium to longer-term, ageing-related spending pressures may point to the need for further fiscal consolidation combined with structural changes to the pension/benefit system. (OECD 2006: 119)

The magical 3 per cent figure (of the Stability and Growth Pact) has been exceeded at a time when the economy is relatively buoyant, though the output gap figures of the UK Treasury suggest that the economy is currently at the trough of the cycle (Treasury 2005). The OECD's measure of the output gap for the UK for 2005 is –0.5 per cent and forecast gap for 2006 of –0.8 per cent (OECD 2006).

It can first be noted that there is a notion here of a regular(ish) business cycle, and although it is not anywhere spelt out it would seem that the expectation is of a cycle of the order of 4 to 8 years in length. It can be seen that the 'golden rule' seeks to build in the notion of a balanced current budget position over the business cycle, which runs counter to the precepts of 'functional finance' which 'rejects completely the traditional doctrines of 'sound finance' and the principle of trying to balance the budget over a solar year or any other arbitrary period' (Lerner 1943: 355). There is a sense of viewing fiscal policy in passive terms as an 'automatic stabilizer', with budget surpluses emerging during the upswing and deficits in the downswing. Cyclically adjusted budget deficits are regularly calculated on such a basis in that adjustments are made to the actual budget deficit to allow for the effects on public expenditure and tax revenues of the difference between the actual level of economic activity and that, which would occur at a specified level of activity. One matter, which is not clearly laid out, is what is perceived to be the mechanism underlying the business cycle. If the cycle were driven by government expenditure, then deficits would appear in the upswing, and hence it must be presumed that the cycle is perceived to be driven by swings in private expenditure. The old-fashioned Keynesian-style explanation would come from an accelerator–multiplier type mechanism whereby the business cycle would be driven by investment demand. From the equation of $G - T = S - I + M - X$, fluctuations in investment (I) would impact on the budget position such that high levels of investment and low levels of savings would be associated with budget surpluses.

The Chancellor has recently argued that

> The Budget 2006 projections for the public finances are broadly in line with the 2005 Pre-Budget Report and show that the Government is meeting its strict fiscal rules:
>
> - the current budget shows an average surplus as a percentage of GDP over the current economic cycle, even using cautious assumptions, ensuring the Government is meeting the golden rule. Beyond the end of the current cycle, the current budget moves clearly into surplus including, by the end of the projection period, the cyclically-adjusted current budget in the cautious case; and
> - public sector net debt is projected to remain low and stable over the forecast period, stabilising at a level below the 40 per cent ceiling set in the sustainable investment rule. (Treasury 2006: 3)

From Table 13.2, it can be noticed that the current budget is projected to return to surplus from 2008/09 onwards. This return to surplus is based on two crucial assumptions. On the revenue side, tax receipts rise relative to GDP by around 2 percentage points between 2004/05 and 2006/07 and thereafter rise by 0.5 per cent through to 2010/11. On the expenditure side, it is based on real public expenditure rising at 1.9 per cent per annum from 2008/09 onwards, significantly below the trend rate of GDP growth (Treasury 2005: 213). The source of the revenue

*Table 13.2* Meeting the fiscal rules

| | *2004–2005* | *2005–2006* | *2006–2007* | *2007–2008* | *2008–2009* | *2009–2010* | *2010–2011* |
|---|---|---|---|---|---|---|---|
| **Golden rule** | | | | | | | |
| Surplus on current budget | –1.6 | –0.9 | –0.1 | 0.0 | 0.5 | 0.7 | 0.8 |
| Average surplus since 1997–1998 | 0.2 | 0.1 | 0.0 | 0.0 | 0.1 | 0.1 | 0.2 |
| Cyclically-adjusted surplus on current budget | –1.3 | –0.3 | 0.4 | 0.7 | 0.7 | 0.7 | 0.8 |
| **Sustainable investment rule** | | | | | | | |
| Public sector net debt | 35.0 | 36.4 | 37.5 | 38.1 | 38.3 | 38.4 | 38.4 |

*Note*: Outturn estimate projections (per cent of GDP).
Debt at end March; GDP centred on end March.

*Source*: Treasury (2006).

rises is not increased tax rates and comes from an assumed buoyancy of corporation tax and the success of anti-avoidance measures. The expenditure side suggests an intended squeeze, particularly when compared with the recent rises in public expenditure.

The presumed nature of the current business cycle is that (as measured by output gap) the cycle began during 1997/98, peaked during 2000/01 with a negative output gap from 2001/02 onwards, with an upswing forecasted for the next two to three years, with the output gap forecast to end in 2008/09. The forecast effects on the (current) budget deficit show that with the reduction of the output gap bringing the current budget position back into surplus such that broadly over the cycle from 1997/98 to 2008/09 the current budget position will have been in broad balance (Treasury 2006: Charts 2.5 and 2.6).

> Some slowdown is, however, to be welcomed, given signs of capacity constraints. OECD measures of the output gap, as well as those based on survey evidence, suggest the economy is operating at, or slightly above, capacity...; however, the government's view is that the economy retains some slack. (OECD 2005b: 26)

There has been much recent debate as to whether the 'golden rule' has been met and whether the present size of budget deficit at over 3 per cent of GDP is consistent with the future achievement of meeting the 'golden rule'. The argument is over how the budget deficits should be cumulated (e.g. in nominal or real terms and then summed, in percentage terms). More significantly has been the issue of the dating of the business cycle.

> If the deficit were not to improve in line with the official forecast, then adjustments to current plans may be needed to ensure that the Government meets its own fiscal rules. Meeting the government's 'golden rule' – that over the course of the cycle the public sector should only borrow to invest – depends on the timing of the cycle. Following substantial revisions to national accounts data the Treasury recently revised its judgment regarding the beginning of the current economic cycle; it now judges that the cycle began in the first half of 1997 rather than in mid-1999... Combining fiscal years 1997 and 1998 the government current budget was in surplus by the equivalent of 1% of GDP. If the cycle is judged to finish at the end of 2005 as assumed by the Treasury, then on OECD projections the average current balance over the cycle will be close to zero by the end of fiscal year 2005... On the other hand, if the current cycle has already finished (as suggested by OECD calculations) then the golden rule has already been met. (OECD 2005b: 30)
>
> Given that the margin by which the golden rule will be achieved (or not) over the past cycle is likely to be small, a binary 'success' or 'failure' judgment seems inappropriate. A more important implication of the OECD projections is that the persistence of a deficit on the current balance of around 1% of GDP suggests that action will be needed to avoid substantially missing the golden rule over the next cycle, as well as to significantly reduce the overall government deficit below 3% of GDP. (OECD 2005b: 31)

The historic record on budget deficits and debt is given in Table 13.3. It can be readily seen that budget surpluses accrued in the early years of the Labour government under the impact of restraints on government expenditure, falling savings and booming investment.

Given the extent of the budget surpluses in the early years, the 'golden rule' has so far had little constraining effect on the operation of fiscal policy. However, from the present position this would no longer appear to hold.

*Table 13.3* Budget deficits (percentage of GDP)

| | *Public sector current budget* | *Cyclically adjusted surplus on current budget* | *Public sector net borrowing* | *Cyclically adjusted public sector net borrowing* |
|---|---|---|---|---|
| 1989/90 | 1.4 | –1.4 | –0.2 | 2.6 |
| 1990/91 | 0.4 | –1.2 | 1.0 | 2.6 |
| 1991/92 | –2.0 | –1.5 | 3.8 | 3.3 |
| 1992/93 | –5.6 | –3.6 | 7.6 | 5.6 |
| 1993/94 | –6.2 | –4.1 | 7.8 | 5.6 |
| 1994/95 | –4.8 | –3.5 | 6.3 | 4.9 |
| 1995/96 | –3.4 | –2.7 | 4.8 | 4.0 |
| 1996/97 | –2.8 | –2.3 | 3.5 | 3.1 |
| 1997/98 | –0.2 | 0.0 | 0.8 | 0.7 |
| 1998/99 | 1.2 | 1.1 | –0.4 | –0.3 |
| 1999/2000 | 2.2 | 1.9 | –1.7 | –1.4 |
| 2000/01 | 2.2 | 1.6 | –1.7 | –1.0 |
| 2001/02 | 1.0 | 0.8 | 0.0 | 0.2 |
| 2002/03 | –1.2 | –0.8 | 2.3 | 1.9 |
| 2003/04 | –1.9 | –1.4 | 3.1 | 2.7 |
| 2004/05 | –1.6 | –1.3 | 3.3 | 3.0 |
| 2005/06 (estimate) | –0.9 | –0.03 | 3.0 | 2.4 |

*Source*: Treasury (2006: Tables 2.5 and C25).

The Private Finance Initiative (PFI) has been given a substantial role in stimulating public investment. We have discussed elsewhere (Sawyer 2003, 2005) the desirability or otherwise of the PFI, and specifically pointed to the spurious nature of the argument that PFI increases public investment. Here, we focus on its implications for the budget deficit and public debt. The PFI in effect replaces expenditure financed by debt with the consequent future interest payments by expenditure undertaken by private firms for which they are repaid by leasing agreements over a period of up to 30 years. At the time at which the investment in capital equipment is undertaken by a private firm, there is no public expenditure incurred, but rather the future stream of public expenditure is increased (by the leasing and management charges). The overall effect of a move from 'traditional' public sector investment to PFI is to increase public expenditure over the lifetime of the project (essentially because the implicit cost of finance under PFI is higher than the cost under 'traditional' financing through sale of bonds) and to understate the scale of public liabilities. The obligation to make future payments (for leasing, maintenance, etc.) under PFI is a liability of the public sector and as such should be included in the public debt (as it would be in a comparable situation in the private sector). The outstanding obligation under PFI as of December 2005 amounted to £143.6 billion, and applying a real rate of discount of 2 (3) per cent amounts to a debt of £117.5 billion (107.2 billion).[2] The public sector net debt position at the end of 2004/05 was £416.7 billion. The inclusion of PFI would then raise the public debt position by the order of one quarter and put the debt to GDP ratio closer to 50 per cent (and under the Maastricht Treaty definitions around 5 plus per cent). The use of the PFI has fluctuated, but generally reduced the budget deficit by the order of 0.3 per cent of GDP. Over the next few years the estimated payments under PFI contracts rise from £6.4 billion in 2005–06 to £7.2 billion in 2010–11, which is of the order of 0.5 per cent of GDP.

It can be seen from above that the net debt position is currently around 36 per cent of GDP and is projected to rise toward 38 per cent over the next few years, against a ceiling of 40 per cent. The inclusion of an allowance for the debt obligations under PFI would take the outstanding debt position well over 40 per cent.

Fiscal policy has been operated since 1997 in a clear framework with an underlying view that fiscal policy should be operated subject to constraints on budget deficits, and specifically the current budget position balanced over the cycle. The near-achievement of the 'golden rule' owes much to the surpluses generated in the late 1990s by the investment boom and lower savings, to reduction in nominal interest rates lowering interest payments on public debt, to use of the PFI and to the re-dating of the cycle.

## Monetary policy

The first economic decision of the incoming government was on monetary policy in the form of moving interest rate decisions from the Treasury to the Bank of England. Monetary policy is now operated by an 'independent' Bank of England (strictly the Monetary Policy Committee) with the objective of achieving an inflation target. Initially the target was cast in terms of the retail price index at 2.5 per cent +/–1 per cent, and later the HICP was used and the central figure modified to 2 per cent. There would seem to be two sets of reasons for this decision. First, it could be seen as a 'signal' that the incoming government gave the control of inflation as its first priority, seeking to assure the City and financial markets that rising inflation would not be a problem (in contrast with the previous period of Labour government). Second, acceptance of the arguments for an 'independent central bank' in terms of the enhanced credibility of such institutional arrangements with favourable impacts on inflationary expectations through the perception of greater commitment to low inflation.

The inflation record can be seen from Table 13.1. The immediate impression could be that the policy has been successful in the sense that inflation has remained within the target range throughout the period (in contrast, for example, with the record of the ECB where inflation in the Euro area has persistently exceeded, albeit by a relatively small margin, the inflation target range). But inflation over the period since 1997 has been rather similar to inflation after 1992. This conforms to a more general finding that the inflation record of countries adopting inflation targeting (which the UK policy since 1997 has been) is rather similar to those, which do not adopt inflation targeting (Arestis and Sawyer 2006).

A quick look at Table 13.3 suggests that within a general climate of low inflation, the UK's inflation record since 1997 (here based on the Harmonized Index of Consumer Prices measure, whereas the Retail Price Index has been used in Table 13.1) has been similar to, and

*Table13.4* Comparative inflation rates

| | *UK* | *USA* | *Euro area* |
|---|---|---|---|
| 1991 | 7.5 | 4.2 | 1.8 |
| 1992 | 4.2 | 3.0 | 4.6 |
| 1993 | 2.5 | 3.0 | 4.0 |
| 1994 | 2.0 | 2.6 | 3.2 |
| 1995 | 2.7 | 2.8 | 2.9 |
| 1996 | 2.5 | 2.9 | 2.4 |
| 1997 | 1.8 | 2.3 | 1.7 |
| 1998 | 1.6 | 1.5 | 1.2 |
| 1999 | 1.3 | 2.2 | 1.2 |
| 2000 | 0.8 | 3.4 | 2.2 |
| 2001 | 1.2 | 2.8 | 2.5 |
| 2002 | 1.3 | 1.6 | 2.3 |
| 2003 | 1.4 | 2.3 | 2.1 |
| 2004 | 1.3 | 2.7 | 2.1 |
| 2005 | 2.0 | 3.4 | 2.2 |
| 2006 (forecast) | 2.2 | 3.3 | 2.1 |

*Notes*: HICP measure used.

*Source*: OECD (2005a, 2006).

perhaps a little better than, inflation in the USA and the Euro area. However, Table 13.4 suggests that nominal interest rates in the UK have been consistently higher than in the USA and Euro area over that period (and real interest rates even more so).

A major reason for doubting that monetary policy and how it is conducted has much impact on the rate of inflation (and more generally on the macroeconomy) comes from the results of simulation exercises undertaken on macroeconometric models. A recent illustration of this comes from the Bank of England's new macroeconometric model. In Bank of England (2005), Figure 13.1 indicates that the effects of a 1 per cent increase in nominal interest rates held for a year (and then with interest rate policy following a simple Taylor's Rule) on inflation would be a maximum decline in inflation of 0.3 per cent. This result is in line with other finding, which we have surveyed in Arestis and Sawyer (2004). This conclusion may be modified by the reflection that

> The simulation shown... is based on the assumption that the unexpected change in interest rates does not affect agents' long-run inflation expectations. But the response of the economy to a change in interest rates depends on the credibility of the inflation target. In particular, as inflation expectations become more firmly anchored

*Table 13.5* Short-term nominal interest rates (percentage)

| | *UK* | *USA* | *Euro area* |
|---|---|---|---|
| 1991 | 11.5 | 5.9 | |
| 1992 | 9.6 | 3.8 | 11.2 |
| 1993 | 5.9 | 3.2 | 8.6 |
| 1994 | 5.5 | 4.7 | 6.3 |
| 1995 | 6.7 | 6.0 | 6.5 |
| 1996 | 6.0 | 5.4 | 4.8 |
| 1997 | 6.8 | 5.7 | 4.3 |
| 1998 | 7.3 | 5.5 | 3.9 |
| 1999 | 5.4 | 5.4 | 3.0 |
| 2000 | 6.1 | 6.5 | 4.4 |
| 2001 | 5.0 | 3.7 | 4.3 |
| 2002 | 4.0 | 1.8 | 3.3 |
| 2003 | 3.7 | 1.2 | 2.3 |
| 2004 | 4.6 | 1.6 | 2.1 |
| 2005 | 4.7 | 3.5 | 2.2 |
| 2006 (forecast) | 4.5 | 5.1 | 2.7 |

*Source*: OECD (2005a, 2006).

> around the inflation target – the target becomes more credible – a change in the short-term interest rate is likely to have less impact. (Bank of England 2005: 131)

This can be linked with the argument that the success of monetary policy with an 'independent' central bank comes from the creditability in the achievement of low inflation, the belief that the authorities will and do act to restrain inflation and the favourable impact which these have on inflationary expectations.

At one level, monetary policy since 1997 could be judged a success in that it was set a single objective in terms of a target rate of inflation, and the actual rate of inflation has been within the permitted +/–1 per cent of the target throughout the period. In this regard, the Bank of England's track record is clearly superior to that of the ECB, where inflation in the Euro area has often been above the 2 per cent upper limit set for inflation. Clearly the question is whether the conduct of monetary policy and its institutional framework can take the credit for that achievement, and to answer that question would require the setting of some counterfactual episode of what would have happened under some other form of policy. We are not able to construct that counterfactual but offer the following comments. The inflationary climate (as illustrated in Table 13.4) has been favourable, particularly when compared with the climate in the 1970s and 1980s. Most countries have experienced low inflation, and this does not appear to be related to the institutional arrangements (and, specifically, when a country has adopted inflation targeting; Arestis and Sawyer, 2005). The effects of interest rates on inflation, as discussed above, appear small, and the effects of say a ¼ per cent change in interest rates (which has been the typical change) would be miniscule. The policy regime change in 1997 inherited a benign inflationary climate (cf. Table 13.4), and it may have helped to consolidate low inflationary expectations, which in turn fostered lower inflation.

## The (un)employment record

Table 13.1 has indicated the continuous fall in unemployment from 1993 to 2005. The rate of unemployment on the basis of the unemployment benefit claimant count in 2004 at 2¾ per cent was lower than at anytime since 1974. The figures on unemployment on the ILO definition of those actively seeking work were not quite so impressive, but had fallen below 5 per cent in 2004 though with a subsequent rise. In their report on the UK, the OECD wrote that

> [i]n international comparison labour utilisation rates are high, with activity rates only clearly exceeded by a small number of Nordic countries where female participation is particularly high. However, while the unemployment rate has fallen to its lowest level in three decades and by nearly 7 percentage points from a peak in the mid-1980s, there has been little fall in the inactivity rate... Indeed, while the activity rate of women has risen substantially, the male inactivity rate has shown a consistent upward trend accompanied by a similar rise in men reporting long-term sickness or disability as the main reason for inactivity. In 1980 the number claiming disability-related benefits was less than the number claiming unemployment benefit, whereas currently the former are three and half times as great. While increasing numbers on disability-related benefits is common in many OECD countries, the United Kingdom stands out as having a relatively high concentration of disability among prime-age males. (OECD 2005b: 39)

> Seven per cent of the 25–54-year-old men are now inactive outside the labour market, many more than three decades ago. Solid growth since the late 1990s has brought down unemployment but not inactivity, with 2½ million currently claiming incapacity benefit. (OECD 2005b: 99)

*Table 13.6* Severe disability and invalidity benefits

| | *Severe Disability and Invalidity Benefit* | | *Invalidity Benefit* | |
|---|---|---|---|---|
| | *Number (thousands)* | *Per cent of working age population* | *Number (thousands)* | *Per cent of working age population* |
| *May 1997* | | | | |
| Claimants | 2,507.7 | 7.3 | 2,192.8 | 6.4 |
| Beneficiaries | 1,887.6 | 5.5 | 1,560.4 | 4.5 |
| *February 2005* | | | | |
| Claimants | 2,638.4 | 7.4 | 2,386.9 | 6.7 |
| Beneficiaries | 1,695.6 | 4.7 | 1,444.8 | 4.0 |

*Source*: Incapacity Benefit and Severe Disablement Allowance Tables from website of Office of National Statistics.

Table 13.6 indicates recent trends in the number of recipients of incapacity benefits. The significance of the numbers receiving incapacity benefits arises from the general perception that one method used during the 1980s to keep down the figures on unemployment (based on the benefit claimant count) had been the encouragement of placing some of those without employment and with poor prospects of securing employment on the then form of incapacity benefits. It has also been argued that the proportion of people receiving incapacity benefits is higher in regions of higher unemployment. Both of these suggest that incapacity benefits can to some degree take the role of unemployment benefits, and that many (but by no means all) of those on incapacity benefits could be considered as 'hidden unemployed'.

The record on unemployment appears laudable. We would argue, however, that full consideration does need to be given to the measurement of unemployment, and that there is at least a case for considering perhaps half of those receiving incapacity benefits as 'hidden unemployed'. The doubling of those receiving incapacity benefits since the mid-1980s is unlikely to reflect a worsening health situation in the UK, though it clearly could reflect a more relaxed approach to the award of such benefits (for example, application of less stringent medical tests), and a lack of job prospects. Particularly when regard is given to the inactivity rate (as mentioned above) the record on unemployment is not quite so good.

A particular important question is: why did unemployment (as recorded) fall continuously from 1993 to 2004 (with some upward movement in the past 15 months)? The two competing explanations would be the aggregate demand one and labour market 'reforms' and increased 'flexibility'. We could first note the lack of cross-country correlation between labour market 'flexibility' and unemployment (see, for example, Baker *et al.* 2004). Indeed, we may generalize the argument by referring to more recent evidence on the degree of labour market flexibility in Europe and economic performance. A recent OECD study (Brandt *et al.* 2005) makes the point vividly. In Table 13.7 we cite the degree of labour market reforms (score) and the ranking in view of the score, in a number of European countries. Given the UK's economic success, perhaps at the top of this group of countries, its 11th position in so far as labour market reforms does not sit comfortably with the argument that the two are so strongly correlated if at all! Moreover, Germany and Italy, to take another obvious example, with their relatively high position in Table 13.7 cannot claim much of an economic performance recently. We can also note that the decline in

*Table 13.7* European labour market reforms

| *Country* | *Score* | *Rank* |
|---|---|---|
| Denmark | 29.3 | 1 |
| Netherlands | 25.7 | 2 |
| Finland | 25.0 | 3 |
| Germany | 23.9 | 4 |
| Italy | 21.7 | 5 |
| Belgium | 21.4 | 6 |
| Austria | 17.8 | 8 |
| Ireland/Sweden | 17.4 | 9 |
| UK | 16.7 | 11 |
| Portugal | 15.9 | 12 |
| Norway | 15.2 | 13 |
| France | 14.5 | 15 |
| Luxembourg | 14.4 | 16 |
| Greece | 13.8 | 17 |
| Spain | 10.5 | 24 |

*Source*: Brandt *et al.* (2005).

unemployment is consistent with what was happening to demand in that there were no marked changes in productivity growth. There are also specific episodes, notably in the recent years, when the rise in employment can be clearly linked with expansion in public sector demand for labour.

## The lucky chancellor?

There are at least two ways in which 'luck' can be considered. The first is whether a combination of the inherited economic conditions and the general world economic climate is favourable. In terms of inflation, that has clearly been the case. The inherited economic conditions (Table 13.1) were generally good and rather better than the conditions which previous Labour governments had inherited. The investment boom of the late 1990s was a further favourable factor.

The second is whether policy decisions taken for essentially political reasons have turned out to be good economic decisions. An example of the reverse situation from a previous Labour government comes to mind. The Labour Party rather unexpectedly formed a government in March 1974, and came into power with a commitment to increase public expenditure and with an inherited commitment on indexing wages. In the immediately aftermath of the sharp oil price increases in late 1973 these may well have been inappropriate policies. The new Labour government came into office with a commitment to maintain the previous Conservative government's spending plans for the coming two years, even though those spending plans were very tight. It is likely that the Conservative government would not have kept to those spending plans if they had continued in office. The effects of restraining public expenditure in macroeconomic terms depends on the buoyancy of private expenditure, and we will argue below that Brown was fortunate in that the restraints on public expenditure did arise when private expenditure was booming. In a similar vein but in the opposite direction, public expenditure, particularly on education and health was boosted from 2001 onwards.

It can be seen from Tables 13.8 and 13.9 that there was a substantial squeeze on public expenditure in the second half of the 1990s. Total expenditure (the last column of Table 13.8) indicates a fall in the ratio of public expenditure to GDP from 42.3 per cent in 1995/96 to 37.0 per cent in 1999/2000. The slow annual growth (and indeed decline in 1997) of public expenditure on goods and services is clear in Table 13.9.

Exports and investment expenditure could be seen as having maintained the expansion of final expenditure. Whilst the ratio of invest-

*Table 13.8* Trends in public expenditure (percentage of GDP)

| | *Public sector current expenditure* | *Public sector net investment* | *Public sector gross investment* | *Total managed expenditure* |
|---|---|---|---|---|
| 1989/90 | 35.7 | 1.2 | 4.0 | 39.7 |
| 1990/91 | 36.1 | 1.4 | 3.9 | 40.0 |
| 1991/92 | 38.4 | 1.8 | 3.9 | 42.3 |
| 1992/93 | 40.2 | 2.0 | 3.9 | 44.2 |
| 1993/94 | 40.0 | 1.6 | 3.4 | 43.4 |
| 1994/95 | 39.7 | 1.5 | 3.3 | 43.0 |
| 1995/96 | 39.1 | 1.4 | 3.2 | 42.3 |
| 1996/97 | 38.3 | 0.7 | 2.3 | 40.6 |
| 1997/98 | 36.8 | 0.6 | 2.1 | 38.9 |
| 1998/99 | 35.8 | 0.8 | 2.2 | 37.9 |
| 1999/2000 | 35.1 | 0.5 | 1.8 | 37.0 |
| 2000/01 | 35.9 | 0.6 | 1.9 | 37.7 |
| 2001/02 | 36.2 | 1.0 | 2.3 | 38.5 |
| 2002/03 | 36.9 | 1.1 | 2.4 | 39.3 |
| 2003/04 | 38.0 | 1.2 | 2.5 | 40.5 |
| 2004/05 | 38.6 | 1.6 | 2.9 | 41.4 |

*Source*: Treasury (2005: Table B31).

*Table 13.9* Growth of components of demand (percentages)

| | *Growth of consumer expenditure* | *Growth of investment expenditure* | *Growth of expenditure public on goods and services* | *Growth of exports* | *Growth of final expenditure* |
|---|---|---|---|---|---|
| 1992 | 0.59 | 2.25 | 0.73 | 4.32 | 1.55 |
| 1993 | 3.10 | 2.43 | –0.71 | 4.38 | 2.60 |
| 1994 | 3.07 | 8.63 | 1.04 | 9.21 | 4.69 |
| 1995 | 1.66 | 2.66 | 1.38 | 9.26 | 3.44 |
| 1996 | 3.63 | 3.20 | 1.06 | 8.72 | 4.29 |
| 1997 | 3.59 | 8.22 | –0.49 | 8.25 | 4.67 |
| 1998 | 3.99 | 13.25 | 1.09 | 3.11 | 4.58 |
| 1999 | 4.43 | 2.93 | 3.97 | 4.25 | 4.09 |
| 2000 | 4.56 | 2.70 | 3.66 | 9.14 | 5.13 |
| 2001 | 3.03 | 2.83 | 1.70 | 2.90 | 2.82 |
| 2002 | 3.46 | 0.98 | 4.44 | 0.24 | 2.58 |
| 2003 | 2.55 | 0.97 | 4.49 | 1.17 | 2.35 |
| 2004 | 3.61 | 5.06 | 3.06 | 3.44 | 3.67 |

*Source*: Calculated from National Statistics (2006: Table 1.3); and Treasury (2006).

ment to GDP has tended to decline in current prices after 1997 (18.2 per cent in 1998 falling to 16.7 per cent in 2004), in constant price terms investment after 1997 has been significantly higher than before 1997. A fall in the household savings ratio has also been instrumental in maintaining the expansion of expenditure (for example, down from 9.2 per cent in 1997 to 4.2 per cent in 2004), which raises questions on the future expansion of consumer expenditure. The growth of exports is noteworthy as it was taking place against the background of a rising exchange rate. When the growth of investment and exports was particularly low in 2002 and 2003, those years saw the highest rates of growth of public expenditure in the past 15 years.

> An expansionary fiscal policy has been an important factor supporting demand since the global downturn; between 2000 and 2004 the cyclically-adjusted balance declined by 4½ per cent of GDP, which was only exceeded by the United States. Over the same period over half of new jobs have been created in the public sector, which has experienced average employment growth of 2% per annum (about six times the growth rate in private sector employment). (OECD 2005b: 29–30)

Our general argument here is that Brown has been a lucky Chancellor in two related ways. First, whilst the varying growth rates of public expenditure have been driven by some political imperatives, they have been complemented by the varying growth rates of private expenditure. When the growth of public expenditure was restrained (as in the early years in office), investment and consumer expenditure were particularly buoyant. When public expenditure growth speeded up, this came at a time when private expenditure was slowing. Second, fiscal policy rules were set (as detailed above) which appeared to place significant constraints on the size of budget deficits. However, in the outturn there does not seem to have been an effective constraint on the fiscal deficit as compared with what would be required to sustain a high level of employment. The budget deficits in 2004 and 2005 were at levels (relative to GDP) comparable to those of the 1980s and were only low by comparison with the figures of the early 1990s. From a 'functional finance' perspective the appropriate budget deficit is one, which supports the highest achievable level of demand. On occasions (perhaps in the late 1990s) when investment expenditure is high and savings low, then a budget surplus can arise (and be appropriate). The test for the 'golden rule' is likely to come over the next few years. Starting from the present position of a budget deficit exceeding 3 per cent of GDP with output gap close to zero suggests that over the whole of a cycle with the present fiscal stance the budget deficit would average close to 3 per cent, and significantly away from zero. Further, any significant slowdown in economic activity would lead to substantial increases in the budget deficit. A budget deficit position compatible with the 'golden rule' would require some combination of rise in investment, fall in domestic savings, or improvement in the current account.

We could also add that there has been a third way in which the Chancellor has been lucky – the UK has not been a member of the Euro area. If the UK had been, then monetary policy would have been conducted in a less transparent manner. But, more significantly, the Stability and Growth Pact would have been in operation, and the UK would clearly have broken the budget deficit rules of the SGP. It could, of course, be argued that since France and Germany similarly ran budget deficits outside the rules and no effective action was taken against them – though they were censured, and a smaller country, Portugal, was forced to cut public expenditure with a consequent rise in unemployment, the UK would have probably gone through a similar experience. However, at the same time, the UK would have gone through a round of embarrassing pressures to lower the budget deficit, without at the same time the independent Bank of England being able to help in any way whatsoever. Evidence of the argument advanced here is the current demand by the European Commissioner of the UK Chancellor, Gordon Brown, to breach the UK deficit below the 3 per cent SGP limit (believed to be 3.4 per cent). This despite the UK Treasury insistence that 'This year we expect to have a treaty deficit of 3%, falling to 2.7% next year, and down to 1.5% by 2010', and that 'The UK continues to have the lowest average debts and deficits of any other major European economy'; also 'We make no apologies for investing in vital public services' (reported in the *Guardian*, 12 January 2006). Despite the UK deficit being less worrying for the European Commissioner (12 countries out of 25 in the European Union, and a number of them members of the Euro area, are now running deficits in excess of the 3 per cent of GDP limit), the UK is now considered as having an 'excessive deficit' and will be asked to correct it. Such directives would not be applied in the case of Germany and Italy, which do have higher deficits, but find them now justified by the new SGP rules.

## Conclusions

We have argued in this chapter that the benign economic conditions in the UK in the past decade or so might be due to luck rather than to the effectiveness of the economic policies pursued over the period. In any case, there are serious problems looming on the horizon. The main force behind the economic growth since 1997 has been aggregate demand, and consumer spending in particular; its faltering in 2005 is the main reason of the current slowdown (GDP growth was 1.8 per cent for 2005 as opposed to a trend GDP of over 2.5 per cent). The rise in consumer spending, however, has been responsible for the unparalleled expansion in consumer debt at the back of a boom in house prices. This development contains the seeds of a potentially serious downturn should sharply increase interest rates. The budget deficit and the current account of the balance of payments deficit are evident.

## Notes

1. This refers to the current target set in terms of the HICP to which the figures in Table 13.1 refer. For much of the time the target was set in terms of the RPI and used the figure of 2.5 per cent.
2. Calculated from Treasury (2005: Table B25).

## References

Arestis, P. and Sawyer, M. (2004) 'Can Monetary Policy Affect the Real Economy?', *European Review of Economics and Finance*, 3(3): 9–32.

Arestis, P. and Sawyer, M.C. (2006) 'Inflation Targeting: A Critical Appraisal', *Greek Economic Review*, (forthcoming).

Baker, D., Glyn, A. Howell, D. and Schmitt, D. (2004) 'Labour Market Institutions and Unemployment: A Critical Assessment of the Cross-country Evidence', in D.R. Howells (ed.), *Fighting Unemployment: The Limits of Free Market Orthodoxy* (Oxford: Oxford University Press).

Bank of England (2005) *The Bank of England Quarterly Model* (London: Bank of England).

Brandt, N. Burniaux, J.-M., and Duval, R. (2005) *Assessing the OECD Job Strategy: Past Developments and Reforms*, Economics Department Working Paper No. 429, 11 May (Paris: OECD).

Brown, G. (1999) 'The Conditions for Full Employment', *Mais Lecture*, City University London, 19 October.

Gow, D. (2006) 'EU to Give Brown 15 Months to Sort Out Britain's Budget Deficit', *The Guardian*, Saturday 7 January.

Labour Party (1997) *New Labour: Because Britain Deserves Better* (London: Labour Party).

Lerner, A. (1943) 'Functional Finance and the Federal Debt', *Social Research*, 10: 38–51; reprinted in M.G. Mueller (ed.) (1966), *Readings in Macroeconomics* (New York: Holt, Rinehart and Winston).

OECD (2005a) *Economic Outlook* (Paris: OECD).

OECD (2005b) *Economic Survey of the United Kingdom* (Paris: OECD).

OECD (2006) *Economic Outlook*, preliminary edition (Paris: OECD).

Office of National Statistics (2006) *National Income Blue Book* (London: HMSO).

Sawyer, M. (2003) 'The Private Finance Initiative: A Critical Assessment', in D. Coffey and C. Thorley (eds), *Industrial and Labour Market Policy and Performance* (London: Routledge).

Sawyer, M. (2005) 'The Private Finance Initiative: The UK Experience', in W. Rothengatter and G. Ragazzi, 'Procurement and Financing of Motorways in Europe', *Research in Transportation Economics*, 15: 239–53.

Treasury (1997) *Pre Budget Report 1997*, Cmnd. 3804 (London: HMSO).

Treasury (1999) *The New Monetary Policy Framework* (London: HMSO).

Treasury (2005) *Britain Meeting the Global Challenge: Enterprise, Fairness and Responsibility*, Pre-Budget Report, December 2005, Cm 6701.

Treasury (2006) *Budget 2006. A Strong and Strengthening Economy: Investing in Britain's Future*, HC 968 (London: HMSO).

# Index